Shakespeare
in the Theatre:
The National Theatre,
1963–1975

SHAKESPEARE IN THE THEATRE

Series Editors
Peter Holland, Farah Karim-Cooper and Stephen Purcell

Published titles
Patrice Chéreau, Dominique Goy-Blanquet
The American Shakespeare Center, Paul Menzer
Mark Rylance at the Globe, Stephen Purcell
The National Theatre, 1963–1975: Olivier and Hall, Robert Shaughnessy
Nicholas Hytner, Abigail Rokison-Woodall
Peter Sellars, Ayanna Thompson
Trevor Nunn, Russell Jackson
Cheek by Jowl, Peter Kirwan
Peter Hall, Stuart Hampton-Reeves
Yukio Ninagawa, Conor Hanratty
The King's Men, Lucy Munro

Forthcoming titles
Sir William Davenant and the Duke's Company, Richard Schoch and Amanda Eubanks Winkler
Sarah Siddons and John Philip Kemble, Fiona Ritchie
Phyllida Lloyd, Elizabeth Schafer

Shakespeare in the Theatre: The National Theatre, 1963–1975

Olivier and Hall

Robert Shaughnessy

THE ARDEN SHAKESPEARE
LONDON • NEW YORK • OXFORD • NEW DELHI • SYDNEY

THE ARDEN SHAKESPEARE
Bloomsbury Publishing Plc
50 Bedford Square, London, WC1B 3DP, UK
1385 Broadway, New York, NY 10018, USA

BLOOMSBURY, THE ARDEN SHAKESPEARE and the Arden Shakespeare logo
are trademarks of Bloomsbury Publishing Plc

First published in Great Britain 2018
This paperback edition published 2020

Copyright © Robert Shaughnessy, 2018, 2020

Robert Shaughnessy has asserted his right under the Copyright, Designs and Patents
Act, 1988, to be identified as the author of this work.

For legal purposes the Acknowledgements on p. x constitute an extension of this
copyright page.

Cover design: Dani Leigh
Cover image © Zoë Dominic

All rights reserved. No part of this publication may be reproduced or
transmitted in any form or by any means, electronic or mechanical,
including photocopying, recording, or any information storage or retrieval
system, without prior permission in writing from the publishers.

Bloomsbury Publishing Plc does not have any control over, or responsibility for,
any third-party websites referred to or in this book. All internet addresses given
in this book were correct at the time of going to press. The author and publisher
regret any inconvenience caused if addresses have changed or sites have
ceased to exist, but can accept no responsibility for any such changes.

A catalogue record for this book is available from the British Library.

Library of Congress Cataloging-in-Publication Data
Names: Shaughnessy, Robert, 1962- author.
Title: Shakespeare in the theatre : Shakespeare and the National Theatre,
1963-1975 : Olivier and Hall / Robert Shaughnessy.
Description: London : The Arden Shakespeare, 2018. | Series: Shakespeare in
the theatre | Includes bibliographical references and index.
Identifiers: LCCN 2018006303| ISBN 9781474241045 (hb) | ISBN 9781474241038
(pb) | ISBN 9781474241052 (epub) | ISBN 9781474241069 (epdf)
Subjects: LCSH: Shakespeare, William, 1564-1616–Stage
history–England–London. | National Theatre (Great Britain)–History. |
Olivier, Laurence, 1907-1989. | Hall, Peter, 1930-2017.
Classification: LCC PR3106 .S56 2018 | DDC 792.09421/65–dc23 LC record available
at https://lccn.loc.gov/2018006303

ISBN:		
	HB:	978-1-4742-4104-5
	PB:	978-1-4742-4103-8
	ePDF:	978-1-4742-4106-9
	eBook:	978-1-4742-4105-2

Series: Shakespeare in the Theatre

Typeset by Integra Software Services Pvt. Ltd.

To find out more about our authors and books visit www.bloomsbury.com
and sign up for our newsletters.

For Nat

CONTENTS

List of Illustrations viii
Series Preface ix
Acknowledgements x
A Note on the Text xi

Introduction 1

1   Olivier 9

2   1967 57

3   Translations 97

4   Hall 143

Conclusion 187

Appendix 190
Notes 191
Bibliography 221
Index 235

ILLUSTRATIONS

I.1 Frank Barrie and Jo Maxwell-Muller in *Rosencrantz and Guildenstern are Dead*, directed by Derek Goldby, 1967 — 6

1.1 Maggie Smith and Laurence Olivier during a break in rehearsals for *Othello*, directed by John Dexter, 1964 — 33

2.1 Jeremy Brett, Charles Kay and Ronald Pickup in *As You Like It*, directed by Clifford Williams, 1967 — 76

3.1 Wolf Kaiser, Ekkehard Schall and Helene Weigel in the Berliner Ensemble *Coriolanus*, 1965 — 128

4.1 The set for the masque in *The Tempest*, directed by Peter Hall, 1974, with stage-hands sitting in for Juno and Ceres — 160

4.2 Simon Ward, Albert Finney and fight director William Hobbs in rehearsal for *Hamlet*, directed by Peter Hall, 1975 — 184

SERIES PREFACE

Each volume in the *Shakespeare in the Theatre* series focuses on a director or theatre company who has made a significant contribution to Shakespeare production, identifying the artistic and political/social contexts of their work.

The series introduces readers to the work of significant theatre directors and companies whose Shakespeare productions have been transformative in our understanding of his plays in performance. Each volume examines a single figure or company, considering their key productions, rehearsal approaches and their work with other artists (actors, designers, composers). A particular feature of each book is its exploration of the contexts within which these theatre artists have made their Shakespeare productions work. Thus, the series considers not only the ways in which directors and companies produce Shakespeare, but also reflects upon their other theatre activity and the broader artistic, cultural and socio-political milieu within which their Shakespeare performances and productions have been created. The key to the series' originality, then, is its consideration of Shakespeare production in a range of artistic and broader contexts; in this sense, it de-centres Shakespeare from within Shakespeare studies, pointing to the range of people, artistic practices and cultural phenomena that combine to make meaning in the theatre.

Series editors: Peter Holland,
Farah Karim-Cooper and Stephen Purcell

ACKNOWLEDGEMENTS

My thanks, first and foremost, to the series editors, Bridget Escolme, Peter Holland and Farah Karim-Cooper, for inviting me to write this book, and to the Arden Shakespeare's Margaret Bartley for commissioning it. I am particularly indebted to Peter for his astute comments on the final draft, and the book is much the better for them. I started this project under the auspices of the University of Kent and finished it under those of Guildford School of Acting, University of Surrey, and I acknowledge the support of both institutions, as well as the companionship of those colleagues and friends who have followed and facilitated its progress. For Bloomsbury, Susan Furber's editorial guidance has been assured, tactful and firm.

The book could not have been written without the generous co-operation of the staff at the National Theatre Archive. Erin Lee arranged access to the closed materials that have enabled me to tell the stories behind the stories that are a matter of public record, and Jennie Borzykh has tirelessly provided resources and responded to my many queries. I am privileged to have felt very much at home in the reading room with a view of the Waterloo Road, and of the theatre in which the events recounted here took place.

The other scene of writing has been very happily shared with Nickie, Caitlin, Gabriel, Erina and Nathaniel, to whom this book is dedicated.

A NOTE ON THE TEXT

All quotations from Shakespeare's plays are taken from *The Arden Shakespeare: Complete Works*, Revised Edition, eds Ann Thompson, David Scott Kastan and Richard Proudfoot (London: Arden Shakespeare, 2011).

Introduction

In the beginning, it was all about Shakespeare. When the radical publisher Effingham Wilson issued the first manifesto for a British National Theatre in 1848 he entitled it *A House for Shakespeare* and advocated the founding of a theatre wherein the works of 'the world's greatest moral teacher may be constantly performed', and which would be funded by government; along the principles established with the creation of the National Gallery in 1824.[1] The proposal was received with enthusiasm by eminent literati and theatre people but went nowhere; sixteen years later, it resurfaced amidst plans to commemorate Shakespeare's tercentenary, and the initiative passed from London to Stratford-upon-Avon where what began as a modest plan to commission a monument led, a decade later, to the creation of the first regional (many would say parochial) centre dedicated to the fulfilment of Wilson's mission, in the ungainly shape of the Shakespeare Memorial Theatre (SMT). The SMT opened on 23 April 1879; a month later, the Comédie Française brought Molière and Racine to London's Gaiety Theatre. 'There is no company of actors in the world', reported *The Times* of the visit, 'the charm of whose performance consists so much in the perfection of its *ensemble*';[2] and Matthew Arnold was inspired to write an essay calling for a theatre that would perform Shakespeare, established modern classics and new plays, powered by the slogan '*The theatre is irresistible; organize the theatre!*'[3] Meanwhile, the actor-manager Henry Irving lent his support to the movement ('With regard to its desirability, I have little, if any, doubt') whilst balking at the idea of state funding: 'The institutions of this country are so absolutely free that it would be dangerous – if not destructive – to a certain form of liberty to meddle with them.'[4] For the next ten years, Irving's productions of Shakespeare and of Romantic and historical dramas at the Lyceum Theatre offered one model of what a National Theatre might look like: led by himself and Ellen Terry these were star-centred, extravagantly picturesque and, until the venture ended in financial collapse in the 1890s, successful on both popular and middlebrow terms.

Irving's ideological antipathy to state funding was not shared by the critic William Archer and theatre all-rounder Harley Granville Barker who in 1904 jointly authored *A National Theatre: Schemes and Estimates*, which was published in 1907. This secured the support of Irving and presented plans and costings for the institution in some detail, including its projected repertoire: the theatre would launch with all four plays in the Second Tetralogy of Histories (*Richard II*, *1 Henry IV*, *2 Henry V*, *Henry V*), followed in time by *The Tempest*, *The Taming of the Shrew*, *Romeo and Juliet* and *As You Like It*. Archer and Barker reasoned that once outliers (*Titus Andronicus*, *Henry VIII*, *Timon of Athens* and the like) were stripped out, there remained a core canon of twenty-five plays: 'If six, on an average, were revived in every season, the whole list (save one) would be gone through once in four years; while in each season certain plays, carried forward from the season or seasons before, would be considered, not as revivals, but as belonging to the permanent substratum of the repertory'.[5] They even provided cast lists for the first season populated by fictitious actors whimsically named (for the men) after London landmarks and (for the women) after the place-names of deep England so that 'Mr Kingsway' played Richard II, Prospero, Hamlet and Jaques, and 'Miss Tintagel' Katherine and Juliet.[6]

By now, the National Theatre (NT) movement had joined forces with the London Shakespeare League (established in 1902), and in 1908 the Shakespeare Memorial National

Theatre Committee was created, with the aim of raising the funds that, it was now assumed, would not be provided by the state. In 1909 the Committee published its aims, and 'to keep the plays of Shakespeare in its repertory' headed the agenda.[7] Proponents of the National Theatre (among them George Bernard Shaw, J. M. Barrie and Arthur Wing Pinero) looked towards the tercentenary of Shakespeare's death in 1916 for its opening; the First World War put paid to that, although a private member's bill pledging government support was passed in the House of Commons in 1913 and the first site (in Bloomsbury) was acquired the same year.

It would take fifty years for the dream of a National Theatre to be realized and a further thirteen for the reality of the longed-for new building to materialize; in the interim, Shakespeare was the adhesive that prevented the whole ramshackle crusade from falling apart. In 1912 Lilian Baylis prepared the ground for a house for Shakespeare that would soon outclass that of Stratford, when she assumed management of the Old Vic. Over the course of the next three decades, as the site of the projected National Theatre shifted from Bloomsbury to Cromwell Gardens, Leicester Square, Belgravia and elsewhere, the Old Vic got on with the business of staging (almost) every play in the canon and nurtured the talents of the century's greatest Shakespearean actors, among them John Gielgud, Peggy Ashcroft, Ralph Richardson and, one of the main subjects of this book, Laurence Olivier. By the end of the Second World War Olivier had been identified as the NT's leader-in-waiting, and in 1946, in his capacity as one of the three co-directors of the Old Vic, he wrote that the theatre had 'for some time been, in people's minds, the National Theatre; it is now destined to be in fact'.[8] Not long after this he was sacked, but the foundations for state funding of the arts had been laid during wartime in CEMA (Council for the Encouragement of Music and the Arts); the forerunner of the Arts Council. In 1949 the National Theatre Bill passed without opposition in the House of Commons prompting one member to fantasize a complex that, in addition to a theatre, would also accommodate 'a small model cinema' in which the Shakespearean presence of its putative director would be ubiquitous: 'It would be interesting to see Sir Laurence Olivier in *Hamlet* on the stage and then go downstairs and see him in *Hamlet* on screen'.[9] Yet the National Theatre was deferred again creating the opportunity for this book's co-star, Peter Hall, to shift the initiative back, initially it seemed decisively, to Stratford-upon-Avon. In 1960 Hall became artistic director of the Shakespeare Memorial Theatre, and in no time he set about transforming what many regarded as an ailing cultural backwater into a national theatre in all but name: acquiring a Royal Charter, renaming the Shakespeare Memorial Theatre as the Royal Shakespeare Theatre, instituting a permanent ensemble company (the Royal Shakespeare Company, or RSC), acquiring a London base in the Aldwych Theatre, expanding the repertoire beyond Shakespeare to incorporate recent European drama and commissioning new playwriting.

A year later, in the context of continued inaction on the part of Harold Macmillan's increasingly enfeebled Conservative government, the Labour-controlled London County Council pledged to meet half the construction costs of the South Bank complex, and the Labour opposition committed a future government to match the funding. Macmillan's chancellor, Selwyn Lloyd, confirmed his government's commitment to the project on the condition that 'the Stratford, Old Vic and Sadler's Wells organisations merged, and only if an opera house was built on the South Bank under the same roof'.[10] This ambitious scheme was soon abandoned and the National Theatre Board was established, with Olivier named as artistic director in 1962. After a try-out season at the Chichester Festival Theatre, the National Theatre Company began operation at the Old Vic in 1963.

This book tells the story from this point until the company moved to the South Bank, which is that of the National Theatre during the most Shakespeare-intensive period in its history. To an extent, the reality of the RSC's assumption of the responsibility of providing a 'house for Shakespeare' set the National on a different path to that envisaged by its originators nearly a century earlier; in theory, at least, the institution was freer to pursue its non-Shakespearean objectives, and it certainly never aimed for the kind of consistency of purpose that was evident in the early years of the RSC. But the Shakespeare work was, nonetheless, a distinctive and in many ways central component of its output during this period. Of the ninety-four in-house shows mounted at the Old Vic eleven were main-stage productions of Shakespeare, three were Mobile (small-scale touring) versions and one was a hugely successful offshoot (*Rosencrantz and Guildenstern are Dead*); between them, they account for nearly 16 per cent of the theatre's output. They include some of the NT's biggest hits of the period – *Rosencrantz and Guildenstern*, Olivier's *Othello* and *The Merchant of Venice*, Franco Zeffirelli's *Much Ado about Nothing*, the all-male *As You Like It* – and some of its best-forgotten flops, among them the inaugural production of *Hamlet*. The chapters that follow consider this work from four angles. Chapter 1 addresses the productions directed by or starring Olivier; Chapter 2 focuses on a single remarkable year (1967) and its aftermath; Chapter 3 looks at the contribution made by visiting European practitioners; and Chapter 4 brings the story to a close with the work of Peter Hall.

The title of this book suggests a study in Shakespearean contrasts between the last of the great, heroic actor-managers and the man who became celebrated (or notorious) as the theatre politician-director to his fingertips, and its narrative traces the passage from the dominance of the one to the ascendancy of the other. Some of the work has been documented at length before (notably, of course, Olivier's two performances); some will be less familiar. In the interests of economy, I assume some familiarity with the broad outlines of the biographies of the key players and of the National Theatre itself in the period; the latter has been told numerous times, but the reader need look no further than Daniel Rosenthal's monumental, definitive *The National Theatre Story* for the context and background to the productions discussed here.[11] I have also paid attention to the stories that lie hidden behind those of the stars, and the image on the facing page (Figure I.1) is one place to start.

FIGURE I.1 *Frank Barrie and Jo Maxwell-Muller in* Rosencrantz and Guildenstern are Dead, *directed by Derek Goldby, 1967. Photograph by Antony Crickmay, courtesy of the V & A Theatre and Performance Collections.*

Few readers will have difficulty placing it: one actor in a dark doublet and another in a spreading white dress can spell only Hamlet and Ophelia in a production dating back, the period styling suggests, some decades. A second look, however, reveals that all is not what it seems: the picture records a scene that in *Hamlet* is described (Ophelia's account of how 'He took me by the wrist and held me hard' [2.1.87]) but not staged, one that is rarely seen in productions of Shakespeare's play.

Actually, the moment is not from *Hamlet* but from the original NT production of *Rosencrantz and Guildenstern are Dead*, a play and a production that contains Shakespeare within it even as it is contained within Shakespeare.

The plot thickens, for Hamlet and Ophelia here are not even the 'original' actors but Frank Barrie, the third to take on the role in the course of a three-year lifespan that took the production through twelve cast permutations, and Jo Maxwell-Muller, its fourth Ophelia.[12] No other trace of their performances in Stoppard's play survives but, in a further twist, Maxwell-Muller's excellent, unnerving Ophelia in Shakespeare's play does. In 1964, Christopher Plummer led a television version filmed at Kronberg Castle, Helsingør; at his insistence Maxwell-Muller was cast as Ophelia, and her mad scene is readily accessible to view online (this version also features Michael Caine's only filmed Shakespearean performance as Horatio). The untold stories of theatre history provide one of the subthemes of this book; another is its counterfactuals, the things that did not take place to allow those that did. These include a film of *Rosencrantz and Guildenstern are Dead* starring Laurence Olivier as the Player, a 1971 production of *Antony and Cleopatra* led by Joan Plowright and paired productions of *The Tempest* and Edward Bond's *Bingo*, both starring John Gielgud; none of these happened, all might have.

The story begins and ends with *Hamlet* and also with two sharply contrasting cultural moments. The National was launched in a climate of optimism, as the product of a political consensus that accounted support for the arts part of a programme of modernization and liberalization that was to some extent reflected in the Shakespearean work it fostered. It ended its stay at the Old Vic at the point when that consensus was on the verge of disintegration, and when the future of the National Theatre itself looked far from certain. Shakespeare's position, at least, was secure but never again would it be so significant.

1

Olivier

Curtain up

The first words belonged to Richard Hampton (Barnardo) and Dan Meaden (Francisco): 'Who's there?' 'Nay, answer me ...' (*Ham*, 1.1.1–2). Spoken just after 6.30 pm on Tuesday 22 October 1963, the lines marked the moment when the National Theatre finally began what was hoped would be a fairly brief residency at the Old Vic, before the move to the as-yet-unbuilt new complex on the South Bank, which would take place 'not before 1967',[1] as rumour had it (and which in the event did not happen until 1976). For the opening night of such a prestigious national cultural venture, it was a low-key affair: according to one report a handful of well-known theatre figures were in attendance, but the 'great first night celebrities were being reserved for the opening of the National Theatre proper', and in the absence of royalty the British establishment was represented by former Conservative chancellor Selwyn Lloyd, 'arriving in a lone shaft of glory from his Treasury days', and showbiz glamour was provided by the popular singer Shirley Bassey, who, 'in a voluminous gold and white theatre coat', could 'not be missed'.[2] The sense of occasion was created more by the awareness that the moment was fraught both with the hopes, dreams, arguments and plans, thwarted and realized, of the past 100 years and with the equivalent hopes and fears for the theatre's future; since the story of the National Theatre thus far had been (and would continue to be) one of deferral and delay, *Hamlet* might have seemed an inevitable opening choice. Two men in the audience, at least, registered the propitiousness of the moment: J. C. Trewin wrote of how the curtain rose to reveal 'Francisco at his watch upon a ramp, massive in hewn stone, curving upward across the stage. The sentry climbed until he was almost out of sight, then Barnardo (Mr Hampton) appeared at the foot of the slope. Silence for a few seconds; suddenly he turned in fear with a shattered, breath-caught cry …'.[3] There was plenty to be nervous, and uncertain, about; and Harold Hobson, likewise, felt the sense of anticipation and foreboding: 'when … I saw the mounting curves of Sean Kenny's dangerous rocks, and the poised figures of the sentinels against the sky, I had a great and perilous emotion of peril, as of one venturing into realms of threatening ambush'.[4] National Theatre, stand and unfold yourself.

As most of the first-night critics agreed it would have been satisfying to report that the NT's opening production, directed by Laurence Olivier himself, was an achievement commensurate with the occasion. This was not at all the case. There were a couple of raves. 'Let those vain minds who vaguely criticise this Hamlet beware the march of time' warned one reviewer, who found the show 'magnificent, beautiful, triumphant, noble', 'brilliantly sane and madly lovely' and 'a milestone in the theatre … a moment when critics in their future greyness will rest their minds when they search for a comparison for some Hamlet yet to be'.[5] Less hyperbolically the *Yorkshire Post* hailed 'the most exciting "Hamlet", I believe, that I have ever seen', and praised its 'superb costumes' and 'tremendous drive, purpose, and poetic intensity'.[6] Other responses were more muted. B. A. Young noted 'a kind of super Old Vic production' of the sort familiar from decades of the theatre's history;[7] and Bamber Gascoigne recorded 'seeing an efficient and at times a most imaginative version', in which Olivier 'is not trying to prove anything new about the play'.[8] For some, this studied neutrality was a virtue; Bernard Levin wrote that there was no 'underlying conception of Shakespeare such as, for instance, informs Mr Peter Hall's work with the Royal Shakespeare', that it was a 'handsome, careful but inescapably superficial reading', and that this was exactly the '*Hamlet* of a kind that the National Theatre ought to be giving us to start with: that is, a meticulously careful, uninterpreted, uncomplicated version'.[9] Hobson concurred, praising Olivier's 'outstanding daring' in shaking 'a rebellious fist in the face of the reigning school of Shakespearean interpretation' by presenting 'a *Hamlet* which will assault the emotions by the sheer force of its acting rather than by its curious titillation of the intellect'.[10]

Olivier attempted to inject a sense of the contemporary in a programme note that compared Shakespeare's protagonist to Jimmy Porter, the verbose anti-hero of John Osborne's *Look Back in Anger* (1956), but the setting and costuming were broadly period-traditional in the most tasteful way imaginable: Kenny's multi-location set, dominated by a large semi-circular ramp that embraced the central acting area and swept up into the flies, was reassuringly monumental and the court was dressed eclectically, 'mostly rich gold-encrusted Caroline, with flashes of Elizabethan ... or 19th-century (hunting habits for the ladies, with smooth Young-Victoria or Lampedusa-period hair do's)'.[11] Trewin admired the arresting visuals,

> the set's wheeling curve; the mounting of the haunted ramparts; the sight of Hamlet, his back against the tower, as he delivers the marking-time 'dram of eale' speech high above the stage; or Fortinbras, his back to us, on the sunlit crest, while below him, Hamlet speaks 'How all occasions'; or Ophelia, as she rushes in her madness, prepared to hurl herself from the stage.[12]

Such moments were almost filmic, and overall both the pictorialism and the gymnastics were not unrelated to the chiaroscuro style and occasional physicality of Olivier's 1948 film ('there is even background music to some of the speeches', it was noted);[13] as Trewin reflected, 'one should not first think of a *Hamlet* for its visual qualities'.[14]

As *The Times* summarized, the production 'bears the stamp of having been put on as a means of exhibiting a number of big names in the most famous and popular work in the classical repertory'.[15] In a starry production (Michael Redgrave as Claudius, Diana Wynyard as Gertrude, Max Adrian as Polonius, Rosemary Harris as Ophelia, and the up-and-coming Robert Stephens, Derek Jacobi and Frank Finlay as, respectively, Horatio, Laertes and First Gravedigger), none was starrier than Peter O'Toole in the lead. Already less stage actor than film star O'Toole acquired the part, Olivier recalled, on a whim; late in 1962, with *Lawrence of Arabia* still running in London's cinemas, he turned up hoping 'to play Hamlet for a short season in the West End some time in the following year' with Olivier directing; 'I said no ... but if he would like his Hamlet to be the opening number for the National Theatre in October I could fix that; so we shook hands on it.'[16] There was some praise for O'Toole's performance, with Levin stating that he 'fits the production effortlessly', and that 'his presence is always princely, his grief finely done, and the rest of his moods almost always convincing',[17] and Gascoigne thought that as 'a Hamlet of action' O'Toole was 'convincing and at ease when there is something for him to do'.[18] O'Toole had a physical swagger that emulated some of Olivier's virtuoso athleticism in the 1937 Old Vic production and subsequent film; but for many, he had not much else. The *Guardian* reviewer described him as 'slightly uncouth' with his 'Adam Faith haircut', 'not innerly poetic' and lacking 'the trick to make the poetry, the reflective poetry, issue from his mouth as is he had just thought of it', but 'found him often very moving all the same'.[19] *The Times*, however, noted the 'hollow laughs, lachrymose delivery, and dejected stance' which 'all seem imposed from without', and 'the brittle staccato rasp which is the stock-in-trade of all Hamlets', all of which were 'conventional' and 'well-worn'.[20] The *New Statesman*'s Roger Gellert was blunter, seeing 'a soppily traditional creature, ravaged and suffused with self-pity' and concluding that it was 'a mess', the result of 'too much fame too quickly come by' which 'have left him unprepared, mentally and technically, for such a part'.[21]

The *Sunday Telegraph*'s Alan Brien was scathing: 'All over the world young men are now acting Hamlet in the bathroom', he declared, and while such 'narcissism' is 'understandable in private' the actor 'who allows himself to fall in love with the role cannot avoid wallowing in self-indulgence. And this is the central weakness of Peter O'Toole's performance':

> he is begging for our affection. An overgrown schoolboy in a Little Lord Fauntleroy suit several sizes too small, with blonde, enamelled hair over shiny blue eyes in kohl-black sockets, his face is screwed in a mask of childish self-pity. He is in search of a mother, not a father, and curls in a foetal ball on the laps of both Ophelia and Gertrude. He is the most cuddlesome of Hamlets.
>
> When Mr O'Toole is not suffering, he is laughing. The first player's concern for Hecuba seems to him such a joke that he can hardly speak for guffaws and he announces 'I die, Horatio' through a cheerful grin. Whenever some speech or action recalls him to his grievances, he signals the melancholy mood by a stiffening of his dangling arms, a rigidity in the half-bent legs, and the gradual focusing of his pupils on the end of his nose.[22]

'This', Brien concluded, channelling Dorothy Parker, 'is the famous running the gamut from A to B'.

Out of his depth in his own vanity project O'Toole was also, some noticed, semi-detached from the rest of the cast; if the intention was to portray a Porter-type misfit, wrote T. C. Worsley, 'he only succeeded in seeming somehow distant from everyone else on the stage – there was no communication with them – and very little with us'.[23] Interviewed just before opening night, O'Toole seemed to admit to his isolation; 'If you want to know what it's like to be lonely, really lonely, try playing Hamlet ... everyone, every other man in the cast, every man in the audience, knows in his heart that he's a better

Hamlet than I am.' It's an original line, at least, and O'Toole had a strategy for dealing with it: 'I know that, with one exception [i.e. Olivier], I'm a better Hamlet than anyone else who will be in that theatre next week.' This attitude, he rather implausibly concluded, was 'not arrogance' but 'the proper kind of irreverence for an actor to have'. Maybe, but the interview suggests another factor in O'Toole's solipsism: depicted leaning 'broodingly on the piano at the back of the saloon bar', he ends 'star[ing] thoughtfully into his glass for a moment' and confesses to seeing his part 'through a glass, darkly'.[24] Already a fully-fledged member of the self-mythologizing class of male actor (there is no female equivalent) known as the 'hell-raiser' (or, more accurately, boorish, tiresomely-indulged drunk), O'Toole appears not to have endeared himself to at least some of his colleagues; recalling the production four decades later cast members depict him 'wallowing in drink' and 'terrifying Derek Jacobi' who, as Laertes, had to fight him in the last scene. 'If he gave me a wink, and he usually did, this wild Irishman, it meant a very hard fight. It was even dangerous to be sitting in the front row'.[25]

According to Robert Stephens, Olivier was all too aware of O'Toole's shortcomings:

> Larry said about three weeks into the run of the opening *Hamlet* that it was the worst production of anything he'd ever seen. And he was the director. I asked him why, and he replied, 'Because I don't have a Hamlet.' Nonetheless O'Toole, who had shot to international screen stardom in the previous year as Lawrence of Arabia, was the most tremendous draw, and tickets were changing hands on the street outside for £60 a piece, a lot of money in those days. Peter simply walked through the role, and didn't really bother with it.[26]

Rumour had it that either O'Toole or the production appealed to a gender-specific audience base: an item in the *Daily Telegraph* a month after opening reported that 'Female interest is very strong. At the "Hamlet" matinee on Saturday nearly three-quarters of the audience were women and girls, and I have heard of two women with stalls for every performance of "Hamlet" since the season started.'[27] Like the audiences, some of the actors were prepared to be wowed; among them Michael Gambon, one of the production's twenty-two-strong supporting cast of 'Soldiers, Court Ladies, Courtiers and Servants', who described O'Toole as 'a god with bright blond hair'.[28]

Whatever its muted significance as an event, Olivier and O'Toole's *Hamlet* probably deserves little further scrutiny as either a directorial or an acting achievement; and to this extent it serves mainly as prologue to the main action of this chapter, and of this book. Before moving on to this, however, I want to take the opportunity to reflect upon two of its untold stories – stories which, writ large, stand for the hidden narratives that lie behind the events recounted in the pages that follow. The first of these involves a return to the production's first moments. As noted above J. C. Trewin was very taken with the opening ('no one with the smallest grain of theatrical imagination can fail to have felt the pulse of excitement') and in particular with Richard Hampton, 'a splendid young Shakespearean', who 'will have much to do in years ahead' but would be unlikely to 'know again a moment so exciting'.[29] Trewin was both right and wrong: Hampton would, indeed, find much to do but as far as his Shakespearean acting career was concerned the words that he roared from the foot of Kenny's ramp were its high point. Hampton, who was sturdy enough to understudy Jacobi's Laertes, had various small parts during the first NT season and composed the music for *The Recruiting Officer* and *Othello*; thereafter, he worked mostly in television and film.

His partner in the opening exchange, Dan Meaden, fared a little better garnering walk-on roles in the first season and returning as a member of the Watch in *Much Ado about Nothing* in 1965; beyond the NT he had steady employment as a screen actor and worked for many years at the RSC, graduating from the ranks of spear-carriers to play Williams in *Henry V* and the Host of the Garter in *The Merry Wives of Windsor* (both 1975); and, more noticeably, a drag Mistress Overdone in *Measure for Measure* (1974). He was seen in *Hamlet* again, first as the Norwegian Captain in the BBC/Time-Life Television Shakespeare (1980) and then as Claudius in an ill-fated production led by Edward Fox at the Young Vic (1982). When he died in 2011 his obituary referred to his appearance in the Bond film *Never Say Never Again* (1983) as a career highlight (he is credited as 'Bouncer at Casino'), but asserts that Meaden was 'most proud of his stage appearances'; and that from start to finish he was 'passionate about the work of Shakespeare and did all he could to dispel the view that the playwright was somehow elitist'.[30] There is no reason to doubt his commitment, and it is in its own way evidence that the story of Shakespeare at the National Theatre is as much that of Richard Hampton, Dan Meaden and dozens of unmarked others as it is of Laurence Olivier, Maggie Smith, Anthony Hopkins and Joan Plowright. Olivier, to his credit, intuited this: there are many anecdotal accounts of his efforts to bring what Simon Callow calls 'a little touch of Larry' to company life by, for example, lunching in the canteen, 'generally choosing to sit with the ushers or the box-office staff, in his kindly bank-manager persona, taking an interest, trying valiantly and not entirely successfully to remember each one'.[31] A decade later, the director John Dexter credited Olivier with 'an unspoken sense of the need for community within the theatre which would enable the company to become a social unit as interloving and hating as family'; but while 'always inspiring', he was 'often ignorant of the sacrifices of personal life that were made and often cavalier in his treatment'.[32]

Dexter's differences with Olivier were more sharply manifested during the production which is the subject of the next section, *Othello*. Following one early performance, Dexter gave notes which castigated the cast for 'lack of focus, sloppiness, and many other faults'; confronted by a furious Olivier ('How dare you speak to my company that way'), Dexter responded: 'It is not your company. It is the National

Theatre Company, and the sooner you stop regarding it as yours, the better.'[33] Both, in their own way, were right: for the NT to achieve its historic mission of becoming a 'national' theatre in anything like the sense originally envisaged, the institution had to matter more than the individual leading it; yet it was unquestionably Olivier's energy and example that drove the work during the first ten years. It did not help that by the time that the NT opened at the Old Vic there was already a *de facto* national theatre in operation across the river at the Aldwych, and on the banks of another river in Stratford-upon-Avon in the form of the three-year-old Royal Shakespeare Company led by Peter Hall. Placing Shakespeare at the centre of its activities, assiduously cultivating a permanent ensemble while also paying attention to ongoing actor training and fostering both contemporary European work and new British playwriting, the RSC was already fulfilling most of the functions of a national theatre, and more. What, in these circumstances, was Olivier's National for? Dexter's characterization of Olivier as 'cavalier', perhaps unconsciously, echoes the terminology used by NT dramaturg Kenneth Tynan to distinguish his own theatre's work from that of his rivals; 'We are the Cavaliers, Stratford ... the Roundheads',[34] as he said more than once. For Tynan, this meant an adventurousness and flamboyance of style that was lacking in what he saw as the dour, puritanical and risk-averse work of the RSC. Whether this was sufficient as a definition of the NT's own output is open to debate; and the historical analogy is not the most fortunate since it was, after all, the Roundheads that prevailed.

Hamlet, arguably, was more Hampton's and Meaden's than it was O'Toole's; for not a few spectators it was even more the *Hamlet* of Rosemary Harris who, as Ophelia, appears to have acted the leading man off the stage. Reporting at the end of 1964 the New York Drama Critic of *The Times* reviewed her in an off-Broadway Shaw revival where, in the 'minor role of Violet', she 'persuaded many that *Man and Superman* is fundamentally a play about a girl called Violet', which was 'not very different from her brilliant work at the National Theatre a year ago, when many came away with the impression that *Hamlet* is a play about Ophelia'.[35] Played as a lady-in-waiting to Gertrude, Harris's Ophelia was 'a violent and marvellous departure from the traditional reading'; a 'figure of frustrated sweetness to begin with', who in her madness became 'a creature of sexual vindictiveness who approaches the King like a prostitute and accompanies the exit line "Goodnight sweet ladies" with an obscene hand gesture'.[36] For Gascoigne, her mad scene was 'done without a trace of balletic wispiness' and thus 'extremely touching';[37] B. A. Young admired the 'really noteworthy' depiction of 'a deb with a suppressed taste for the bawdy that is embarrassingly set free when madness overtakes her';[38] and Trewin traced the move from 'a curious early greyness' to a mad scene that was 'both unexpected and uncompromising'.[39]

How much more contemporary, and dangerous, was her performance than that of the star is evident from David Pryce-Jones's identification of Harris as the 'one person who was never operatic', 'a waif and a courtier, whenever she entered the scene, the human element and the tragedy came with her. This was real at last'.[40] Noting how she 'appears in a loose buff bodice and tucked-up skirts, rubs herself amorously against Claudius and treats Gertrude with vicious spitefulness', Harris's 'harrowingly unsentimental' performance, wrote Gellert, was 'the best of the evening'. A comparison with the lacklustre O'Toole ('the most limp-wristed Hamlet of recent years') was inevitable: the 'nunnery scene, on Ophelia's side at least, is played with considerable feeling, like a frustrated love scene, and her madness is suggested as beginning from that point'.[41] For Robert Speaight,

> the performance – indeed the event – of the evening was Miss Rosemary Harris's Ophelia. Far from turning 'hell itself' to 'favour and to prettiness', her mad scene showed the fury of sexual frustration working on a nature too delicate to sustain the double shock of her father's death and Hamlet's repudiation. She revealed Ophelia as a tragic contrast and

companion to Hamlet himself – the one succumbing to total madness, the other taking refuge in a feigned lunacy, both unhinged, and both defeated in their struggle with unkindly fate. Miss Harris not only played the part with superb originality, but she raised it to a new importance.[42]

What the production's women-dominated audiences made of this unprecedentedly frank exploration of female desire cannot be known, but it calls to mind contemporary accounts of the sexual frenzies unleashed in pop-concert auditoria as discussed by historian Dominic Sandbrook: noting that press coverage 'focused on the way in which teenage girls responded to their idols, which most observers described simply as "hysteria"', he writes that 'Since there had already been several long debates in the press about teenage sexual precocity, it was no surprise that some commentators chose to interpret the girls' "hysteria" as a sexual phenomenon.'[43] Perhaps Harris was giving a voice and a body to something larger, and much more immediate, than Ophelia's character and Shakespeare's play. Harris, at least, did have a bright future ahead of her but it was not to be realized at the National. In addition to Ophelia she completed her first season playing Ilyena in *Uncle Vanya* and the First Woman in Beckett's *Play*, and then moved to New York for a long and distinguished Broadway and film career. It was New York's gain, and the National Theatre's loss.

Blacking up

They might have got away with it if it hadn't been filmed. If, as for most of the Shakespeare productions staged during the NT's history, the only traces to survive of Olivier's *Othello* were the verbal and visual production records, the reviews, and other writings from memory (including Olivier's own autobiography) we might have a very different picture of the production and, crucially, its central performance. Filmed in

1965, while the stage production still had more than a year to run, Stuart Burge's record of John Dexter's staging mercilessly exposes what most viewers now regard as an embarrassing, offensive, hideously unwatchable racist travesty; a portrayal that, as Barbara Hodgdon puts it, 'confirms an absolute fidelity to white stereotypes of blackness, and to the fantasies, cultural as well as theatrical, that such stereotypes engender'.[44] Olivier, as we shall see, believed he was doing quite the opposite; we can begin to position this production historically by recognizing that, in the first instance, a significant number of his contemporaries appeared to agree with him.

Olivier's *Othello*, which opened at the Old Vic on 21 April after two weeks of preview performances on tour in Birmingham, had been long awaited and no commentators saw anything awry in the casting of Britain's leading white male actor in the role. Interviewed by the *Daily Mail*, Olivier admitted that he had 'put it off because I think it's pretty well unplayable. It's a terrible study and a monstrous burden for the actor', and, quoting Anthony Quayle declared that it was 'as bad as Titus Andronicus, only you have to black up as well'.[45] The assumption that Othello is a part for a white actor is shared in, for example, W. A. Darlington's *Daily Telegraph* review which situates Olivier in a pantheon of greats that includes Frederick Valk, Donald Wolfit, Orson Welles, Jack Hawkins, John Gielgud, Ralph Richardson, Wilfred Walter and Godfrey Tearle ('easily the greatest Othello of my experience'), but not Paul Robeson, who had returned to England to play the role at the Shakespeare Memorial Theatre only five years previously. Darlington was one of those who thought that 'Moor' should be parsed as 'Arab' since it enabled the actor to 'retain his own personality', whereas 'as a Negro, he must disguise himself elaborately': 'generally, you expect a Negro in the grip of a violent emotion to lose control of himself'.[46]

Such casual and overt racism was not widespread but the nature and range of critical reactions to Olivier's blacking up, which most saw as in no way problematic, suggest its subtler manifestations. For a handful of reviewers, race did not feature; in a lengthy notice Trewin did not mention it at all, stressing rather that in his appearance Olivier was 'an Othello who fetches his life and being from men of royal siege'.[47] Levin, similarly, completely ignores the issue in his account of 'Sir Laurence's masterpiece' wherein 'every line, every gesture, is fresh-studied, freshly meaningful'.[48] Even so, there was a tendency for raced vocabulary to emerge in code: Trewin refers to the 'barbaric music' and 'deities of a primeval darkness', and Levin writes that in Othello's raging 'it is as though a wild beast has been sewn up inside him and is clawing to get out'; while the *Spectator* reviewer invoked a discourse of primitivism, animality and savagery in his impression of Olivier 'being about to spring like a black panther', roaming a set that 'gives him a far exit either to bedroom or to castle wall, a retreat like the inside kennel of a zoo-house'.[49]

Some addressed Olivier's makeup and vocal and physical work directly. *The Times* noted the 'measured deliberation and a new lower resonance' and the 'range of movements organically related to the part: a stance with feet apart and trunk thrown forward, and a use of oblique arm gestures and flattened palms of the hand' (a gesture, palm-up, that Olivier had frequently deployed in the past);[50] the *Guardian* the 'negroid speech and easy, generous, frank and easily articulated gait and physically imposed authority';[51] and the *Observer* the 'hairless shins, drooping eyelids, the stipulated "thick lips" of the text'.[52] The *Observer*'s Bamber Gascoigne was among those who worried that this was potentially offensive but, like Ronald Bryden in the *New Statesman*, he was persuaded that what 'could have been caricature, an embarrassment' was anything but: 'after the second performance', Bryden reported, 'a well-known Negro actor rose in the stalls bravoing'.[53] The comment is presumably well-meant, but it is telling that Byrden does not afford this actor the courtesy of a name the mere fact of his blackness being sufficient to define him. For Gascoigne, Olivier's Othello was 'firmly real' but for Bryden ('He was the continent, like a figure of Rubens allegory') and others the power of the performance stemmed from its capacity to transcend the real and occupy the realm of myth: 'larger than life', as Levin put it, 'bloodier than death, more piteous than pity'.[54]

Yet Bryden also commended Olivier for the precisely-observed accuracy of his portrait, speculating that the actor 'had made it difficult and interesting for himself by studying ... how an African looks, moves, sounds' to 'turn himself into a coastal African from below the Senegal: dark, thick-lipped, open, laughing'.[55] The combination of stereotyping generalization ('an African') and faux-authoritative specificity ('a coastal African from below the Senegal') is found in other descriptions, which (sometimes simultaneously) identify Olivier's Moor as African, West Indian and black American: 'a handsome black ebony statue that comes to life with a sauntering graceful walk and the faintest lilt of a West Indian accent',[56] 'the easy hip-swinging lope of the African ... the bent, bizarre vocals of some Caribbean tongue',[57] 'a prince of darkest Africa on whom the veneer of Venetian manners has only a precarious hold ... moving with a rhythmic, loose-jointed gait more West Indian than African';[58] 'sinuous movement, the pendulous limp, the head lowered in anger like a buffalo about to charge – these are Negro in origin, certainly, but they owe as much to Africa as to the West Indies', even if Olivier's first entrance, 'trailing a flower in his hand, leaning idly against a doorpost and giggling under his breath, certainly owes more to Harlem than Mauretania'.[59]

Challenging as it is to imagine Olivier inhabiting this hybrid diasporic multiple identity anywhere outside a racial imaginary wherein a critic can refer to 'the very essence of what it means to be born with a dark skin',[60] the responses are informed both by the conflicts and anxieties of a nation struggling with its own experience of decolonization and immigration and by white British culture's difficulty with envisaging blackness other than in terms of spectacle, masquerade and mimicry. The year 1962 saw the passing of the Commonwealth Immigrants Act, the first-ever Act of Parliament aimed at limiting the numbers of migrants from Britain's former colonies, and when Labour in 1964 succeeded the Conservative government that had introduced it the decision to retain it indicated the consensus across the two parties over the issue. That year, with *Othello* in the NT repertory, the electoral contest in the Midlands constituency of Smethwick became a by-word for the state of race relations in Britain, with the Conservative candidate Peter Griffiths notoriously trading on the slogan 'If you want a n—— for a neighbour vote Labour.' In 1965, in the context of a programme of liberalization that also led two years on to the abolition of the death penalty, the decriminalization of sex between men and the Abortion Act, the first Race Relations Act was passed, which 'enshrined the principle of ending discrimination against black immigrants on the grounds of race'.[61] Meanwhile, the long-running stage celebration of blackface minstrelry, *The Black and White Minstrel Show*, was in the third of the ten years that it ran at the Victoria Palace Theatre; the television version, which started in 1958, ran until 1978. The September 1964 issue of *Plays and Players* featured a cartoon depicting a smartly-dressed, middle-aged couple emerging arm in arm from the Old Vic, with the woman, rolling her eyes heavenward, saying 'You know, I don't think I'll ever be able to enjoy the Black and White Minstrels again!' while her husband looks on in bemusement. The joke is not entirely clear (is Olivier being sent up, or the Minstrels, or both?), but the broad sentiment seems to be that blackface and the racism that sustained and was sustained by it needed at the very least another look. It would take a long time for majority opinion to come round to this view.

The reviewers' contradictory reactions to Olivier's racial impersonation to some extent mirrored his own conflicts. In his autobiography he professes that the decision to black up, taken in agreement with Dexter, was motivated by liberal anti-racism (though he doesn't use this term): 'the modern trend towards a pale coffee-coloured compromise, a natural aristocrat ... was a cop-out, arising out of some feeling that the Moor could not be thought a truly *noble* Moor if he was too black and in too great a contrast to the noble whites; a shocking case of pure snobbery'.[62] In *On Acting*, he documents the cosmetic work that this entailed:

> On the first night, I was in the theatre several hours before, creating the image which now looked back at me from the mirror. Black all over my body, Max Factor 2880, then a lighter brown, then Negro Number 2, a stronger brown. Brown on black to give a rich mahogany. Then the great trick: that glorious half yard of chiffon with which I polished myself all over until I shone ... if you use this wonderful bit of chiffon, it gleams a smooth ebony. The lips blueberry, the tight curled wig, the white of the eyes, whiter than ever, and the black, black sheen that covered my flesh and bones, glistening in the dressing-room lights ... I am ... I am, I ... I am Othello ... but Olivier is in charge. The actor is in control. The actor breathes into the nostrils of the character and the character comes to life. Othello is my character for this moment in my time – he is mine. He belongs to no one else, he belongs to me.[63]

Commenting on this passage Hodgdon writes that Olivier's efforts to achieve 'an ultimate cultural impersonation', 'as though mimicry might efface notions of difference', produce a power relationship in which Othello ('He belongs to me') virtually becomes 'colonial property'.[64] Certainly this is what Olivier attempts to assert, but even within his own account there is a countervailing insecurity: the harder he works to claim the other as self the more it reveals its resistance, the absolute alterity of 'the image which now looked back at me from the mirror'. For Olivier blackness is a gestural repertoire, a vocal register and, crucially, a skin colour that can be precisely commoditized and branded (Max Factor 2880, Negro Number 2); he represents himself reaching *down*, lowering both his voice ('he had a deeper voice than mine. Bass, bass part, a sound that should be dark velvet') and his centre of gravity ('He should grow from the earth, the rich brown earth, warmed by the sun'),[65] by blacking *up*, paradoxically searching the deep truth of character through the painstaking accumulation of layers.

The term that dominates the account is 'control': 'Olivier is in charge. The actor is in control'; 'Come back to the text, do not drift. You are only good if you are in control. Every moment you must be in complete control';[66] it hardly needs stating that the insistence on control, mastery and ownership suggests a degree of uncertainty as to who is actually in charge. There are, Olivier reflects, moments 'when I think I am Othello, when I think am convinced I am black', and also moments when 'I begin to think that Shakespeare is playing Iago and I am playing Burbage.'[67] At another level, this recasts the participants in another power struggle: Olivier and Kenneth Tynan. At the beginning of his essay on Othello, Olivier reveals that his dramaturg had made it a condition of his appointment that he would play the role within five years and that it 'had never occurred to me': 'I felt that Othello was a loser from the word go ... It's a very badly designed role', and it was 'Iago's piece'.[68] Although he accepted the challenge of necessity, Olivier indicates that he never felt that he had full ownership of it: his piece ends with a salutation: 'Dear Ken, your contract is fulfilled ...'.[69] To put it another way: 'Will you, I pray, demand that demi-devil / Why he hath thus ensnared my soul and body?' (5.2.300–1).

Tynan himself kept a rehearsal diary for the two months from first reading to first night, and at times his narrative of the process is couched as an Iago–Othello dynamic: recalling that it had not been easy to lure Olivier into the part, he speculates that 'perhaps, deep in his personal labyrinth, where the minotaur of his talent lurks, he had already decided, and merely wanted to be coached'[70] ('As if there were some monster in thy thought / Too hideous to be shown' [3.3.110–11]). Tynan states that Dexter had announced at the first reading that the production drew upon F. R. Leavis's reading of *Othello*, to the effect that Othello was 'a man essentially narcissistic and self-dramatising ... a pompous, word-spinning, arrogant black general', and almost immediately registers the risks inherent in this: watching Olivier as 'bespectacled and lounge-suited, he fell on the text like a tiger', he wonders if this 'triumphant back despot, aflame with self-regard' might 'verge too closely for comfort to comedy'.[71] Mesmerized by the spectacle of 'a great classical actor in full spate' Tynan discerns a complex, almost metatheatrical, layering in Olivier's performance of race, seeing him before the Senate (1.2) as 'a Negro sophisticated enough to conform to the white myth about Negroes, pretending to be simple and not above rolling his eyes, but in fact concealing (like any other aristocrat) a highly developed sense of racial superiority', so that 'he is at once the Duke's servant and the white man's master'. 'This will not be a sentimental reading of the part, not one that white liberals will necessarily applaud' (though, as we have seen, most of them did).[72] At the same time (and the considerations are interconnected), Tynan worries that the performance of self-dramatization is liable to misreading. 'Query: will the public and critics realise that this is an egocentric Othello, not an egocentric performance? ... it is Othello, not Olivier, who is indulging himself emotionally. Question: yes, but will the audience know the difference?'[73]

Reviewers and audiences would not have been aware of either Olivier's conflicts or Tynan's doubts but between them they highlight the fissures within a performance, and a production, that divided responses in part because they were themselves divided. For all the critics who declared themselves convinced by Olivier's performance, there were others who either harboured doubts or were emphatically unpersuaded. For John Gardner of the *Stratford-upon-Avon Herald*, 'my mind, of its own volition, returned blasphemously to Mr Jack Benny's Rochester, or the physio-vocal picture of *The Black and White Minstrels*'.[74] In an otherwise enthusiastic review, the *Daily Sketch* regretted that when Olivier 'looked at us full face he presented us with the ludicrous picture of Al Jolson in place of the tortured Moor';[75] but Milton Shulman, revisiting the production when it transferred to Chichester for a summer run, was relieved to report that 'the occasional similarities to a Christie minstrel – the slow drawl, the O-shaped grin, the soft-shoe shuffle – had all but disappeared'.[76] Alan Brien, on the other hand, was less concerned with the resemblance to white blackface performance than with the 'perfunctory' echoes of black performers: 'the combination of a Louis

Armstrong guttural voice and a Stepin Fetchit sway'.[77] The second comparison is particularly damning; Stepin Fetchit, the film persona of Lincoln Theodore Monroe Andrew Perry, was (and remains) a hugely controversial black vaudeville and film performer, celebrated in the 1920s for his stereotype-reinforcing portrayal of 'The Laziest Man in the World'.

There is one piece of anecdotal evidence that suggests that Olivier was himself at least partially aware that his performance of race risked offence. Narrating the circumstances that led to his casting as Coriolanus at the National in 1971 (as discussed in Chapter 3), Christopher Plummer recalls visiting Olivier in his dressing room after an *Othello* matinee:

> A dresser was busy removing Larry's black makeup, an ordeal that seemed to take forever. 'You weren't out front today, I hope', Larry screeched, 'Oh myyy Gawd! They booed me, dear! They booed me! They think I'm a racist pig, darling, a racist pig!' When Larry was in an exuberant mood, he would often assume this pseudocamp performance, which was miles over the top. He told a few off-colour jokes and then we fell into silence. His dresser was having the deuce of a time trying to remove the makeup – it wasn't coming off at all easily. What could this mean? Black Equity's revenge?[78]

Given that there is no situation in Plummer's self-narration in which he does not have the upper hand, the story has debatable status as evidence; but, to adopt a formulation established in the heyday of new historicism, whether it is true or false matters less than that it is imaginable: an Olivier trapped within an assumed skin, booed rather than cheered, an actor and an embodiment of an acting tradition whose time had passed.

Having produced great copy in response to O'Toole, Brien rose to the occasion again as one of the few reviewers to slate Olivier's performance; and his grounds for doing so reveal exactly why it was so compelling to everyone else. Brien's opening gambit is that there is 'a kind of bad acting of which only a great actor is capable', and that Othello was 'the most prodigious and perverse example of this in a decade'. Olivier, Brien declares, 'is the romantic gymnast of our stage, the noblest Roman wrestler of them all':

> He can press his own weight in blank verse and hurl a soliloquy like a javelin until it sinks up to the haft in the back row of the gallery ... Olivier is born to action, bred for speed. In *Othello*, he runs the gamut on the spot. It is a spectacular demonstration of static exercise like a man racing up a down escalator or rowing with perforated paddles in a chained skiff ... as the jealousy is transfused into his blood, the white man shows through more obviously. He begins to double and treble his vowels, to stretch his consonants, to stagger and shake, even to vomit, near the frontiers of self-parody. His hips oscillate, his palms rotate, his voice skids and slides so that the Othello music takes on a Beatle beat.[79]

Brien's dialectic of badness and greatness registers the charismatic power of an actor who is at once both black and white, and neither, performing an acting workout that simultaneously encompasses the heights of tragic sublime and the lowest lows of popular performance, unsettling oppositions even in the act of enforcing them. His attentiveness to Olivier's athleticism, his 'hydraulic fluidity of physical grace', foregrounds another important element; one that perhaps even more fully defines the difference between the experience of its live performance and that of watching the film. For Olivier, as far is *Othello* is concerned, the actor–audience relationship is an eroticized power struggle, a game of dominance and submission in which the performer and the spectator alternate the roles of seducer and the seduced:

> An audience will encourage you to show the extent of your powers, willing you and wooing you to do so, but an audience is like Iago himself; once having got you to open your heart, it will eat your entrails. You, the actor, must

always be on top. Show a glimpse, flirt, live dangerously, but never take your trousers off. Let them think that you are always just about to. Let them beg. Let them come back for more. Always the encore.[80]

Aptly for an Othello envisaged as all body the wooing process is a matter of sequenced physical action, 'careful timing and delicate use of rhythm', that lures the audience from the safe space of naturalism wherein Othello makes his first entrance 'as the most real person the audience has ever seen' (Olivier flicking a single red rose), into somewhere much sexier, charged and dangerous, as 'bit by bit, when I'd won their confidence, I would be able to start riding them'.[81]

Olivier's vision of the actor and his public is rooted in bodily co-presence, and to state that to fully apprehend the power of his Othello you had to be in the room seems like mere common sense. I want, however, to reinforce this claim and also attempt to account for that singular power by placing it within a model of the performer–audience relationship that originated within dance studies, and which is increasingly being employed by theatre scholars: kinaesthetic empathy. Dance historian Susan Leigh Foster summarizes:

> Early twentieth century dance theorist John Martin argued for a vital rapport between dancer and viewer and an equally basic connection between movement and emotion. Dance, he explained, conveys meaning because viewers, even though sitting in their seats, feel the movements and consequently the emotions of the dancer. Now at the beginning of the twenty-first century neurophysiologists are likewise claiming an intrinsic connectivity between dancer and viewer based on the discovery of mirror neurons – synaptic connections in the cortex that fire both when one sees an action and when one does that action.[82]

The physicality of performance stimulates muscle awareness and memory in the viewer; the effect on Olivier's audiences, the vocabulary of the reviews suggests, was somatic, visceral, immersive with superlatives like 'stupendous' and 'titanic' wielded without reservation; 'feeling so deeply moved by, and totally committed to, the portrayal', wrote one reviewer, 'I wanted to laugh and cry when Othello and Desdemona laughed and cried';[83] 'As the words flood from his tormented lips we are lost' wrote another.[84] Olivier's bodily commitment instigated an equivalent physical demonstrativeness in his, literally, 'moved' spectators. In the first of two reviews, Trewin reported that at the end of the first night performance 'I never in my life heard such a roar of cheering ... At the back of the Old Vic they were standing to shout ... on Olivier's personal call it swelled to the sustained thunder that is one of the rarest and most exciting sounds in the living theatre.'[85]

It was not only on the first night that this happened: show reports regularly document up to ten additional curtain calls, and when the production visited Moscow in September 1965 the calls were followed by a further ten minutes of applause. Trewin reiterated this sentiment in his second review, stating that 'For many years I have listened to cheering in the theatre; only three nights have ever come within measurable distance of the salute to Olivier.' 'It was not "fan" hysteria', he insists, 'it was the acknowledgment of one performance of genius'. The review that effected the fullest erasure of race, Trewin's notice was also the one that best articulated the sense of an event more akin to musical performance than character acting:

> I think of the third-act 'Farewell' which sounds every clarion, billows out to the skies at 'Jove's great clamour counterfeits', and ends, as Kean ended, on a 'Farewell' lingering and elongated, the cry from a stricken heart. Even finer is the 'Pontic sea', where the icy current and compulsive course ne'er feels retiring ebb, but grows and rages in its desperate flood as the lines, unpunctuated now and magnificently vowelled – observe Olivier's treatment of the reiterated 'o' – swell forward to the Propontic and the Hellespont. Then, suddenly, there is the isolation, the yearning, the agonised

recollection on the two words 'humble love'. Again the flood beats down everything before it: 'Till that a capable and wide revenge swallow them up.'[86]

Oliver's capacity to pass, or not, as a black man was only the starting point, and the springboard for a leap into the beyond.

None of this excuses what remains a deeply problematic performance; but, at the least, it enables us to situate it historically, and, as a phenomenon that was not just seen but *felt*, to find the response of its original witnesses comprehensible (that said, the British tradition of white actors blacking up to play Othello continued after Olivier, for more than a decade, with Paul Scofield at the National itself in 1980 as one the last of the practitioners to do so). It also suggests that by naively supposing that a raw, un-cinematic, 'theatrical' treatment would directly and accurately capture its essence, the decision to film the performance not only missed the point but also actively did Olivier a disservice. Reviewers immediately seized upon the disparity between style and medium (Olivier had 'not attempted to scale his performance down for the camera', commented *The Times*, and the result was 'almost too overpowering'),[87] and upon the offensiveness of a portrayal that, in the words of Bosley Crowther of the *New York Times*, offered

> the by-now outrageous impression of a theatrical Negro stereotype. He does not look like a Negro (if that's what he's aiming to make the Moor) – not even a West Indian chieftain, which some of the London critics likened him to. He looks like a Rastus or an end man in an American minstrel show. You almost wait for him to whip a banjo out from his flowing, white garments or start banging a tambourine.[88]

Unsurprisingly, time has not been kind to Burge's film of Olivier's performance, which remains a touchstone in the ongoing arguments over the casting of the play. Had it never been filmed, it might have been remembered very differently.

Lighting up

Taken during a hiatus in rehearsals, the photograph shown in Figure 1.1 catches Olivier and Maggie Smith apparently off-guard; he in an extravagantly white-trimmed knee-length dressing gown, open almost to the waist to reveal the full body makeup, she in pale, very contemporary shirt and slacks leaning her cheek, as if for much-needed support, against his right shoulder. They are on a cigarette break: she dangles a slim cylinder in her drooping right hand as she stares blankly into the middle distance he, meanwhile, leaning slightly off-kilter, gazes coolly at the camera, meeting the viewer's gaze as he takes a deep drag on a stubby butt held between the splayed fingers of his left hand. At first glance it seems a liminal, in-between moment: Olivier and Smith both as themselves and half-in, half-out of, role, the relaxed intimacy of their wordless tryst bespeaking a sense of colleagues both at ease and hard at work. It looks like a captured, candid, behind-the-scenes moment of spontaneity, but the longer you look the less convincing this seems. There is something about the angle of Olivier's head so that it plunges his eyes into deep shadow and frames the dark centre of his forehead with strips of light, creating an effect of skin that is both black and white, something in the exquisite colour match of the white of the cigarette to the cuffs and belt of the dressing-gown and something about the muscular tension visible in those spread fingers that together suggest that Olivier, at least, is not here, and perhaps never, 'off', whether in role or not.

Fully made up, chiffon-buffed to a sheen, Olivier (perhaps also styling himself after 'the greatest', the boxer soon to rename himself as Mohammed Ali) is already deep in the Othello zone, and there are various ways in which this picture tells the production's story of race. Not the least of these is the consciously-performed, and emphatically masculine, act of smoking itself which, as purveyed by his own-brand filter-tips, was part of Olivier's celebrity persona but also, in this instance, a display of power: I may be caked in Max Factor 2880 and Negro Number 2, the stance says, but by smoking

FIGURE 1.1 *Maggie Smith and Laurence Olivier during a break in rehearsals for* Othello, *directed by John Dexter, 1964. Photograph by Roddy McDowell, courtesy of the National Theatre Archive.*

in and through them I am still the master of, and in, this skin. As objects in themselves the cigarettes in this picture play their whiteness against Olivier's assumed blackness, and also participate in the play's transgressive, diabolical, destructive power, what Richard Klein in his classic study of the representation of smoking calls 'a darkly beautiful, inevitably painful pleasure that arises from some intimation of eternity', whereby 'the taste of infinity ... resides precisely in the "bad" taste the smoker quickly learns to love'.[89]

I want to think about the other story that it tells, which is also central to the production but less commented upon, which is one of gender. Consider Maggie Smith's cigarette, unlike Olivier she is not at that moment smoking but in a gesture that perfectly counterpoints the assertive inhalation exercised by him, it is absently balanced between fore and index fingers, her thumb poised to flick ash floorward. As a woman-who-smokes, Smith occupies a position which, as Klein shows, has a long history of gendered over-determination, in that 'even today, when a woman smokes she is seen as performing a brazen, transgressive act': 'Lighting a cigarette is a demonstration of mastery that violates the assumptions of feminine *pudeur*, the delicate embarrassment women are expected to feel, or at least display, in the presence of what their innocence and dignity are supposed to prevent them from desiring.'[90] But how to interpret Smith's posture, her facial expression? There is, perhaps, a sense of dependency, even submissiveness in her leaning against Sir's shoulder, but her expression is not easy to read: is she lost in thought or exhausted, anxious, fed up? Whatever else she is doing, Smith is not conforming to the standard Desdemona template – certainly not as it was understood in 1964.

Smith subsequently offered some reminiscences of the work she undertook with Olivier, but they are strangely oblique. Confessing that she was 'terrified' of playing her first major Shakespearean part, she remembers visiting him as he applied the makeup, to take notes, and 'to help him put on his false eyelashes'. On one occasion, these two actions unexpectedly converged, when he warned her to 'take care with your vowels'; 'I glued the eyelashes on and we looked at each other in the dressing room mirror. The effect was stunning.' As Smith takes charge of the woman's work of cosmetic prosthetics she stages another mirror-moment, this time involving a sudden, unexpected unsettling of gender binaries; as Smith and Olivier exchange glances with their own and each other's alter-egos, and, for an instant, both are women. What followed was bizarre; a little stung by Olivier's remark, Smith recites the archest, most old-fashioned of elocution exercises: 'How now Brown Cow'; Olivier responds with approval ('much better'), and Smith concedes, 'Well, it was a weak joke ... why should he find it funny?' Weak or not, it was apt: racialized, feminized and animalized, the butt of the gag, the 'Brown Cow', is Olivier. The ultimate pay-off is even more of a non-sequitur. Later, when it came to the line 'Honey, you shall be well desired in Cyprus' (2.1.203), Olivier – according to Smith – suddenly got the joke, and dried: '"Honey you shall be well desired in ..." his eyes rolled and his mind had gone quite blank ... and then he said with full force and total conviction and courage: "... PARIS!"'.[91]

In the light of the foregoing, the best (or the worst) I can do with this anecdote is that it suggests the Bogart and Bacall of *Casablanca*, another iconic, nicotine-rich romantic couple for whom Paris will always be a treasured shared memory. A better option, probably, is to regard it as another of those moments in the life of the production when the mask slipped, on this occasion when Olivier was wrong-footed by the actor who had better claim than most (certainly better than the production's Iago, Frank Finlay) to be regarded as his co-star. The majority of the reviews were, inevitably, dominated by Olivier and either briefly addressed Smith's work or did not mention it at all. Some found in Smith the conventional feminine virtues that quietly complemented Olivier's rampages: Levin admired a 'near-perfect wife' of 'great sweetness, that never cloys', and 'a beautiful, still certainty that turns into more heart-rending loss';[92] the *Yorkshire Evening Post* saw 'a wife as true as she is genuinely enchanting';[93] and Alan Dent recorded a 'tall, sweet and very loving Desdemona'.[94] Others registered someone less submissive, more contemporary and more interesting. B. A. Young thought that her 'regal carriage and steely voice' were 'well suited to this tough lady who, listening to Othello's tales, sighed first for the pity of them, and sighed then that she could not take part in them', and while the part was 'a very tearful one for a potential Amazon', Smith 'comes out like a trumpet with "By Heaven, you do me wrong!"'[95]

The *Times* critic, by contrast, registered the assertiveness but disapproved, complaining that as 'a mettlesome girl who would not for an instant have endured domestic tyranny', Smith 'introduces facetious modern inflections' that 'clash destructively with the character'.[96] For Bamber Gascoigne the performance was 'a most spectacular triumph', and he identified 4.3 as a highlight wherein Smith's 'stillness, the very opposite of her style of comedy, seemed to make auditorium holds its breath in the willow song scene; even the most ordinary words, such as "Nay, that's not next", when she sings a wrong line, became inexplicably poignant'. In this Smith was strongly supported by Joyce Redman's Emilia, who 'with Desdemona kneeling at her feet, managed brilliantly to speak her polemic about men's infidelity in such a way as even then not to break the mood'.[97]

One critic went as far as to state that the pair between them gave the production's 'most satisfying performances', Smith being 'an actress able to run chills up and down her spine every time she drops her voice' and Redman's Emilia 'a three-dimensional figure' who 'in her final scene with the dying Desdemona ... proves able to provide the climax of the performance'.[98] It is a strong claim, and an outlier in terms of critical opinion, but it can be tested against the evidence of Burge's film, which in this respect performs the service of documenting two performances that have aged rather better than Olivier's, though some viewers now might find Smith's cut-glass diction a touch quaint. Like that of Rosemary Harris in *Hamlet* (and, indeed, like those of many of the twenty-two women that acted in the seventy-seven-strong first season company), Redman's is one of the largely untold stories of early NT Shakespeare: in most of the reviews, she is barely mentioned. On film, however, Redman erupts in the final scene as Olivier's nemesis, in acting as well as narrative terms. Commanding the centre of the performance space, she forces Olivier and Finlay to the sidelines; up against the bravura physicality and vocal bombast that kinaesthetically thrilled audiences at the Old Vic, Redman's righteous fury embodies emotional truth and moral authority. Yet the film version conceals as well as reveals; the dialogue between Redman and Smith that so held audiences at the Old Vic is cut at the point where they begin to weigh the cost of infidelity and Emilia bawdily names her own price (4.3.60–104); the scene ends on Desdemona's 'These men!' (4.3.59), possibly because it would have compromised the film's U-certificate; racism, misogyny, suicide and murder, meanwhile, were 'universal, suitable for all'.

Although Maggie Smith's Desdemona is captured in the film version, the role was not hers alone. As early as August 1964, it was also played by Whitelaw, who had been part of the 1963–4 intake and who, like Smith, had little Shakespearean experience, having in her own words been previously typecast as 'a battling working class lass, usually seduced by the boss's son, in what I called "trouble up at t' mill plays"'.[99] Given this, it is a pity that Whitelaw's performance is largely undocumented, but what she has to say about the production sheds further light on it. First, with regard to Olivier: intimidated by the prospect of the role, Whitelaw went to see the show, and found, to her surprise, that she 'actually had doubts about his own performance':

> What I saw was technically brilliant, but I could find no real emotional involvement. That being my first impression, I hoped to correct it the following night. To my astonishment what I saw was *exactly what I'd seen the night before*. Later, when I came to play Desdemona with him, I witnessed three or four performances in which Olivier was unforgettable, but only a handful of people ever saw him at his very best.[100]

Whitelaw echoes Plummer, who, more positively, recognized that Olivier 'overwhelmed us into being moved, and though we could see through the whole process, it didn't matter a damn because it was still shamefully exciting'.[101] Perhaps it takes an actor to intuit the vacuity of technique without conviction, and it is also evidences Olivier's struggle with the character that he was determined to master, the character that he feared would master him, and the audience that he rightly imagined would judge them both. Olivier 'at his very best' was, I hazard, Olivier with an audience at its most energized and energizing.

Whitelaw was well aware of her position in the show, telling herself 'that as long as she stood in the right places and didn't wriggle around too much, as long as she didn't get in his light or in his way, the cat could have gone to play Desdemona; Olivier wouldn't have minded'.[102] Intriguingly, she describes her own work of light(en)ing up, revealing that Desdemona's whiteness was as much a product of stage cosmetics as Olivier's blackness:

> To make my own skin look 'as white as alabaster' as the Bard says, I had alabaster make-up all over my body. Once, as I knelt at his feet, I put my hand on his knee. He glared down at me; there was a white mark on his black knee! Some of my white alabaster had come off on his beautiful black make-up. I felt like a naughty girl at school.[103]

Paul Menzer has written of the almost identical, but photonegative, contamination effect in the well-known head shot, used in the production publicity, of Olivier and Smith in the final scene, where a trace of his black makeup is visible on her face, 'the infamous "dirty still" – in which Olivier's makeup has left a smudge on Smith', whereby 'the daub on Smith's forehead triggers the underlying panic, the famous "one drop of blood" anecdotally alchemized into a smudge of Max Factor'.[104] Whitelaw's naughty-schoolgirl anecdote, by reversing the cosmetic racial and gender polarities, rewrites this history as *St Trinian's* comedy, so that this time it is masculinity that is under threat; rather like Smith's 'Brown

Cow', it serves for Whitelaw to subvert Olivier's 'impregnable' self-regard (the adjective speaks volumes), and also to highlight the generation gap between the 35-year-old actress and the patriarch who, though 'only 57', struck her 'as a man getting on years'.[105]

Smith played Desdemona at the last performance on 4 February 1967, and then took leave of absence from the company; the circumstances of her departure were far from happy. To a degree, there was only so much that Olivier, Tynan, Dexter and the rest could have done to enhance opportunities for the company's women, at least as far as the National's Shakespearean repertoire was concerned. In the ten plays staged in original productions at the Old Vic only thirty-eight, or less than 20 per cent, of just over two hundred roles are female, and most of these are minor ones. Some of the non-Shakespearean classic revivals provided good roles for Smith and Joan Plowright in particular, among them Smith's Sylvia in *The Recruiting Officer* and Hilde in *The Master Builder* in 1963–4, Plowright's Saint Joan in Shaw's play during the same season and Smith's Miss Julie in Strindberg's play at Chichester in 1965. But there was a persistent bias towards male-oriented plays; the Board minutes of 13 January 1964, for example, record that a projected production of Middleton's *A Chaste Maid in Cheapside* had been dropped in favour of Marston's *The Dutch Courtesan* due to 'the former having too many female parts'.[106] Opening in 1964, The National's first big contemporary hit, Peter Shaffer's epic drama of Inca history, *The Royal Hunt of the Sun*, has twenty-four name parts, two of which are female (and non-speaking), plus an unspecified number of Peruvian Indians; Tom Stoppard's *Rosencrantz and Guildenstern are Dead*, which followed in 1967, has only the miniscule name parts of Ophelia and Gertrude in a cast-list of sixteen, plus 'Courtiers and Attendants'.[107] Irving Wardle reported in 1967 that there was 'a large number of junior actors (some twenty-five out of a total strength of sixty-eight) who have been underemployed for the past year',[108] and, though he does not pursue the gender implications, this was even more the case for the women in the company than the men.

By the time that the all-male *As You Like It* and the nearly all-male *Rosencrantz and Guildenstern* were up and running, the imbalance was becoming embarrassingly obvious, and with Plowright leading the way, efforts slowly began to be made to redress it. The minutes for the meeting of the NT Board on 11 May 1970 note that *Antony and Cleopatra* was being considered for the 1970–1 season;[109] had it happened (perhaps with Plowright in the lead role), this would have been the most substantial Shakespearean acting opportunity for a woman since Franco Zeffirelli's *Much Ado about Nothing* in 1965. Instead, the Roman play of that season was *Coriolanus*, which, as I shall discuss in Chapter 3, was a disaster. The NT's first work by a woman playwright, Natalia Ginzberg's *The Advertisement*, premiered towards the end of 1968, and in February 1969 Plowright directed 'An Evasion of Women', a workshop season at the Jeanette Cochrane Theatre of four one-act plays by women writers (all established as novelists): Margaret Drabble, Shena Mackay, Gillian Freeman and Maureen Duffy. On the back of this, Duffy's *Rites*, which boasted an eleven-strong all-female cast, was given a short-run full production at the Old Vic at the end of May. As Plowright recalled, the plays 'made for a fascinating evening and were much enjoyed, though they were not received with a great deal of enthusiasm by male critics. And the writers returned to their novels and didn't write for the theatre again'.[110]

If there was a Shakespearean contribution to be made to this mildly feminist project, Olivier's next production, as director, was not it. *Love's Labour's Lost*, which ran from December 1968 to June 1969 and brought back for a handful of performances in 1970, might conceivably have been a vehicle for Plowright, the most senior female performer in the company, who played Rosaline opposite Jeremy Brett as Berowne; alongside her was Louise Purnell, who had joined the National in 1963 as one of *Hamlet*'s anonymous cohort of Court Ladies, as the Princess of France. The production, however, was memorable largely for stunning visuals, stately pacing, and elegant choreography. Olivier and designer Carl Toms took their inspiration from a fifteenth-century illustration of hunting at the Court of Philip the Good, 'as lovely as a Book of Hours, or a painted missal'.[111] After the pop-art pleasures of the previous year's modern-dress *As You Like It*, this was a self-consciously extravagant, indulgent exercise in pre-1960s period style. In front of a dark green cyclorama on which were etched the outlines of palace and pavilion, slender tree-trunks stretched upwards from a manicured lawn criss-crossed with leaf-strewn pathways; the ending of the play, marking the abrupt transition from spring to winter, and from the words of Apollo to the songs of Mercury, was, reviewers agreed, stunning, as the entry of the black-clad Mercade cued a lighting shift that turned the greenery an autumnal brown, which gave way to a Christmassy effect of gathering darkness, snowfall and the lighting of the lamps.

Within this picture-book setting the cast were sumptuously costumed in blue, scarlet, green and gold. Responding to the play's artifice, Olivier slowed the pace and encouraged a near-musical style of verbal delivery, now and then augmenting rhymed speech with a tinkling instrumental accompaniment, and the costumes dictated a matching formalization of movement, especially for the women. 'Carrying their stomachs forward and lifting their robes knee-high as they advance on out-turned feet', observed Irving Wardle, 'Joan Plowright and Louise Purnell are equally incapable of awkwardness and speed.'[112] This was all that Wardle had to say about Plowright's performance, and few critics had much to add, most being more taken by the quality of movement and the richness of the production's palette. Plowright and Purnell were 'little more than ceremonial ladies with the gait of well-bred Houyhnhnms',[113] and as 'the wimpled women advance with the stately, swollen-bellied grace of a Van Eyck', the 'four blues worn by the Princess of France and her ladies ... blend as delicately as the gowns of Piero della Francesca angels';[114] the effect, for one reviewer, was to render the women 'at times like exotic birds, in their exotic costumes and plumed headwear'.[115] This was a production that few took seriously, and its women, whether etherealized, exoticized or objectified, were taken least seriously of all.

The most interesting responses came from Hilary Spurling in the *Spectator* and Harold Hobson in the *Sunday Times*. Spurling, who had for some time styled herself as one of the National's sternest critics, was impressed by the show in a way that she had not been by the previous season's *As You Like It*, seeing in it a 'sense of teasing and provoking, of hovering between false and spontaneous, ludicrous and solemn' that was found 'nowhere more sharply than in the malicious gaiety of Joan Plowright's Rosaline, or in Louise Purnell's sweet, sharp Princess of France'.[116] Noticing the 'scallops' on skirts that 'twirl and loop or twist in folds, like sticks of barley sugar', Spurling's culinary-themed review (entitled 'Sugar is sweet') characterizes the production as an exquisite confection, and she begins quoting the celebrated first lines of the Bible of Victorian domestic culture, Mrs Beeton's *The Book of Household Management*; 'As with the commander of an Army, or the leader of any enterprise, so it is with the mistress of a house. Her spirit will be seen through the whole establishment; and just in proportion as she performs her duties intelligently and thoroughly, so will her domestics follow in her path.'[117] The allusion is to Olivier, who, in yet another play upon his gender identity, is the master–mistress both of the National, in his role as artistic director, and of the show, possessing 'those qualities of the prudent housewife – elegance, sobriety and orderliness – which Mrs Beeton so admired', and capable administering a recipe of 'agreeable relaxation' in the cast and an 'uncommonly well-regulated' production.[118] Olivier had enjoyed great success playing the army commander, and the part of the prudent housewife was a new one, but as a model of an art of hybrid creative leadership for a director of Shakespearean comedy, it seemed to fit.

Hobson's notice was no less complimentary, and was offered as part of a round-up of the week's performance events that reveals the magnitude of the gap between the National Theatre's Shakespeare and certain aspects of the contemporary theatre scene. 'If there are locutions not immediately understandable in *Love's Labour's Lost*', he posits, 'what can be said of Ed B [Berman]'s two one-act plays, *Sagittarius* and *Virgo* (Institute of Contemporary Arts), except that they are inhospitable to squares?' Hobson answers his own question by having some fun at the expense of a show, intended for an audience of 'bearded boys and moustached girls' that began with 'grunts and groans, squeaks and squawks', and was followed by 'the screen shadow at one end of the hall of a girl who undresses till she is completely naked; whilst at the other a second lady self-sacrificingly represents the Drab Reality by stripping down to her G-string'. 'It was greatly rewarding', Hobson drily observes, 'to watch the eyes of the audience – intellectuals to the last sweater – swivelling like racing cars from one lady to another, obviously keen as mustard not to miss anything Symbolic'. Hobson nonetheless concedes that 'there is more to Ed B than the avant garde manipulation of the pretentiously erotic', not least his 'considerable skill in the integration of the mutually unlike'.[119]

We might say that this is also what Hobson's own juxtaposition of productions achieves (and how it was taken by *Sunday Times* readers over their toast and cornflakes can only be marvelled at), but there is also a sense in which two shows preoccupied with apparently very different kinds of visual pleasure, and in which women are the objects of the male gaze, are, at least in Hobson's imagination, closer in spirit than one would think. *Love's Labour's Lost* was 'delightful to look at', but 'more than once one wishes ... that the stately measure of the endless sarabande, as the beautiful ladies bending backwards with uplifted skirts, move in slow state about the stage, would break into the vulgar vitality of the can-can'.[120] Hobson is nearer kin to the bearded voyeurs at the ICA than perhaps he knows. A female reviewer looks at the production and sees the art of cookery; a male one looks the same way and dreams of women's underwear. You that way, we this way.

Coming down

They filmed it, and this time they more or less got away with it. If the combination of racial stereotyping and blatant staginess was what did for the film *Othello*, John Sichel's 1973 television version of Jonathan Miller's 1970 *The Merchant of Venice*, as least as far as the second aspect was concerned, certainly did not make the same mistake. Adhering scrupulously to the rules of television realism in its *mise en scène*, techniques of filming and, for the most part, its actors' performances, it is offered as a lightly cut (132 minutes, twenty minutes shorter than the stage version), faithful rendering of the original production that is unambiguously a television film rather than a filmed stage play. The setting is late nineteenth-century, nominally Venice and Belmont but mostly England: the action takes place in dark houses stuffed with ornaments, heavy furniture and draperies, in cobbled backstreets that echo to the sound of barking dogs and tolling church bells, and on the marbled patio and immaculate lawns of Portia's country-house Belmont, where the distant sound of parlour piano and string trio playing snatches of a score, composed by Carl Davis, 'redolent of the world of Donizetti and Verdi',[121] is always faintly audible. In this buttoned-up world, men in frock-coats and top hats, and women in bustles, petticoats and corseted, high-necked dresses, give performances that are understated to the point of seeming to signal active repression: Portia (Joan Plowright) is a bored, anxious Victorian heiress who recognizes that a marriage to the caddish chancer Bassanio (Jeremy Brett) will do in the absence of any better alternative; Brett plays his part with a cool arrogance that allows him to take full advantage of the considerably older, and clearly infatuated, Antonio of Anthony Nicholls.

Richly textured, detailed in realization, the world of the film like that of the stage production is not just a decorative backdrop to its central performance, Olivier's Shylock, but a context and rationale for it. The difference in approach to *Othello*, on the part of both Olivier as actor and Miller as director, was marked: Dexter's production, rooting Olivier's Moor in racial fantasies that produced a white man's imagining of how a black man should move and speak, pitched his performance into a void space that could exist nowhere but in a theatre; Miller, by placing Shylock with some historical and cultural precision, anchored the play's world in history. The result is a performance, like Olivier's Othello preserved for all time on screen, that has generated none of the controversy of its predecessor, and that has worn remarkably well; and it has done so, I suggest, partly because of the real-world framing, and partly in spite of it. As much as Olivier's Shylock belongs within the production's Victorian world picture, it is nonetheless in crucial respects at odds with it.

In Olivier's account of the role's genesis and evolution, he claims to have been clear from the outset about both the ethical stakes and his determination to eschew caricature. Stating that his Shylock 'owed more to Benjamin Disraeli than to Fagin', Olivier started by dismissing 'the long, matted hair, invariably red, the hooked nose and the bent back' as 'a easy way out, not only making mock of the Jewish race but also of Shakespeare himself', and imagines this stock figure as 'begging to be hissed from the gallery, the more boos the better; the audience backing Gratiano, that embryonic fascist'. Bent on 'the old search for reality', Olivier, wanted a setting 'which would give it a feeling of dignity and austerity' and 'hit upon 1880–1885, that period when the Victorians had found their maturity. Tall hats and frock coats, a time of clean and polished fingernails'. 'Fortunately', he concludes, 'Jonathan and my other associates agreed with my vision.'[122]

Miller remembers it differently. He claims credit for the setting, which, he states, was inspired by 'hearing certain speeches, in my mind's ear, delivered in a way that was incompatible with a sixteenth-century setting', by thinking of Bassanio and Antonio in terms of 'the relationship between Oscar Wilde and Bosie where a sad old queen regrets the opportunistic heterosexual love of a person whom he adored', by the Count de Primoli's late nineteenth-century photographs of Venice, Trieste and other northern Italian cities, and by the 'rather dull, Adriatic mercantile life that Italo Svevo re-creates in his novels, and the footling young men who frequented the waterside cafés'.[123] While the detail of who came up with what, and when, seems a trivial issue (and I am not really that interested in trying to determine whose recall is more reliable), the discrepancy is worth noting not only insofar as it conveys a discreet struggle for ownership, raising the question of whether the production was conceived to serve the star actor's performance, or vice versa, but also because it points towards a tension between them that remained (to my mind productively) unresolved.

According to Miller, Olivier began with a version of Shylock that was very close to the caricature the actor says he rejected from the start: envisaging 'a grotesque, ornamentally Jewish figure', he 'bought himself very expensive dentures, a big hook nose and ringlets'. Gradually, however, Olivier realized that while he 'could have given *his* performance regardless ... either he or the production could then have looked absurd', and he learned to tame and contain his instinctively larger-than-life theatrical energies within the frame of a 'nineteenth-century character', rather than offering 'a ridiculous pantomime dame in the midst of the rather ordinary nineteenth-century set' (O, the gendered terminology ...). Except for the teeth, Olivier surrendered the 'excrescences' that Miller regarded as excessively theatrical, and worked with the notion that Shylock was trying to look 'much more like everyone else, as it is this crucial question of difference that lies at the heart of the play'.[124] In this version of events, Olivier dutifully takes his place within a strong directorial reading, and surrenders to what Peter Hall irritably characterized as Dr Miller's habit of 'directing plays as if he were advancing a theory for the *New York Review of Books*'.[125]

In Olivier's account, having distanced himself from the stereotype that Miller claims he had to be persuaded to abandon, he began his fieldwork, studying his fellow citizens 'in trains, buses, streets, taxis', and rapidly concluding that 'the so-called Jewish nose was to be seen more frequently on Gentile faces than on Jewish ones'. It does not occur to Olivier that the idea that there is such a thing as a recognizably 'Jewish face' is itself an anti-Semitic trope, nor does he explain how he is able to differentiate Jew from non-Jew in the street by sight, but he has the sense to abandon this line, settling instead on the equally stereotypical image of the 'Jewish mouth': 'Larger, more sensitive, much more mobile.' It prompts a classic Olivier physical transformation:

> I had teeth made that totally altered the shape of my face. They pulled my mouth out and pushed my upper lip forward. Suddenly there he was, my Shylock. Months of sitting and staring at noses that didn't exist, and there it was all the time. The mouth was the thing. The moment I saw it in the mirror I knew I was right.[126]

The mouth was indeed the thing, but the cosmetic dentistry worked very differently to the Max Factor 2880 and Negro Number 2, not least because it worked from the inside out, rather than, as with Othello, the other way round. A few reviewers noted the prosthesis: 'Olivier's face has exchanged its familiar contours for a fleshy apoplectic countenance whose very lips have somehow grown thick and flabby';[127] and the teeth 'force his mouth open into a snarling bray of fawning, unconvincing laughter, and leave it drooping when closed in a hungry line like a carp's'.[128] Neither of these reporters thought that Olivier was perpetrating an anti-Semitic caricature, and others barely noticed, ignored or even denied any physical difference; 'he has not even given himself a particularly Semitic cast of feature', claimed B. A. Young, 'In looks he is the least Jewish Shylock ever.'[129]

Olivier's dentures altered the shape of his face and, more importantly, assisted him to adjust his way of speech. Olivier's Shylock voice is a bizarre hybrid of acquired and only part-successfully mastered mannerisms and affectations; in his first scene alone he refers to 'ducuts' (9, 26, 54, 63, 101, 120), to the 'doin' of the deed of kind' (83) and 'hard dealin's' (160), and to 'all are trrribe-uh' (108); as Wardle commented, it is 'a ghastly compound of speech tricks picked up from the Christian rich: posh vowels and the slipshod terminations of the hunting counties'.[130] J. C. Trewin felt that the missing consonants travelled in the opposite direction, so that, for all his efforts 'to ingratiate himself with the Christians', this Shylock was 'probably aware that his carefully nurtured accent can slip into plebeian vowels sounds, and that the game he plays is fruitless'.[131] The conception of Shylock as an alien anxious to assimilate (he dresses identically to the Gentile merchants but for the skull-cap secreted beneath his top hat), and doomed to fail, is thus rendered as a multi-layered act of performance; if the least convincing of Tynan's rationalizations of the performance of blackness in *Othello* was that it was the character acting out stereotypes rather than the actor, Olivier's performance as an Olivier trying not to play Olivier, playing a Jew trying not to play a Jew, is much more interesting. Olivier reports that Miller took him to task in the early stages for being 'Olivier all over', and quotes the director, 'If you want to stamp yourself vocally all over the role, just Olivier being Olivier, then go ahead. You don't need me for that.' 'I'd made a mountain out of mannerisms,' Olivier ruefully reflects, 'and had ended up impersonating myself'.[132] He claims that 'from that moment I stopped living in my own image and began afresh',[133] but it is at those moments in the performance when Olivier plays Olivier (or, alternatively, when Olivier plays Olivier playing Shylock) that it is most powerful and affecting.

It has long been recognized that, despite Miller's efforts to domesticate Olivier within the production's realist scheme, there is a tension between this, his style, and that of his co-actors; as Michael Billington put it, Olivier 'offers the terrifying and exhilarating spectacle of a full-scale piece of heroic acting being given in an orderly, mercantile late-nineteenth century setting'.[134] The first sign of this was in his first scene, which progresses naturalistically enough up to 'For suff'rance is the badge of all our tribe' (1.3.114); Olivier has been pretending to check the finance pages of his newspaper (*Il Tempo*, naturally) while Antonio addresses Bassanio, and on this line he methodically folds it. The gesture announces a tonal shift: turning and taking a couple of paces upstage, as if to create space around himself for something much less fastidious, much bigger, he then spins on his heel: '"Sh*ylock*, we would have *mon*eys", *you* say so …' (1.3.114), hitting the first ringing top notes, and creating the show's first crescendo. The sense is both of a man briefly releasing simmering rage, and of an actor unleashed, and it simultaneously sits within the production's emotional-realist scheme and shakes it to the foundations. Pointing his silver-topped cane imperiously at Antonio, Olivier briefly thunders as Olivier as Henry V, a ghosting effect that is also even more unexpectedly felt in 3.2, when, fashioning a hood from his tallit as part of the prayer ritual on 'I will have the heart of him if he forfeit' (ll. 118–19), he becomes his former self on the night before Agincourt.

In this scene, especially, Miller was alert to the possibilities of intertextual allusion and metatheatre: directing Olivier to enter 'with Jessica's dress in his arms', he suggests

> that when she leaves the house wearing men's costume she would have left her dress behind her – like a snake shedding its skin – for Shylock to find in her absence. Shylock coming in with the dress draped in his arms has a wonderful overtone of Lear carrying Cordelia. In *King Lear*, as in *The Merchant of Venice*, a daughter who betrays her father seems, in his eyes, to die when she denies him her love. Holding the empty dress, Olivier appeared to be carrying the corpse of the departed daughter, as Shylock wishes when he says, '*I would my daughter were dead at my foot, and the jewels in her ear! would she were hearsed at my foot, and the ducats in her coffin!*'[135]

Writing of this moment, Hilary Spurling found it perfectly encapsulated Olivier's 'frenzy', 'when, clutching Jessica's discarded dress or dashing it to the ground, he circles the stage with cries which have the operatic grandeur of a hounded, robbed and vilely baited Rigoletto'.[136] As with Othello, affect is tied to musicality; and also, though to a lesser extent that reflects the reduced capabilities of a significantly older man, the actor's physical grace and even, occasionally, athleticism.

One such moment is seen in another of the bits of business that Miller offered to replace the 'excrescences', when Shylock learns from Tubal that Antonio's ventures have miscarried (3.1.94): transported with glee, Olivier executes a little skipping dance, which, the director reveals, was taken from newsreel footage of Hitler 'in the railway carriage, at Compiègne, at the surrender of France' (for me, there are also shades of Chaplin in *The Great Dictator*).[137] I assume that Miller knew what he was up to by turning Shylock, momentarily, into Hitler, but the association is perverse and not a little troubling. There is a rupture of a different kind earlier in the scene when, following a lengthy pause punctuated by the ominous tolling of a bell, Olivier delivers 'let him look to his bond' (3.1.43) straight to camera; the fourth wall is broken, and Olivier completes his compendium of self-quotation by becoming Richard III. Lastly, there was the unforgettable final offstage cry following Olivier's devastated exit from the trial scene, 'sharp and intense at first and then barbarically extended – that reminds one of a wolf impaled on a spike and dying a slow death'.[138] Olivier details the Method-style commitment that this entailed: 'I used to leave and deliberately lose my footing in the wings. I'd fall forwards and smash my hands on the concrete floor. Then the real pain would make me cry and sob like a child.' He wanted, he says, 'something to remain ringing in the ears long after I was in the dressing room. Something that would stay with the audience through the sweetness and light of the final romantic comic scene ... Beneath the humour there should be a sad shadow of a destroyed man. For me the cry did it.'[139]

Sweetness and light, and romance and comedy, were in short supply. The Venice and Belmont that is realized in the film was indicated in the stage production through a combination of suggestiveness of setting, and precise and profuse local detail in terms of costumes, furniture and props. Within a framework of colonnades, arches and church architecture, with 'two Palladian loggias' upstage, 'mirror images of each other, which swung open to reveal the interiors of, respectively, Shylock's house – tastefully sober in its deep-grained woods, bookcases and busts – and Portia's house, all golden draperies, overstuffed furniture, and Victorian bric-à-brac'[140] (the sign of 'a greedy philistine society whose real life goes on in counting houses and legal chambers').[141] For Spurling, Belmont was a place of 'buttoned sofas and opulent golden light', Venice one of 'high, crumbling walls, balconies, a covered gallery, a portico and pillars' that has 'exchanged its first splendour for a patina of rust, mould, decay, a kind of grand decrepitude achieved by centuries of use. Dusty sunlight falls on brown and purple stucco, stone medallions, scalloped ironwork'.[142] The city was well-populated: 1.1, envisaged as 'A Quay in Venice', had a café ('Florian's', equipped with 'tables, chairs, waiters'),[143] and 'Loggia umbrellas, Extras coming from church, P side, carrying wreaths, Extras in background carrying parcels with sacks over heads'.[144] This was all very realistic (though B. A. Young noticed a neat metatheatrical in-joke in the form of a 'tattered poster advertising *Otello* at the Fenice'),[145] and picturesque, and Miller rather regretted this: 'I would have preferred to make it resemble Svevo's Italy, and set it in a rather boring, unscenic, un-Venetian world of the kind that you find in Trieste.'[146]

This was symptomatic of Miller's determination to stage the play against the grain of tradition, and there were fewer concessions in the characterization, with the Christians ranging from the merely dislikeable (Portia, 'a bored, neurasthenic Victorian millionairess with tight little gold curls and the bossy impatience of the rich')[147] to the odious (Derek Jacobi's Gratiano, 'a strikingly nasty piece of work, full of repressed malice and violence'); Olivier's Shylock, in this setting, was 'a profoundly emotional being in a world where emotions embarrass people'.[148] The reviewers' largely negative reactions to Plowright's Portia matched her own initial response to the part. Portia, she felt, was 'maliciously arrogant', 'positively racist', 'nasty', 'vengeful' and 'bereft of any of that quality of mercy she has urged on other people'; in rehearsal, though, she developed a character that was 'rueful and wry, ironic and provocative, and prone to ecstasy when she falls helplessly in love'.[149] The trio of marriages of convenience had never seemed so doomed to result in lifetimes of unhappiness. At the end of the play, Antonio and Jessica (Jane Lapotaire at the Old Vic, Louise Purnell on film) were left alone on stage, both holding pieces of paper documenting their new-found financial good fortunes, both wondering at their awful cost; as the lights faded, the sound of the Kaddish was heard in the distance. It was a rare eruption of raw emotion, matched by the moment at the end of the trial when, hearing Olivier's offstage wail, the Christians stared at each other in horror, appalled by the consequences of their own actions.

At times, however, the repression of feeling becomes almost comical as in the first two suitor scenes wherein both the Princes of Morocco and Arragon react to the outcome of the casket-tests with little more than mild disappointment. At least, this is how these play in the film version; but this is a less serious matter than the casting of the first of these roles. In 1969, the NT had taken a step towards atoning for *Othello* by engaging its first black British actors in Peter Nichols's state-of-the-nation play *The National Health*; among them Cleo Sylvestre in a leading role, and Norman Beaton.[150] Less than two months after *Merchant* opened, Miller himself directed the first British postcolonial production of *The Tempest* at the Mermaid Theatre; with Beaton and Rudolph Walker playing, respectively, Ariel and Caliban. In *Merchant* Morocco was a white actor, Tom Baker, in blackface. Played flat-out for cheap laughs, Baker's Morocco was 'a property negro',[151] 'a wild refugee from the minstrels who draws a shriek from the two girls',[152] and 'a fugitive from the Black and White Minstrels – "Aw, hell! What have we here?"'[153] In the film version Baker (who was about to assume his best-known television role as the eponymous lead in *Doctor Who*) was replaced by Stephen Greif and the burlesque is toned down, but what remains still looks and sounds like a bad impression of Olivier's Othello. For a production otherwise highly sensitive to the politics of race, both the casting and the treatment are crass and offensive choices.

In *Confessions of an Actor*, Olivier acknowledges that during the run of *Othello* he had his first experience of a debilitating stage fright that would last for five years; it led him to 'beg' Frank Finlay not to leave him alone for his soliloquies, 'but to stay in the wings downstage where I could see him, since I feared I might not be able to stay there in front of the audience myself'.[154] To imagine a supposedly superhumanly powerful performance being placed in a state of almost infantile dependency is painful enough, but for Olivier the stage fright was made even worse by manifesting itself as physical vulnerability; once it had taken hold, he found himself backstage 'lurching so badly that I was ricocheting from one wall to the other'. Onstage, 'I found it impossible to stop myself staggering; all too soon I had to lurch further downstage and, sure enough, the hissing whispering started out front, the content of which I could well imagine: "You see? Look at him, I wondered how long it would be before he had one too many, didn't you?" ... "But isn't it marvellous the way he keeps it out of hiss voice and speech? Oh yesss it certainly issss – marvelloussssss!"'[155] Olivier's morbid characterization of his audience as a nest of snakes indulges paranoid imaginings that are apt in context ('Where is that viper?' [5.2.286]), and it provides an insight into just how personally testing and painful playing Othello really was. In his discussion of stage fright, Nicholas Ridout identifies the condition as 'a phenomenon of modernity' that arises from the actor's contradictory positioning within an alienating, technologized apparatus, that is defined by the 'narcissism of the recently elevated public personality, whose intimacies are public property, who is isolated in the visibility of the electric light, who simulates the involuntary disclosure of emotion through the reanimation of his own'.[156] For a condition that can afflict any actor at any time it seems acutely relevant to the predicament of an actor who was simultaneously the NT's boss, its most valuable asset,[157] and an employee trapped in a role in which he felt fundamentally *wrong* (perhaps fearing that, deep down, he was a 'racist pig'), and which mandated an extreme degree of emotional nakedness that was physically co-figured and colour-matched through the nightly display of his fetishized, blacked-up body.

As with Othello, so too with Shylock. Halfway through Olivier's account (in *On Acting*) of his work on the role, it takes a sudden, unexpected turn and he reveals that during the run he suffered from 'the actor's nightmare' and wonders whether it 'had anything to do with my performance becoming fresh, open and naked again'.[158] If, as I have suggested, the reality of Olivier's playing was far more layered than this claim to candour and simplicity indicates, what follows reveals the vertiginous instability at the heart of what appears to be one of his most assured performances. Promising a 'brief insight' into stage fright that actually occupies half the length of the essay, Olivier charts in excruciating detail the day-to-day (and, worse, night-by-night) experience of the condition; which is 'the character in *The Turn of the Screw* who never appears: he is always waiting outside the door, any door, waiting to get you … I'm alone, oh God, how alone I am. Nobody understands this … nobody'.[159] Olivier then spends two pages anatomizing his first entrance and the scene's first ten lines (1.3.1–10), a sequence that in the television film occupies all of twenty seconds:

> I have given instructions to the other actors not to look me in the eyes. My company, what a thing to do to them. But I had to. The one thing an actor must do is look his fellow actors in the eyes and I have asked my fellow players not to.
>
> SHYLOCK
> *Three thousand ducats; well?*
> I've said it … the line's out. I've said the first line. God, supposing I fall over. I've got the feeling I'm going to fall over.[160]

The fear of falling, which is presumably more than literal, persists as does the obsession with 'lack of balance .... Lack of sense of balance ... Balance ... come on balance'; and then:

SHYLOCK
Three thousand ducats, for three months, and Antonio bound.
I've done it ... That's the right line. I've done it.[161]

For Olivier doing the 'horrid and cruel' *Merchant* was, ultimately, the way to restore a sense of equilibrium and he had 'much to thank the play for': 'It finally put down my stage fright. Now I can say, "I have been there. I have looked over the edge, and I have returned."'[162] As he took that self-choreographed tumble in the wings Olivier both mastered and surrendered to his fears of falling, of loss of control, producing a cry that was a wail of pain and also, at some level, the sound of a man released. Shylock was not the last time that Olivier acted at the Old Vic,[163] but it was the last Shakespearean role he played on stage.

2

1967

Heads ...

Tom Stoppard, the story goes, was enjoying a quick smoke on the sidewalk, after one of the first Broadway performances of *Rosencrantz and Guildenstern are Dead*, when he was accosted by an audience member who asked him what the play was about. Without missing a beat, Stoppard replied: 'it's about to make me rich'.[1] It is a riposte on a par with the crosstalk of one of his own plays: flipping an innocent phrase on its head, Stoppard simultaneously delivered a bon mot that might have equally appealed to Wilde and Wittgenstein, executed a masterly deflection of the actual question and provided an accurate prediction of what would come to pass. But it is also an unusually blatant statement of the normally not acknowledged: that an apparently art-house venture might harbour no higher purpose than to make money, that its originator was candid enough to admit that he was prepared to take his audience for a ride, and the play, like its author, was more than usually self-aware of the means necessary to make this happen. Even before it opened in the United States on 16 October 1967, *Rosencrantz and Guildenstern* was a hit, having opened to rave reviews at the Old Vic on 11 April; and it would remain in the NT's repertory until 1970. The rest, as readers will probably know, is history: Stoppard's career as a playwright and screenwriter went from strength to strength, as he accumulated awards and honours that included a knighthood in 1997, and it became one his most-produced plays – most recently, at the time of writing, in the fiftieth anniversary production that opened at the Old Vic in February 2017. As we shall see, Stoppard was right: making him, and a fair few others, rich was *exactly* what the play was, and is, 'about'.

Stoppard's witticism suggests cool flippancy but the reality was that he had worked long and hard to become an overnight success. *Rosencrantz and Guildenstern* was not, as some reviewers believed, Stoppard's first play. Having first worked as a journalist in Bristol, Stoppard moved to London in 1962 at the age of twenty-five to freelance as a theatre critic and to write (mostly unperformed) scripts; two radio plays were broadcast in 1964 and a third in 1966; he wrote two television plays, *A Walk on the Water*, shown in 1963, and *A Separate Peace*, in 1966; and in the same year was commissioned by the RSC to re-work the translation of Sławomir Mrożek's *Tango* for production at the Aldwych. *Rosencrantz and Guildenstern* underwent a lengthy development process that began in 1964 when Stoppard was awarded a Ford Foundation scholarship to undertake a six-month writing residency in Berlin. The first, one-act, version, more an extended sketch than a play, was a twenty-five-minute skit based on the idea of Rosencrantz and Guildenstern meeting King Lear, who turned out to be the unnamed English king who receives the order for their execution. In the draft text, the meeting with Lear was a minor incident, and the action consisted mostly of the pair's voyage to England.

Directed by Stoppard for a work-in-progress evening at the Forum Theatre in Berlin in September 1964, it attracted the attention of *The Times* as the 'strangest piece', a 'rhythmic jamboree ... with the morose Dane uttering characteristic platitudes'.[2] Stoppard engaged four actors from the amateur Questors' Theatre in Ealing for the show, and on 4 October a further reading was given at that venue, which convinced Stoppard that it didn't work and that he needed to start again. A revised version, which shifted the focus from Hamlet to

Rosencrantz and Guildenstern, and which was closer to the first two acts of the final three-act script, was submitted, unsuccessfully, to Questors' in March 1965; Stoppard then committed the faux pas of sending a revised version to the RSC's Literary Manager, Jeremy Brooks, who was known to have 'a certain aversion to plays dealing with secondary characters in Shakespeare, which he believed was "a favoured device of unperformed playwrights"'.[3] Fortunately, Brooks sufficiently overcame his aversion to recommend it to Peter Hall, and to agree a one-year option on the now three-act play. A decade later, as he was about to premiere his production of Stoppard's *Every Good Boy Deserves Favour* at the Royal Festival Hall, Trevor Nunn recalled that the intention was to cross-cast the play with Hall's *Hamlet*, planned for 1965, but that financial pressures meant that the 'experimental season' had to be abandoned, and 'we gave the rights in *Rosencrantz* to a group of Oxford students who were in desperate need of a play for the Edinburgh Festival'.[4] On 24 August 1966 the play opened at the Cranston Street Hall in Edinburgh. Two days earlier, Stoppard's novel *Lord Malquist and Mr Moon* had been published and, sitting amidst an audience of 'a couple of dozen people' for the first night,[5] he was still pinning his hopes on that rather than on a play he thought of little consequence. He reckoned without the presence in the audience of the *Observer*'s Ronald Bryden, who the following Sunday published a strongly supportive review with the by-line 'the most brilliant debut since John Arden's'. Bryden sensed big ideas in play ('is this our relation to our century, to the idea of death, to war?') and Shakespeare-sized talent: like '*Love's Labour's Lost* this is erudite comedy, punning, far-fetched, leaping from depth to dizziness'. Harold Hobson also liked the play, which though it offered 'neither guarantee nor bar to Mr Stoppard's future as a dramatist ... should be seen'.[6]

Bryden's review caught the attention of Kenneth Tynan, who immediately made a grab for what seemed like the play for which the NT had been waiting since the success of Shaffer's *The Royal Hunt of the Sun* in 1964. As far as risky, controversial new writing was concerned, the Royal Court and the RSC appeared to have the edge: the Court had recently experienced the furore of Edward Bond's *Saved* (1965), and the RSC followed the 1965 season's premieres of Harold Pinter's *The Homecoming*, and Peter Weiss's *The Investigation* and *Marat / Sade* (both directed by Peter Brook) with Brook's devised anti-Vietnam War piece *US* in 1966. Despite Tynan's Brechtian allegiances, it was evident that the RSC and the Court were engaging with political drama in ways that the NT was not, and probably could not; in 1967, when Tynan and Olivier attempted to push through Rolf Hochhuth's indictment of Winston Churchill, *Soldiers*, the NT Board blocked them. Opportunity was at hand, thanks to the unexpected gap in the NT's schedule that opened up when the planned all-male production of *As You Like It* was postponed to the autumn. Interviewed by the *Guardian* the day after opening night, Stoppard acknowledged the role of chance in the chain of events, by stating that 'it would never have seen the light of day ... if *As You Like It* had not gone wrong and they needed something in a hurry'.[7]

Possibly, possibly not; but the idea that things could have gone one way or the other until *Rosencrantz and Guildenstern* won the toss resonates not only with the play's game-play metaphysics but also with its author's own deeply personal investment in the possibility of its success. As his biographer records, Stoppard knew all too well the gut-wrenching urgency of financial insecurity, and of living on borrowed time: when his *Guardian* interviewer referred to a previous Stoppard radio comedy about 'a man who has to keep riding round in a taxi because he daren't tell the driver he hasn't got the fare',[8] he was presumably unaware that this rooted in painful personal experience.[9] Money, particularly when coupled with gambling and risk, is one of the things that *Rosencrantz and Guildenstern*, to coin a phrase, is 'about'. Its paradigmatic opening scene, which has the duo betting on the toss of a coin, with Rosencrantz calling 'heads' and winning every time ('Eighty-five in a row – beaten the record!')[10] while

Guildenstern grows visibly more impoverished, reads clearly enough as an absurdist opening gambit ('Don't be absurd',[11] warns Guildenstern, just to underline the point), but it harbours ironies that even Brecht might have appreciated. Take the act of coin-tossing itself: on- or off-stage, it is that treasured moment in a coin's existence when its monetary value is functionally subordinate to its materiality, when what is worth, and in what currency, are irrelevant to the question of which side it ends up on (it matters not whether it is a penny, a pound, a groat or a dime, and Stoppard later confessed that he hadn't bothered to check the Danish currency, which is why the pair gamble with guilders rather than kroner). Stoppard may not have intended to juggle with Marx's theory of commodity fetishism but he was very alert to the dynamics of theatrical risk in this scene. While for both actors and audience the outcome of the toss is neither here nor there – since in the play-fiction it is always heads – both parties would probably prefer the manoeuvre to be skilfully executed. Consider the scale of the challenge Stoppard sets his actors: between them Rosencrantz and Guildenstern are required to toss and catch sixteen times while simultaneously sustaining the rhythm and phrasing of forty-eight lines of rapid-fire badinage, double entendre, philosophical speculation and metatheatrical provocation, all in the crucial opening five minutes. The scene, like the play as a whole, is in multiple senses a gamble and one that paid off handsomely.

The Edinburgh production had a cast of eleven; at the Old Vic this expanded to thirty-two, including seventeen courtiers and attendants. It was still a relatively inexpensive show to mount: Board minutes from December 1966 account for the substitution by emphasizing the thriftiness of the production and pointing out that *As You Like It* had been postponed 'in order to give the Director and designer time to re-conceive the production, as the original designs were proving too costly'.[12] Reflecting the inverted hierarchy of the play's dramatis personae the cast drew upon established, but not leading, members of the company: John Stride (originally cast as Orlando in *As You*

Like It) as Rosencrantz, Edward Petherbridge as Guildenstern and John McEnery (who had joined the NT in 1966 in walk-on parts in *The Storm* and *Royal Hunt*) as Hamlet. Of particular importance was the casting of the Player. Stoppard stipulated in the script that the '*resemblance between HAMLET and the PLAYER is superficial but noticeable*',[13] but he was overruled by Olivier, who cast Graham Crowden, an actor physically and temperamentally as unlike McEnery as it is possible to imagine. Six-foot-three Crowden was already well known for what one of his obituaries termed his 'extra-terrestrial' qualities ('a mix of the ethereal eccentricity of Ralph Richardson and the Scottish lunacy and skewiff authoritarianism of Alastair Sim'),[14] and had memorably originated the lead role of Groomkirby in N. F. Simpson's classic of the English absurd, *One Way Pendulum*, at the Royal Court in 1959. His performance was one of the few in the production that found favour with the *Spectator*'s Hilary Spurling, who wrote that he stood out from the players, 'a grubby, tawdry band, at once weird, outlandish and wretchedly hard up', as a 'gaunt, chalk-white Pagliaccio with carmine lips and downturned mouth', Crowden had 'a sardonic authority and … a rare poignancy in the drooping of an eyebrow, in the flick of his bony wrist'.[15]

A couple of the cast were in the Olivier–O'Toole *Hamlet* (Stride had played Fortinbras, and Peter Cellier, Polonius in Stoppard's play, Rosencrantz), and, as if to further amplify the metatheatrical resonances, some of the costumes from that production were re-used, with Rosencrantz in 'beige felt, slashed tunic' and 'trick trunk hose – to fall down', Guildenstern in 'blue velvet padded tunic and trunk hose', Hamlet in 'white shirt, off-black velvet tunic and breeches' and the Player, splendidly, in 'painted, slashed ribbon breeches and tunic of orange cut velvet and old plum velvet with slashed sleeves, lined with silver lurex, old plum suede boots, crown and dagger'.[16] Desmond Heeley's set, an asymmetrical platform flanked by low steps, over which loomed mouldy Gothic archways, pillars and latticed windows, embodied director Derek Goldby's desire 'to create a mysterious, dream-like aura'[17] while nodding towards Olivier's

Hamlet film (which, one critic pertinently observed, removed Stoppard's protagonists 'with almost no one regretting their departure'),[18] and conveyed the impression of a quaintly old-fashioned production of Shakespeare's play, one that might have been seen at the Old Vic twenty years previously.

The six-week rehearsal period began in early March 1967, and it soon became evident that Goldby and Stoppard approached the play very differently: the former seeing it 'from a kind of dream point of view', the latter in terms of 'arguments'.[19] Fortunately, the pair managed to effect a rapprochement whereby Goldby was responsible for the visuals and choreography while Stoppard worked with the actors on the text, which retained a number of unresolved problems until a disconcertingly late stage. The ending, in particular, went through several quite radical revisions, including a version (included in the first edition of the play but subsequently cut) which follows Fortinbras's final words ('Go, bid the soldiers shoot' [5.2.410]) with twenty lines of dialogue between the two ambassadors, interrupted by a furious knocking on the door of a man '*shouting, obscurely, two names*' and one of them deciding to 'Better go and see what's it's all about …'.[20] In the extant play, the action ends with Horatio's reprize, 'all this can I / Truly deliver' (5.2.392–3) and a slow fade to black.[21]

This is a riskily downbeat ending for a play that, Stoppard insisted, should be seen first and foremost as a comedy. In an interview published just before opening night, he declared: 'Almost everything I've written works on a comic level … I'm afraid of losing the audience if I say something serious, I don't trust my credentials – and humour is a universal cement.'[22] The extent to which *Rosencrantz and Guildenstern* conformed, or not, to audience expectations of a fun night out can be measured by a look at the London theatre listings of the time, which catalogue a West End heavily dominated by musical theatre, mildly risqué comedies, and broad farce. Consulting the weekly satirical magazine *Punch*, the barometer of middle-England sense of humour, taste, and political orientation, and thus useful index of NT audience sensibilities, we learn that, in the week that *Rosencrantz and Guildenstern* opened, work on offer included *Big Bad Mouse* at the Shaftesbury ('cowed clerk becomes office sex symbol by mistake. Jimmy Edwards and Eric Sykes ad lib, forget their lines and treat the original script as a trampoline'), *Cactus Flower* at the Lyric ('middle-aged dentist's tedious affair with mod girl runs into trouble') and *There's a Girl in My Soup* at the Globe ('cool young miss disrupts the comfortable philandering life of a middle-aged, globe-trotting, food and drink expert'); as well as the long-running musicals *Come Spy with Me* (Whitehall; 'Danny La Rue impersonates a dozen virile women ... Jokes and situations as you'd expect') and *Hello Dolly!* (Drury Lane; 'Famous for the scene when twenty waiters cry Hello! To Dolly [Dora Bryan]'). With the RSC out of town, the Aldwych hosted the Noh Theatre of Japan as part of its fourth World Theatre Season, and at the Royal Court the revival of D. H. Lawrence's *The Daughter-in-Law* had just closed, with William Gaskill's production of *Three Sisters* due to open on 18 April. Amidst all this was a revival of a play that transgressively straddled the divide between the commercial and art theatres, Joe Orton's queer-leaning death-and-robbery farce *Loot*, which had been running for six months, and which the *Punch* listing described as 'not to be missed if you enjoy heartlessly comic adventures with coffins and bank robbers and roguery triumphant. Might agitate the sentimental'.[23]

As it happened, Orton was present at the dress rehearsal of *Rosencrantz and Guildenstern* and was not impressed. In his diary, he wrote that it was a 'wonderful idea' but that 'the only drama in the play is by Shakespeare', and that the treatment was a formulaic synthesis of angry-young-man and theatre-of-the-absurd: 'the usual dialogue between two bored people waiting for something to happen ... *Look Back in Anger* and *Waiting for Godot* in equal parts'.[24] A few first-night critics shared this view, including the *Telegraph*'s W. A. Darlington who conceded that 'it is all very clever, I dare say', but 'happens to be the kind of play that I don't enjoy and would in fact much rather read than see on stage'.[25] Elsewhere, reactions ranged from the enthusiastic to the ecstatic. 'As a first stage play it is an amazing piece of work',[26] wrote Irving Wardle, and Peter Lewis announced that the NT's 'biggest gamble to date ... wins at 66 to 1'.[27] The play ('a compound of Shakespearian criticism, Beckett-like cross-talk, and ... mathematical nonsense-comedy'), Wardle stated, was 'highly literary' with 'frank debts to Pirandello and Beckett; but in Derek Goldby's production, these sources prove a route towards technical brilliance and powerful feeling'.[28] For Lewis, the lead roles were 'brought to life with brilliance'[29] by Stride and Petherbridge, who were 'masterly' according to B. A. Young, with Rosencrantz played as 'a rather pathetic simpleton whom an insurance company would describe as "accident prone"' and Guildenstern 'sharper, more likely to start ideas, though no more likely to carry them through'.[30] The production, which 'comes out of the dark like a spotlit jewel, full of vibrations',[31] was highly praised.

By the time the Sunday papers appeared, the consensus had sufficiently cemented for Ronald Bryden to hail 'the most brilliant dramatic debut of the sixties'[32] and Harold Hobson to welcome 'the most important event in British professional theatre for the last nine years' in the shape of 'the best first London-produced play written by a British author since Harold Pinter's *The Birthday Party* in 1958':

> Its ingenuity is stupendous, and the delicacy and complexity of its plot are handled with a theatrical mastery astonishing in a writer as young as Mr Stoppard, who, whilst demonstrating a spirit deep, foreboding and compassionate like Beckett, shows a sleight of hand as cunning as Feydeau.[33]

The namechecking of forbears and influences here and elsewhere (Beckett, Feydeau, Pirandello, Sartre, Cocteau, Giraudoux) seems to reveal a British press readier than it had ever been to embrace a European sensibility (it was, after all, three months since the United Kingdom had launched its application for membership of the European Economic Community), and to find in the play an allegory for The

Human Condition, with both Lewis's and Hobson's reviews demonstrating how pervasive the language of coffee-bar existentialism had become: 'in failing they come to stand for any of us, summoned, we know not why, to live in an Elsinore not of our choosing, playing the parts people expect of us, and watching death approach with incomprehension';[34] the pair were 'equally baffled and helpless before the blank, terrifying, and unanswerable wall of life. It is a situation many people know well'.[35] As Hobson judged, there was a palpable sense that this was a National Theatre event – maybe even a national event – and a hit that to a certain extent atoned for its to date all-too-frequent misses. As a play set, as the programme put it, 'in and around the action of *Hamlet*',[36] *Rosencrantz and Guildenstern* looped back to the opening of the first season, and as it unfolded amidst the haunted ruins of the inaugural showcase, 'the sound of the bravos'[37] and of 'an audience laughing constantly for nearly three hours'[38] loudly redeemed that production's quiet failure.

Another week and nine performances into the run, and the weeklies had their turn. *Punch* put the play on a par with the best of the European avant-garde, finding that 'it works on the mind in the manner of Pirandello's plays, the stories of Kafka and *Waiting for Godot*', and praising Petherbridge and Stride for 'beautifully' suggesting 'two-dimensional characters struggling to acquire a third dimension'[39] (the play was described thereafter in the magazine's listings as 'altogether fascinating').[40] Hilary Spurling of the *Spectator* was less impressed. Granting that the production ('an evening of dazzling versatility') showed the National 'back on form, its old suave, comic self', she dismissed the play's protagonists as 'a pair of green undergraduates trotting out all the clichés of the last ten years, as thick as they come and viewed without irony by their author', and suggested that 'it is this quality – of being so comfortably second-rate – which has made for the play's extraordinary success'.[41] At the other end of the political spectrum, over at the *New Statesman*, the no less rebarbative D. A. N. Jones also weighed in, affording *Rosencrantz and*

Guildenstern one dismissive sentence ('straw men from *Hamlet* are the principals of ... the National Theatre's curious addition to their thin modern repertoire') in a review article that lambasts the 'extras, the rhubarb men ... messengers, spear-carriers character-cameos, and attendant lords' that were, allegedly, 'taking over'.[42]

Two weeks later, Jones warmed to his theme in a review of the published play:

> This is just the kind of play that is thought safe and suitable for our National Theatre – where I briefly noticed, in a recent theatre review, its grand staging and apparent feebleness of language. Quite remote from anything that could disturb or excite an audience into thought, dismay or loud laughter, it indicates threateningly to rival nation-states that we can still select formidable officer-material and brain-drains, culture graduates who have learned how to dispose, amusingly, of Britain's more subversive specialities – poetry and philosophy – and degrade them to examination.[43]

Jones' targets are multiple – Stoppard, the 1950s verse dramatist Christopher Fry, the National Theatre, 'the kind of Frenchman who would begin a play: "There's not going to be a Trojan War, Cassandra"' – but he especially despised the play's likely audience, amused by 'tiny, unfunny' jokes 'to comfort Aunty ("A bit over my head, I'm afraid") and Nanny ("Mazed with book-learning") and give them a chance of a giggle'.[44] Spurling and Jones represented a minority view, but between them – the one with her swipe at 'undergraduates', the other with his scorn for middlebrow theatregoers – they articulated different aspects of a wider disquiet concerning the identity and direction of the National Theatre. From the perspective of both right and left, *Rosencrantz and Guildenstern* (and, by implication, the NT itself) seemed designed to cater simultaneously for a new audience and an established one, both of which could be condescended to in class terms. Jones conjures the dread spectre of 'Aunt Edna', that complacent and conservative petit-bourgeois arbiter of theatrical taste and sensibility that had held sway since Rattigan coined the term in the early 1950s; Spurling invokes her earnest nieces and nephews, the undergraduates belonging to the group that Tynan, a decade previously, had in his review of Osborne's *Look Back in Anger* labelled the 'non-U intelligentsia';[45] that is, the Redbrick middle and lower-middle class types studying the arts and humanities, buying Penguin paperbacks, and subjecting Bob Dylan's lyrics to intense scrutiny.

Both groups were vital components of the National's audience base, and the interests and priorities of the latter would become increasingly important to the institution's sense of what it was, and could be. More broadly, these were implicated in the changing relationship between the new consumers of culture, and in competing definitions of what culture actually is, what standards of taste are, and what deserves to be taken seriously and what doesn't. In this respect it is worth noting that, with the incidental exception of *The Times*,[46] none of the periodicals that reviewed *Rosencrantz and Guildenstern* paid any attention to the other major cultural event of the week of its premiere (but one with which it can be fruitfully compared): the release, on 8 June 1967, of the Beatles' eighth studio album, *Sgt. Pepper's Lonely Hearts Club Band*. That week, the *New Statesman*'s music column preferred a disquisition on the Polish composer Krzyzstof Penderecki ('the pin-up boy of the musical avant-garde'), and on his relation to Carl Orff and Schoenberg;[47] in the *Spectator*, Charles Reid reviewed a double bill of one-act pieces staged by the English Opera Group at the Aldeburgh Festival.[48] The music reviews in the *Guardian* the day after *Sgt. Pepper* was released covered classical and jazz;[49] on Sunday, Benny Green's regular jazz column in the *Observer* offered an appreciation of the singer Blossom Dearie.[50] According to one's news source of choice, these activities, rather than pop, were among those that defined the cultural context of Stoppard's play. Yet the record and the play had more in common than anyone, at the time, recognized: as a brilliantly sustained exercise in musical pastiche that combined, amongst other things, vaudeville, music hall and the avant-garde, *Sgt. Pepper* shared elements of the form and style of *Rosencrantz and Guildenstern* and also, conceptually, something of its back-to-front logic, as it projected a modern sensibility into a retro-period setting (early modern, cod-Edwardian) and reinvented the four most famous men on the planet as a bunch of nobodies. Stoppard was more a Rolling Stones man at this moment, not least because his Mick Jagger face and louche charm helped him to slip effortlessly into the role of pop-celebrity playwright, but his play was still very much in tune with its times.

The suspicion that there was a widening gap between the critic's perspective and that of the *Rosencrantz and Guildenstern* audience surfaced again in a review published in the June issue of *Plays and Players*. Wondering if drama critics 'are the last people who ought to be reviewing drama', John Russell Taylor worried that most contemporary drama 'seems to be directed, perhaps from painful necessity, at people who do not normally go to the theatre', and it was their response, rather than that of 'the inured theatregoer', that ought to be taken as a measure of success or failure. As a consequence, he reports, he found himself scrutinizing the Old Vic audience as closely as he did the play, characterizing them as

> people who go to the theatre as a special event, and rely on the National to provide it; you can be pretty sure that there you will get a substantial, well-written play, probably classic, with a stellar cast; you are not likely, or have not up until now been likely, to be affronted with anything too difficult or 'modern'.

Having rumbled the play in the first five minutes, Taylor realized that 'for the audience around me it was quite otherwise':

> In the first long interval ... speculation was rife on all sides. People were asking each other with every show of excitement

> What it was All About. Some said that it had taken them a long time, but they thought they were beginning to get the hang of it now. By the second interval a lot more had got the hang of it, or resolved that even if they didn't understand it, at least a lot of it was jolly funny along the way. Only one dissenting voice did I hear: the man immediately behind me said loudly: 'Of course, I tend to turn and run a mile at the first hint of anything *clever*!'[51]

He had, Taylor concedes, a point, as the play was 'undoubtedly clever'. But, as he elaborates, this cleverness was shallow and meretricious: there was 'no denying the ingenuity with which Mr Stoppard spins out his material', and a lot of the dialogue was 'agile and funny', which made for 'a quite interesting unusual evening in the theatre'. But Taylor had seen it all before: 'know your way round Beckett and early Pinter', and it was 'all too familiar and uneventful'. The NT audience, whose taste and intelligence he regarded as fair game, would see it differently: if '*Hay Fever*, *The Master Builder* and *Much Ado about Nothing* are usually your mark in the theatre, you will find *Rosencrantz and Guildenstern are Dead* an intriguing and probably an enjoyable experience'.[52]

The condescension was all in a day's work for the author of *Anger and After*, who was accustomed to breezily sweeping aside the concerns of 'conventional, old-fashioned theatregoers' to embrace the 'bright new talents' of the New Wave, who, 'if they can keep their freshness of vision intact', should 'go on for ever'.[53] Taylor envisages an audience packed with Aunt Ednas, but there is evidence, albeit limited, that the play was beginning to find favour not only with the NT's established clientele but also with its next generation of playgoers. On 9 May the play was offered as part of the Theatre for a New Audience initiative, an occasional programme of free performances for young people. The stage manager's report records a 'very appreciative audience' and a 'smooth show',[54] and the play earned much the same response when repeated for this constituency the following January ('excellent reception').[55] In any case,

Taylor's view made little difference, as the play had already entered the next phase of its life. In May it was announced that *Rosencrantz and Guildenstern* would be transferring to Broadway in the autumn, the first NT production to do so, where it would be produced by David Merrick. Arrangements were put in place for Goldby and his team to fly to New York at the end of July; in a sign of how quickly those involved detected the scent of big money, the director's agent wrote to the theatre's General Manager, George Rowbottom, regarding his client's living expenses, and requesting a $40 per diem: 'The normal is $30 a day, but these boys and girls must be free to devote their time to the production and not have to economise unduly on food, taxis, accommodation etc.'[56]

Unsurprisingly, the news of the lucrative transfer was not universally welcomed. On 1 August, Mr G. A. Haw from Huddersfield wrote to Rowbottom:

> Looking through the new brochure, covering the period Sept 5th – Nov. 11th it seems that the play 'Rosencrantz and Guildenstern are Dead' will not be staged after Sept. 28th. Is this because it is to be staged on Broadway? If so, I feel it wrong that a play I and others have not been able to obtain tickets for is being done commercially in New York, whilst British playgoers (and taxpayers) are denied the chance to see this play. What has David Merrick done for the British theatre? In my opinion, all he has done is made himself a rich man by cashing-in on certain British plays. I am angry about this because I think that British playgoers, who support the National Theatre, in London, and when on tour, are not being treated fairly.[57]

Haw's complaint was groundless, since the Broadway production was mounted with an entirely new cast, but his attitude represents an important strand of British public opinion at the time, and points to the National's financial double-bind: make a loss, and it was charged with wasting 'taxpayers' money'; make a profit, it was accused of exploiting its protected position. Rowbottom's assistant replied to Haw, reassuring him that the Broadway production had 'nothing to do with the number of performances of our own production' and that 'there will certainly be more performances ... in future booking periods'.[58] There would be more performances of *Rosencrantz and Guildenstern* over the next three years (181 in total) than of any other play during the entire Old Vic period, and, once back in the repertory from 17 November, it was the most-frequently seen until 31 May. It is to be hoped that Mr Haw managed to secure a much-sought-after ticket for Stoppard's play, but for the time being, like Guildenstern and Rosencrantz, he would have to wait.

... or tails?

Haw would have seen from the brochure that the first booking period of the 1967–8 season, in addition to five performances of *Rosencrantz and Guildenstern*, included eighteen of a new production of *As You Like It*. Had he been following the news, he would have known that this had been in the works for some time. Ronald Pickup recalls that he first learned of the plan for an all-male *As You Like It* early in 1966, when NT associate director John Dexter turned to him during a rehearsal and said 'Get a fucking pair of legs. You're going to play Rosalind in a year's time.' Pickup goes on, 'It seemed absurd at first', and (possibly alluding to Maggie Smith's departure) reports that 'some of the women in the company thought it a bit off'.[59] According to the Board minutes of 20 June 1966, the production had initially been envisaged by the members of the Drama Committee as one 'whereby on alternate performances the female roles would be played boys', while 'the framework of the production would remain unchanged'.[60] This modest proposal was abandoned in favour of the more radical option. Dexter was one of Olivier's more daring appointments, and as a gay man he had a queerer line on the play than either the NT or its audiences were likely to have been comfortable with;

inspired by Jan Kott's Genet-influenced essay, 'Shakespeare's Bitter Arcadia', in *Shakespeare our Contemporary*, he was 'convinced Rosalind was bisexual'.[61]

The production was announced on 24 August 1966, the day that *Rosencrantz and Guildenstern* opened on Edinburgh's Royal Mile. Stating that the all-male casting was inspired by Kott, *The Times* reported that the professor 'has agreed to act as advisor to the production' and named John Stride as Orlando and Dacre Punt as the designer.[62] The production was not mentioned in the press again until mid-December, when it was now slated for the 1967–8 season, still directed by Dexter, with its slot taken by *Rosencrantz and Guildenstern*.[63] Tynan spent some time in the interim trying to persuade Paul McCartney to compose the score, writing that 'there are four or five songs on *Revolver* that ... *are all exactly in the right mood for "As You Like It"* ... we need you because you are the best composer of that kind of song in England'. McCartney initially seemed keen but lost interest, replying 'I don't really like words by Shakespeare',[64] and immersed himself in *Sgt. Pepper* instead.

Unable to settle his differences with Olivier, Dexter withdrew from the production, with *The Times* quoting Tynan to the effect that he was surprised and saddened by his departure: 'if you have a Dexter he's wholly irreplaceable. There has been friction but nobody had any idea that it was going to end like this. He will be missed'.[65] Dexter, however, insisted that he was 'Sacked. Thank you very much' by Olivier, and he recalled letting rip to Joan Plowright over 'the covert undermining of the production, and that betrayal of trust. He could not have feared, as someone has said, that I would be over budget. Over the top, yes. Budget *No*'.[66] Dexter was not that irreplaceable, since Olivier had already secured Clifford Williams to take over the direction, and on 7 August the final cast and creative team were announced: Ralph Koltai had replaced Punt as designer, and Jeremy Brett would play Orlando. It was revealed that the production would be in modern dress as well as all-male, with a note in the press release laying claim to a historical mandate, stating that 'in Shakespeare's own day *As You Like It* was presented with a male cast in costumes of the current time'.[67] With *Rosencrantz and Guildenstern* the NT successfully staged a contemporary text as a traditional-style Shakespearean production; now it was to attempt the trick in reverse order, making over a Shakespeare text as a contemporary one.

Anyone following the personnel changes would have already known that this looked be a production very different to the one that Dexter might have directed. Dexter's only previous Shakespeare production, Olivier's *Othello*, had been a straightforward period-costume piece whose settings (designed by Jocelyn Herbert) had been unobtrusively neutral; Punt was known for restrained, romantic and dreamily suggestive designs for theatre and opera; his sets for a production of Britten's *The Turn of the Screw* in 1966, 'panels of heavy netting, some fixed, some movable', for example, 'could suggest anything from the green innocence of spring to the most horrific sexual symbolism';[68] and those for Berlioz's *Beatrice and Benedick* a few years later were 'simple but imaginative and charming'.[69] Williams, who joined the RSC in 1961, had provided the company with a long-running hit with his lively, colourful *The Comedy of Errors*, which remained in repertoire until 1965; he was a highly competent, respected professional but no iconoclast. Having inherited the all-male scheme, Williams was cautious about it: invited by Olivier in January, he pondered the decision to accept for months, prompting his agent to send him an 'Anxious cable' asking him whether it was true that 'you are going to do the Bard in drag?'[70] Long after the production closed at the Old Vic, he confessed to worrying about Aunt Edna's reaction, and revealed that he had entertained various framing strategies, including presenting the play as a performance in a Japanese prisoner-of-war camp: 'we were apprehensive. We suspected it might offend members of the audience, many of whom are elderly and from the middle class'.[71]

Ralph Koltai had also worked at the RSC and acquired a reputation as an innovator with his design for the Sadler's Wells production of Brecht and Weil's *Rise and Fall of the City of Mahagonny* in 1963, when 'astonished' spectators 'saw a completely bare stage, and a real battered truck and trailer drive on. The sides of the trailer were let down and became the stage ... It was the first time Brecht was shown in England in a non-imitative manner, yet every image was politically appropriate and aesthetically thrilling'.[72] Visually and conceptually, Koltai's setting for *As You Like It* made an equally arresting statement, and one that, intentionally or not, was the antithesis of that of *Rosencrantz and Guildenstern*. Lost in an old-school production of *Hamlet*, Rosencrantz and Guildenstern existed in a chiaroscuro world of gloom and shadows, cobwebs, draperies, soft edges and mist; the inhabitants of Koltai's Arden saw themselves, literally, reflected in a box of mirrors, in which everything – contrary to the greenery-choked version of the play staged almost anywhere and anytime in England since the nineteenth century – was non-organic. Koltai's set was dominated by a suspended sculptural arrangement of translucent tubes flanked by cut-out marshmallow clouds perforated with holes, its materials were plastic, glass and perspex, and its visual logic one of sharp lines and angles, and of solid geometric shapes. The lighting enhanced the aura of unreality, with the stage at one point 'bathed in a golden glow', at others 'in silver, red – or, for the nuptial celebration at the end – an almost psychedelic profusion of colour'.[73] Williams had started with the rather bucolic image of Arden as 'the escape we all need. You know, the week-end cottage in the country';[74] this was closer to Koltai's oneiric vision of an Arden that was 'real to those who dream it'.[75]

The image shown in Figure 2.1, of Swinging London in all its glittering, narcissistic glory (also evoked by a live musical score that hybridized hot jazz, folk-rock, instrumental pop and skiffle), was the play-world that the cast of *As You Like It* inhabited.

How they got there was the subject of an article in the *Sunday Times* published the week before the show opened, which tracked some of the ups and downs of the rehearsal process. Kenneth Pearson pictures the rehearsal room towards

FIGURE 2.1 *Jeremy Brett, Charles Kay and Ronald Pickup in* As You Like It, *directed by Clifford Williams, 1967. Photograph © Zoe Dominic, courtesy of Dominic Photography.*

the end of this period that safely accommodates both macho banter and self-mocking camp:

> Two actors are looking for an astounding poetic move.
> 'What shall I be doing?'
> 'Knitting jockstraps, I reckon?'
> Behind them, in a corner, Robert Stephens, playing Jaques, is softly singing in his best Rex Harrison manner, 'Why can't a woman be like a man?'[76]

The atmosphere was not always this relaxed. Focusing on the four actors cast in the female roles (Pickup, Charles Kay as Celia, Richard Kay [no relation] as Phebe and Anthony Hopkins as Audrey), Pearson tracks their uncertain and sometimes fraught journey from rehearsal to performance, in which the challenges of drag and female impersonation are deeply entangled with an unspoken but ever-present concern with homosexuality. In the year that the Sexual Offences Act decriminalized sex between men, an all-male *As You Like It* was both a welcome symptom of cultural liberalization and a potentially controversial experiment, and its actors' performance anxieties reflect their and the production's careful negotiation of this binary.

Pickup is reported early on 'looking for gestures that spring from the way women are made, from the *inside*; that way he hopes to avoid the camp flicks of the queer'; gradually they learn 'the safety of playing for character as opposed to impersonating women in general'. Overheard in the rehearsal room, Kott had other ideas: 'Even though they are playing the scene as women and developing the relationship as women, you can sense the maleness coming through.' The actor's sexualities were their own business, but it is noticeable that both Richard Kay and Hopkins articulated their worry that playing across gender somehow compromised their own sexual identity. Kay (or Pearson) was keen to signal the actor's straightness by bringing his spouse into the story, though her reaction is not altogether reassuring: 'I wondered what my wife would think. Actually, she was quite cast down for a day or two.' 'The advice of wives in general', Pearson reassures his readers, 'is sought daily', such as when Kay 'sits in the bath and waves a leg': '"Do you think they look like a woman's?" "Er ... mmm ... they *could* be", says Mrs Kaye [sic].'[77]

Anthony Hopkins was at first even more unhappy, and at the start of September was looking for a way out of the production, telling Williams that early rehearsals had 'left him with a complex he cannot overcome'. 'There's a huge wall ... I don't think I can make the sexual leap.' Encouraged by the director to go away and think about it, Hopkins returned after a weekend off with a new strategy: 'he wears a rough shift and it dictates the way he walks. He then adds a wig of long hair and the natural gestures to keep it out of his eyes help to ease the problem'. Ditching the falsetto and keeping his naturally low-pitched delivery, Hopkins was now, pleasingly for Williams, 'Moo-cowish'. Rehearsal photographs show that Hopkins was the only one of the four to shape his physical performance through the discipline of rehearsing in costume, and, perhaps unsurprisingly, his performance of gender turned out the closest to pantomime-style send-up. He was, obviously, more than happy with this; while Pickup and Charles Kay fretted about 'not feeling relaxed like girls are when they are together. Perhaps we need more physical contact', Hopkins cavorted in a corner in a long skirt, 'revealing a pair of stout hairy legs' (what *is* it about these men and women's legs?), while belting out 'Knees Up Mother Brown'.[78] Perhaps it worked as a coping mechanism.

On the Monday of the week before opening night, cast, costumes and set came together on the stage of the Old Vic for a run-through of the first half. The night before, Olivier had thrown a spanner in the works by asking Williams 'Shouldn't the women be wearing breasts?' (answer: no), and Koltai was still making last-minute costume changes. Pickup recalls that Koltai 'wanted to go over the top with it', putting him and Celia 'in leather pants and boots, like a couple of biker girls', with him in 'an awful blond wig': 'It would have been dreadful.'[79] Common sense prevailed, Koltai instead opted for what the costume plot lists as a floor-length white wool dress and belt, white shoes and scarf for Rosalind, and for Celia, white wool dress and shoes and turquoise scarf.[80] That night, an inspired simplification meant that Pickup's performance suddenly fell into place and, in absolutely contemporary terms, made perfect sense: 'Pickup is wigless, his own hair brushed over his forehead ... And suddenly it's Twiggy.'[81] In terms of trendy gender play, the association could not be bettered. The then eighteen-year-old celebrity model Twiggy (Lesley Hornby) was widely seen as the face not only of young fashion but of the 1960s itself, and with her slight build, bobbed hair and boyish looks, and her skill in modelling clothes that blurred conventional gender divisions, she did much to popularize the Ganymede-androgynous look of the time. It would become evident soon enough that the desirable body image and liberated sexuality that Twiggy apparently represented were both, for women, a mixed blessing, the flipside of the new freedom being an eating-disordered body morphology, and pill-facilitated submissive availability; but in 1967 most young people were too busy chasing fun and getting fried to care. When the lightly-built (or as he put it, 'gangly, with these skinny legs')[82] Pickup arrived in Arden sporting a unisex white PVC trouser suit, blue shirt, black ankle boots and white corduroy cap, the identification was complete. 'Don't forget', warned Olivier after the run-through, 'they're all paying fifty bob in the front row to see this'.[83]

A night of mild gender-bending at the Old Vic might have seemed a sound prospect when seen in relation to the comparable delights on offer across London's theatreland. The *Punch* listings for the week of *As You Like It*'s opening had changed little since the *Rosencrantz and Guildenstern* premiere in April, with the comedy of middle-class heterosexual intrigue continuing to hold sway. *Come Spy with Me* had closed in July, as had *Cactus Flower* in September, but taking up the slack were *Let Sleeping Wives Lie* at the Garrick ('mislaid husbands and wives who reappear at just the wrong time and go on doing so for three hilarious acts') and *Uproar in the House* at Whitehall ('four assorted couples spend the night in an absolutely hideous modern house. The bedroom doors never stop swinging'). *Big Bad Mouse*, *Hello Dolly!* and *There's a Girl in My Soup* were still running, and the RSC were back in town with a 'sizzling romp' of a *Taming of the Shrew* and a 'pleasantly unsensational' *As You Like It* that boasted Dorothy Tutin's 'witty' Rosalind, Janet Suzman's 'outstanding' Celia and a 'mighty funny' Touchstone from Roy Kinnear. Still, the NT revival would be in repertory with a

'Tremendously exciting' *The Dance of Death*, the 'very, very funny' *A Flea in Her Ear*, 'magnificent' and 'breathtaking' *The Royal Hunt of the Sun*, 'supremely impressive' *Three Sisters* and the 'altogether fascinating' *Rosencrantz and Guildenstern*, so there was everything to play for.[84]

The show opened on 3 October with the queen of the cross-dressers, Danny La Rue, fresh from *Come Spy with Me*, in the first-night audience. Possibly misreading the mood, he sent the cast a telegram ('COME ON IN THE WATER IS FINE'), but was disappointed by what he saw; 'Well. It's all very interesting, of course', he opined in the Old Vic crush bar during the interval, 'but I don't see the point of it'.[85] The broad, variety-based drag comedy that formed the basis of La Rue's long and successful career was – Hopkins's antics aside – something the production went out of its way to avoid; as Williams insisted, 'we were determined that there should be no female impersonation, no mincing, no attempt to speak in a falsetto, no feminine gesture. In drag it would have been hideous, a very boring travesty'.[86] The production was not altogether successful in this respect: Charles Kay, the *Evening Standard*'s Milton Shulman felt, was 'allowed to teeter into high queerdom',[87] and Ronald Bryden agreed, noting 'straight [*sic*] if muted camping: a comic performance based on masculine imitation of female mannerisms'.[88] Williams also failed to mention the full-on burlesque of Hopkins's Audrey, which was seen by some to reference the entertainment culture of the British armed forces, where the pressures of a men-only environment had long found comic release in transvestism; reminiscent of 'the kind of camp concert resorted to in a battle ship',[89] Hopkins represented 'basic ENSA knockabout',[90] and, for Irving Wardle at least, achieved 'the funniest of all the performances': 'a bass-voiced Brunnhilde who sits expressionlessly through Touchstone's advances and then grasps him in a bear-hug'.[91]

Presumably, Williams cast the butchest male in the company in this role for good reason (it is, incidentally, a rather Stoppardian irony that it took the minor women's parts in *As You Like It* to be played by men to get them noticed), but he nonetheless maintained that the cross-dressing served a higher purpose. True, there was an image of La Rue in the programme, but it was one element of a montage of historical male-to-female transvestites, that ranged from Restoration-era Edward Kynaston through Jack Lemmon and Tony Curtis in *Some Like It Hot*, Alec Guinness in *Kind Hearts and Coronets* and – a cheeky touch – Laurence Olivier as a schoolboy Kate in *The Taming of the Shrew*, to the Peking Opera's Mei Lanfang. Even as it acknowledged the drag traditions of popular entertainment, the production attempted to distance itself from them, and it likewise both deferred to Kott and disclaimed him. Quoted in a lengthy programme note, Kott was simultaneously repudiated by Williams's own programme note, which asserted that *As You Like It* dealt with 'the infinite beauty of Man in love', something that 'takes place in an atmosphere of spiritual purity which transcends sexuality in the search for poetic sexuality'. Somehow, an all-male cast meant 'that we shall not – entranced by the surface beauty – miss the interior truth'.[92] Possibly Williams thought that the distractions of 'beauty' and 'sexuality' were a matter of women's bodies but not men's minds, and that men in any case could not conceivably be the subject of spectatorial desire. He later admitted that 'we read Kott's essay, and decided that it was absolutely daft', and referred to the 'unusually sexually aware' scholar saying 'that his thought had been to use boys about 14 years old'. Kott 'spoke of Shakespeare and pederasty, and said there is in the text a quote from Christopher Marlowe who had a bigger thing about small boys than Shakespeare'.[93] It is little wonder that Williams kept a discreet distance.

These intellectual contortions were ignored by the first-night reviewers, who were not in the least bothered by the production concept. To a man (Hilary Spurling excepted, they were all men),[94] they greeted it with great enthusiasm. Critical attention was split between Koltai's set and costumes and the men acting the women, led by Pickup's Rosalind. Beneath 'a snowflake ceiling … and not a tree in sight',[95] the stage seemed 'to suggest some lunar culture that is yet to dawn';[96] while the costuming suggested 'some sort of timeless era when the garment trade has gone kooky over black leather and white plastic'.[97] Duke Frederick (Frank Wylie), channelling Joseph Losey's cult-hit 1966 thriller *Modesty Blaise*, resembled a drug-dealing pimp; as Jaques, Robert Stephens looked 'like some last of the Bloomsburians in a faded white alpaca suit',[98] and carried a transparent PVC mac and umbrella. The critics agreed that this was lovely to look at, but some, primed by the metaphysical gymnastics and theatrical game-playing of *Rosencrantz and Guildenstern*, suspected that there was more to it than met the eye; that the emphasis on mirrors, surfaces and artifice posed questions about the nature of role-playing, illusion and reality themselves.

For more than one critic, this provided a means of containing the production's paradoxes of gender identity: dazzled by 'the aesthetic pleasure provided by the patterns of a kaleidoscope', Frank Marcus suggested that in this 'rapturous dream' the 'truly staggering surprise of the evening was that the experiment in female impersonation, far from being the most noteworthy facet of the production, became quite unimportant – indeed, almost irrelevant – to it'.[99] A few went still further. While a *Daily Mail* subeditor teased its readers by entitling Peter Lewis's review 'Taking a dream trip with the Bard', its author mused on how 'one entered into a trance …. The Forest of Arden, after all, is a country of the mind … in which the oddest things seemed natural' (his ellipses, not mine), and that this was 'a conception of the play so strange, so visually and aurally hypnotic that the fact that all the girls are really men' is 'merely one of the elements in a dream-like total experience, which you accept with the rest … a dream in which the dreamer glides through layer on layer of different dream personages' (my ellipsis, not his).[100] Those who had figured out what the third track on Side One of *Sgt. Pepper* was 'about' would have needed little prompting; there were no points for guessing what was in this production's water supply.

Lewis was particularly taken with the psychedelic plasticity of this production's girl with kaleidoscope eyes, Pickup's

Rosalind, not least when he watched him 'playing the boy Ganymede pretending to be the girl Rosalind'. Commending Pickup by stating that 'he might as well have been a girl', Lewis speculated whether the show 'would have been less effective had the parts been taken by actresses', but seemed to endorse Williams's line by asserting that the play 'is about love and here love was portrayed as sexless, or rather sexually ambiguous'.[101] There is a distinction to be made between asexuality and sexual ambiguity, but it was not one that Lewis chose to explore; and neither did most of his journalist colleagues. In this respect, the determination to strip Rosalind–Ganymede of erotic allure seems to have paid off: Pickup, most agreed, gave a fine performance but none felt themselves at risk of actually fancying him. He was a 'weedy, gauche creature',[102] according to Shulman; a 'completely non-erotic' 'beaky, long-legged figure in a yachting suit'[103] for Wardle; and Martin Esslin also hailed 'an excellent actor with much wit and feeling' but regretted that 'his long lanky frame is totally devoid of sexuality'.[104] D. A. N. Jones thought that by making 'the boy-girl ... not pretty' the production created 'an artificial reconstruction of what's best in womanhood', and redirected spectatorial desire for Rosalind towards Orlando; 'Normally, a theatre audience, mostly female, identifies with Orlando and gazes at Rosalind; in this production, Rosalind is the impresario and makes you look at her beloved Orlando played by Jeremy Brett.'[105] Whoever 'you' might be – and these comments tell us as much about their authors as about the production – this at least admits that Brett–Orlando might well be desirable, and not just for women. Generally, it was Pickup's skill at executing the double layers of gender impersonation, and, crucially, those moments when he–she *failed* to convince, that captured reviewers' attention. Shulman noticed that Pickup as Rosalind was 'uncertain of what to do with her hands or when to cross her legs' (the slippage of pronouns may or may not be deliberate) but 'naturally comes into his / her own when she wears male clothes as Ganymede'.[106] Jeremy Kingston found the performance 'uncanny in its observation of how, for example, women believe men throw back their arms and laugh'.[107]

The portrayal, as Hobson put it, 'divorces love from sex' as did 'the performances in the other transvestite parts', and the result was 'a purity, a "magical release from material dominion", as Mr Williams himself says, that has probably not been achieved in any professional performance for the last 300 years'.[108] Maybe so, but even if it is too easy to interpret the general insistence on the production's non-sexiness as denial (sometimes a cigar really is just a cigar), the issue of same-sex desire, in a production in which the play's wooing games were played by men, was clearly being skirted. This consideration was underlined by the fact that, both as Rosalind and as Ganymede, Pickup's emphasis on physical mannerisms was not accompanied by any alteration to his customary vocal register. In the audio recording of the production (held in the British Library's National Sound Archive), Charles Kay's wigged and bespectacled Celia preens and trills his way through virtually the entire drag-queen repertoire, while Richard Kay's Phebe adopts the husky purr of a B-movie femme fatale; Pickup, in contrast, sounds at every stage like himself. Perhaps the 'real excitement' that Wardle found 'in seeing this Rosalind and Jeremy Brett's very masculine Orlando being taken unawares by serious emotion'[109] stemmed from the possibility that the love that dared not speak its name had finally, quietly and firmly spoken on the English stage.

The notion that this production was somehow sexless was also given the lie by one of its more rogue elements, Richard Kay's Phebe. The concerns communicated by Kay's wife in rehearsal, as well as his own doubts about whether he could pull it off, were, depending on your angle of view, either absolved or vindicated by the response of the reviewers to the only man in the show to *really* pass as a woman. Bryden saw only 'a nightclub female impersonation: a languorous, lipsticked sexpot with curiously hard muscles',[110] but W. A. Darlington, who was not completely convinced by Pickup ('when he overdid the mincing walk which goes with long skirts we had an impulse to giggle'), wrote that Kay was 'so feminine in voice and gesture that he might have been a woman'.[111] Pickup remembered 'people checking their programmes' when the 'truly womanlike'[112] Kay came on; and for at least one reviewer this was pretty troubling: Esslin contrasted Pickup's lack of sexual magnetism with that of Kay, whom he found 'disturbingly pretty, large but with lovely legs and a fine face', and confessed that it was 'really disturbing if one also becomes aware, at the same time, that this pretty girl is a man'.[113] In the production photographs Kay, barefoot in a classic Mary Quant PVC mini-dress that directs the viewer's gaze towards his long, smoothly-shaven legs, is unquestionably an object of desire.

Whose desire is open to speculation, though the report in the *New York Times* on a first-night house that included 'long-haired boys and short-haired girls among the enthusiastic viewers',[114] provides a clue to the show's appeal; there was a younger, and more socially and sexually diverse, audience for the production than Williams, Olivier and the rest had imagined. As we shall see in the next section, this appeal would be sustained, over the course of a run of ninety-six performances, for rather longer than anyone had expected. On 18 October, *As You Like It* joined the rest of the Old Vic repertory in the *Punch* listings as a production that 'may not achieve all its declared objectives but visually beautiful and most sensitively acted, Ronald Pickup an exquisite Rosalind'.[115] It remained in those listings, on and off, for the best part of two years.

Coining it

Two weeks after *As You Like It* opened, *Rosencrantz and Guildenstern are Dead* was given a pre-Broadway try-out run in Washington. Clive Barnes of the *New York Times* was there, and he was impressed, describing the play as 'Very funny, very brilliant, very chilling; it has the dust of thought about it and the particles glitter excitingly in the theatrical air ... In one bound Mr Stoppard is asking to be considered as among the finest English-speaking writers of our stage'.[116] When the play opened on Broadway, Barnes's *New York Times* colleague Walter Kerr agreed, and, providing some of the production detail that Barnes and the London reviewers had skipped, documented a first-rate play's stunning production: 'a castle that seems so much melted-down wax', 'Hamlet yanking at Ophelia's blond hair to whip-saw her head about, for no known savage reason', 'a dumb-show in which the dead are blown away on the wind like nameless November leaves', 'a sweep of grey cloaks over the field of the dead', 'the preoccupied people from "Hamlet" swirling by in their faintly frosted costumes, the dusty traveling harlequins creeping out of barrels on shipboard to surround Hamlet's two frightened friends in quiet but unhelpful sympathy'. As 'the stage lights turn from an autumnal gold to a tidal wave of blood-red' the total effect was almost synesthetic: 'Richard Pilbrow's lighting seems to swell inside the play and then diminish to the isolated pinpoints on which each of us must stand. The stage is managed as music should be; in time – and despite inevitable reservations – we are overwhelmed by the visual sound.'[117] Music was in the air for *Newsweek* too, which had Brian Murray and John Wood as 'John Lennon and Ringo Starr lost in space' and noticed how, in the opening moments, 'simple Ringo Rosencrantz just keeps pocketing the coins'.[118]

Stoppard and others were soon to discover what *Rosencrantz and Guildenstern* was 'about'; according to his biographer, the playwright had been promised a staggering $6,000 a week from the Broadway run.[119] Exactly one month after the Washington opening, the play returned to the Old Vic repertory for its first three performances since the end of September. The box office receipts for the period from 7 November to 2 December 1967 tell the story: in a repertoire that also included Tyrone Guthrie's *Tartuffe* and the final performances of Zeffirelli's *Much Ado*, the productions of *As You Like It* and *Rosencrantz and Guildenstern* between them accounted for £8,033 (or just over 40 per cent) of the booking period's total takings of £19,498, and almost always played to full houses.[120] For the next twenty-one months, *Rosencrantz and Guildenstern* and *As You Like It* were twin fixtures of the NT schedule. The interweaving trajectories of these shows provide a neat demonstration of the ways in which the changing circumstances and contexts of a production transform what it means to its audiences as it moves through time. Caught between the competing imperatives of the need to sustain its state-underwritten financial viability, the obligation to respond to public demand, the requirement to offer a balanced and varied programme, the wish to preserve what was already proven and valued while allowing opportunities for new work and, occasionally, for risk-taking; the National, as in any period of its history, was faced with multiple challenges. The most pressing concerns at this moment, though, were: first, how to capitalize on the success of two unexpected hits while keeping the work of the theatre as a whole fresh and forward-looking; and, second, in the case of *Rosencrantz and Guildenstern*, how to balance the wish to guard the NT's own financial interest in a valuable asset with its obligations to the wider theatre community.

Long runs at the NT were not unprecedented, and the practice of rolling productions over from one season to the next was during the first decade of the Old Vic period the norm rather than the rare exception it became once the move was made to the South Bank. When Stoppard's play entered the repertory in April 1967, *Othello*, which opened three years previously, had only recently left it, and Shaffer's *The Royal Hunt of the Sun*, from the same season, had more than two months left to run. *Rosencrantz and Guildenstern* was preceded by Strindberg's *The Dance of Death* and followed by *Three Sisters*; these ended, respectively, in July and April 1969, and it outlived them by a further nineteen months. In the interim, the Old Vic opened six new plays and seventeen revivals, including, in addition to *As You Like It*, the Olivier-directed *Love's Labour's Lost* in December 1968 and the Olivier-directed-by-Miller *The Merchant of Venice* in April 1970. The longevity of *As You Like It* is less spectacular, but still impressive. It was one of the two new productions of 1967–8 to carry over to 1968–9 (the other being Marlowe's *Edward II*, which, having had only sixteen showings since opening in April, was afforded the courtesy of a further thirteen over the space of four months), and, opening the season with a run of five performances in a row it accounted for twenty-four of an Old Vic total of over two hundred performances between September and July, which also included thirty-one showings of *Rosencrantz and Guildenstern are Dead*. Taking a cue from the Player's maxim of 'every exit being an entrance somewhere else',[121] every occasion on which performance of either *Rosencrantz and Guildenstern* or *As You Like It* took place was one on which a performance of something else did not. It is impossible to know whether specific productions suffered as a consequence of *Rosencrantz and Guildenstern*'s dominance, but 151 performances at the Old Vic between 1967 and 1970 is more than the combined total (124) of all new plays staged there in the same period; between April 1967 and September 1968, it was the only contemporary play in the repertoire.

The longer they continued, the greater grew the gap between shows born for a particular time and place and the world around them. Of the two, the modern play in period dress probably aged more gracefully, though it seems likely that by the end of its run a production that even when new was a retrofit of another one three years older would have accumulated a patina of backward-looking charm. *As You Like It* might have looked the latest thing in October 1967, but, one imagines, a touch last-season by the same point in 1968. Both underwent alterations during their extended runs, and both would have felt the pressures of a particularly turbulent period of history. In December, Hopkins was granted his wish to leave *As You Like It* and his part was taken by John Stride, who played Audrey until March 1969, when he was replaced by David Ryall; also in December, in the first of many cast changes, Pickup played Hamlet in Stoppard's play. Early in the new year, it was announced that a gala performance of *As You Like It* was to take place on 14 May 'to mark the

150th anniversary of the Royal Coburg Theatre' (as the Old Vic was originally named in 1816),[122] with Princess Marina, Duchess of Kent and President of the Old Vic, in attendance. By the time it took place, the cultural and political scene, both at home and abroad, had shifted considerably. On 17 March, violent clashes between police and demonstrators during anti-Vietnam war protests outside the American embassy in Grosvenor Square showed that the woozy flower children of the Summer of Love had grown some teeth; a month later, Conservative politician Enoch Powell ignited a row over race relations, when he delivered his notorious anti-immigration 'Rivers of Blood' speech in Birmingham. The gala performance on Tuesday 14 May began with some dodgy commemorative verses, composed for the occasion by poet laureate Cecil Day-Lewis and gamely delivered by Sir John Gielgud, and ended with the audience shuffling out to an instrumental reprise of the accompaniment to Hymen's speech (sung falsetto), which sounds oddly reminiscent of the theme music for the science-fiction puppet series *Captain Scarlet and the Mysterons*.[123] Quite what Princess Marina made of the evening is anyone's guess, but it was probably one of the livelier engagements of a week that also included visits to the annual exhibition of the Pastel Society and the 150th anniversary meeting of the British Sailors' Society.[124]

For the British establishment, it was business as usual; meanwhile, in Paris, students chanting slogans that might have been penned by Stoppard himself ('*Soyez réalistes: demandez l'impossible!*') took in their thousands to the streets of the Left Bank, braved the batons and tear gas of the riot police, and occupied public buildings, including Jean-Louis Barrault's venerable Théâtre de l'Odéon. By the end of the week, the noise from France was heard even in the Waterloo Road, with *The Times* reporting that 'About 250' students had marched down Oxford Street on Friday carrying placards 'saying "Down with the bourgeoisie" and "Today l'Odéon, tomorrow the Old Vic"' (the occupation did not take place, and the Saturday matinee and evening showings of *Three Sisters* passed without incident). [125]

Meanwhile, Czech-born Stoppard was keeping an eye upon the even more serious situation unfolding in Prague, where the government was with the broad support of its people attempting a liberalization of the Communist system that Soviet tanks would brutally end three months later, and 'thinking about a possible play on the Romantics'.[126] He was, presumably, enjoying the success of the work that had just won both Tony and New York Drama Critics' Circle awards for best play, and that, since the forced devaluation of sterling against the dollar in December, was earning more money than ever; the Board heard at the start of December that the New York production would cover its relatively modest production costs by the end of January, and was informed that 'a conservative estimate of our likely share of profits to the end of the financial year has been taken at £20,000'.[127] The Old Vic production was taken on a short regional tour to Edinburgh, Leeds and Oxford, and beyond London and Broadway, *Rosencrantz and Guildenstern* was being staged around the world, though not always as successfully. Claude Régy directed a version in Paris in October 1967, but despite the play having, as the *Financial Times* mischievously put it, 'all the elements to make it immensely popular in France – metaphysical frivolity, irreverent logic, and an absurd love of playing games round a subject of towering literary pretension', the production was a 'disaster'.[128] In February, more happily, the week that saw Pickup, Stride and the two Kays back in their frocks at the Old Vic for the first time in over a month, news came of the first (partly) cross-dressed production of the play. Directed by Franco Enriquez for the Compagnia dei Quattro in Milan, it starred Valeria Moriconi as Rosencrantz, opposite Mario Scaccia as Guildenstern; *The Times* reported that within minutes of the opening 'one has already forgotten that the part is being played by an actress', and that 'The theatricality of the play bursts through all barriers.'[129]

In less than a year, Stoppard's play had become not just a classic but also one that, like *Hamlet*, was fair game for radical reinvention. The time was ripe for risk-taking and experiment:

the 1968 Theatres Act, which abolished the censorship powers of the Lord Chamberlain's Office, had already led to an outbreak of iconoclasm, and no small degree of nudity, on London's stages, among the more popular offerings was the hippie musical *Hair* at the Shaftesbury, which opened in September 1968. After May 1968, the more trenchant radicalism rapidly gaining ground among the young British left energized a new generation of activist performance makers, fiercely opposed to the theatre establishment, and positioned in the vanguard of a revolution that, touchingly, they believed to be just round the corner. This was the year that Jim Haynes opened the Arts Lab in Drury Lane, Ed Berman began the community-based work that led to the Inter-Action network, Explosion, and Charles Marowitz, in collaboration with Thelma Holt, founded the Open Space, where he continued the experimental assaults on Shakespeare that began with his collage version of *Hamlet*, staged as part of Peter Brook's 1964 Theatre of Cruelty season at the RSC. It was the year that Brook described most contemporary Shakespearean performance as 'deadly' ('secretly we find it excruciatingly boring – and in our hearts we either blame Shakespeare, or theatre as such, or even ourselves') and declared that he could 'take any empty space and call it a bare stage'.[130] He turned these words into deeds two years later, in his landmark RSC white-box *A Midsummer Night's Dream*, a production that dealt a hammer-blow to the performance tradition in which *Rosencrantz and Guildenstern* affectionately and self-referentially participated.

In this febrile climate, *Rosencrantz and Guildenstern* and *As You Like It* might have looked reactionary and old-hat, but the National's regulars did not seem to mind. By the autumn of 1968, *As You Like It* could be cited as an example of soundly old-fashioned Shakespearean virtues: with its 'strict attention on the text' and 'scrupulous attention to its nuances', one critic wrote, 'the production is much better spoken than many we meet these days'. Thus 'the perspex and plastic of Ralph Koltai's setting, which in other circumstances would please only the trendy, become a valid contribution to the play'.[131] By now, the show was demonstrably a runaway hit. A week of Old Vic performances in September was followed by a tour to Stockholm, Copenhagen and Belgrade; show reports record that every performance earned no fewer than three additional curtain calls, and that one managed six.[132] By the time the production was given its ninety-sixth and last performance on 16 July 1969, additional calls had become routine.

The day before, David Merrick wrote to George Rowbottom from New York with a financial update on *Rosencrantz and Guildenstern*: 'total profit to date $381,604.00. NT share $190,800'.[133] Still touring the United States, the play in London was now a little more accessible; responding to the long-standing complaint that its most sought-after shows tended to sell out on advance bookings alone, the National had started reserving fifty-five day seats for every performance. This was still not enough to satisfy demand, but the seemingly obvious solution of a West End transfer was not pursued. A year previously, Stoppard's agent, Kenneth Ewing, had written to Rowbottom, enquiring about the possibility; Rowbottom responded by deferring the response to the successor in his post, Antony Easterbrook, and the idea died a quiet death.[134] Merrick and the National had also made tentative moves towards negotiating a film version for MGM, to be directed by John Boorman and possibly featuring Olivier as the Player; this fell by the wayside, but MGM paid the National $45,000 (£18,000) for the film rights anyway.[135] *Rosencrantz and Guildenstern* was back for the first week of the 1969–70 season, and there were a further twenty-two performances up until the end of May. The play was slowly loosening its grip on the schedule; this was thirteen short of those given of the NT's next major new play, Peter Nichols's state-of-the-nation *The National Health*, which, coincidentally, also made metafictional (though more politically-charged) play of the relationship between truth and illusion, juxtaposing the grim reality of hospital ward life with the parallel-narrative idealizations of a medical soap opera.

There were signs that some were growing impatient with the NT's continued insistence upon sole ownership of Stoppard's play. In January, the deputy director of the Arts Council, N. V. Linklater, wrote to Easterbrook informing him that there had been reports that the Exeter Northcott Theatre's Tony Church had wanted to stage the play but had been refused the rights:

> We are, as Kenneth Tynan pointed out, anxious to safeguard your interests but I think you will agree that there is a question of policy here that does affect the livliness [*sic*] and wellbeing of repertory theatres whose audiences want to see something while it is still news. The Report of the Theatre Enquiry, which is to be published at the beginning of March, will be recommending a general re-examination of the current practice in this matter.[136]

Easterbrook's reply stated that Stoppard's agents, rather than the NT, were holding out, and tactfully prevaricated, intimating that the 'reason for their attitude is not too clear, but I have a feeling that it may relate to Tom Stoppard's tax situation'. 'However', he continued, 'it does seem more and more inequitable that organisations such as the Northcott … should be denied the possibility of this play'.[137] Ewing relented at the end of April, writing to Easterbrook to confirm a limited release of the play to a selection of regional playhouses that were on the Council of Repertory Theatres 'A' list and located beyond a thirty-mile radius of the Old Vic, and sarcastically signing off, 'It should go like a bomb at Prestatyn!'[138]

There was still no shortage of outside interest. Not long after the play opened, Derek Goldby had written to Ian McKellen's agent, Elspeth Cochrane, to enquire whether her actor would 'be interested to play the part of Guildenstern'.[139] McKellen, at that stage, was not, but in August 1970 (with Ronald Pickup now playing Guildenstern, and Edward Hardwicke Rosencrantz), Easterbrook sent a memo to Olivier and Frank Dunlop letting them know that Prospect Productions had been in touch with Kenneth Ewing, proposing a British and European tour of paired, cross-cast productions of *Hamlet* and *Rosencrantz and Guildenstern*, 'starring Ian McKellen'. Easterbrook quotes Ewing to the effect that 'it might actually enhance our future with the play by reviving interest in it in this slightly gimmicky way', and reports that he told Ewing that 'we would certainly consider it'.[140] Again, nothing came of the idea, although McKellen's Prospect *Hamlet* toured the United Kingdom and Europe in 1972.

The last-ever performance of *Rosencrantz and Guildenstern* at the National Theatre at the Old Vic was on 22 October 1970. Even then, the NT kept its options open; six months later Jill Foster of Fraser and Dunlop wrote to Easterbrook to ask 'what are your plans for R & G and also, if you plan to keep the play in your repertoire, what is your attitude to amateur productions'.[141] Easterbrook wrote back: 'we do hope to keep ROSENCRANTZ in the repertoire bringing it in again probably around the turn of the year. I think it is about time the amateurs had a go, don't you, but of course it is up to you. Perhaps their productions may quicken interest in professional productions'.[142] There certainly was an audience for the play in the regions: a year to the day after the Old Vic production closed, Foster wrote to Easterbrook listing performances in Canterbury, Worcester, Sheffield, Salisbury, Leicester, Ipswich, Birmingham, Bristol, Glasgow and Belfast, as well as a Cambridge Theatre Company tour, and enclosing a rights cheque for £676.07, one third of the total earnings (Stoppard and his agent pocketed the rest).[143] Tyrone Guthrie once wrote that '*Hamlet* is always going on somewhere';[144] in 1971, it seemed that the same could be said of *Rosencrantz and Guildenstern*. Still the NT was reluctant to relinquish the play, and Stoppard's agent was happy to go along with this; the following year, Easterbrook wrote to Ewing expressing 'the strong hope that we would want to produce it in the South Bank Theatre',[145] with Ewing responding, 'we will not grant any West End licences for this play without first consulting with you, as it is our hope that it may appear again in your repertoire'.[146]

As it turned out, *Rosencrantz and Guildenstern are Dead* was not staged on the South Bank until 1995. *As You Like It*, however, enjoyed a second, not entirely successful, lease of life a couple of years after it closed at the Old Vic. In 1974, Williams revived his production for a tour of Canada and the United States. The cast, led by Gregory Floy as Rosalind, was new, but the set and costumes reproduced those of 1967. The show was well received in San Francisco, where it opened on 17 July, and was described as 'utterly beguiling'[147] and 'singularly enjoyable'.[148] Perhaps Williams and the NT hoped to match the global success of Brook's *Dream*, which was still touring four years after opening in Stratford. If so, the wisdom of attempting to resurrect in 1974 what had been groovy in 1967 was sorely tested when the show moved to New York. As Martin Gottfried of the *New York Post* witheringly put it, the production was 'the talk of London six years ago, and it looks it'.[149] Williams became embroiled in a spat with the *New York Times*'s Clive Barnes, who followed a blistering review with a piece in the London *Times* accusing the NT and Williams of shoddy profiteering, and describing this 'sub-standard' revival as 'not at all good for the reputation of the National Theatre'.[150] Williams hit back by referring to the 'glowing' notices the production had received, and sulked that 'either the production, unfortunately, has changed for the worse – or Clive Barnes has'.[151] It is a sad, bitter postscript to the story of one of the NT's greatest Shakespearean successes. It is time, therefore, to draw the curtain, and to remember *As You Like It*, and *Rosencrantz and Guildenstern are Dead*, in the period in which they truly belonged, and as the two sides of a Shakespearean coin that always, always came up heads.

3

Translations

Very choice Italian

When Franco Zeffirelli brought his Italian-language production of *Hamlet* to the National Theatre in September 1964, it was his third encounter with the British Shakespearean theatre. On the two previous occasions the experience had not been altogether happy. In October 1960, he was invited by Michael Benthall to the Old Vic to direct *Romeo and Juliet* having previously worked for the most part in opera; the result was a sultry, sensual, quasi-cinematic neo-realist treatment that, daringly for its time, cast the very young Judi Dench and John Stride in the leads. Importantly, for Zeffirelli, the collaboration between an Italian director and a leading English theatre was conducted in a spirit of forward-looking cosmopolitanism that embraced Shakespeare as a European, rather than exclusively English, writer. In the programme, he wrote that when he received the invitation his instinct had been to refuse, 'because it is so difficult for a foreigner to believe that any but British or American people would be able to touch their own cultural heritage, especially with Shakespearian tradition'.[1] In his autobiography he went further, confessing that when he first took the call from London he was convinced it was an elaborate hoax as 'the Old Vic would never ask an Italian to direct Shakespeare': 'I even thought I recognized the voice of Victor Spinetti, a friend of mine in London who is famous for indulging in such amazingly convoluted tricks.'[2] Thankfully, he pressed ahead with 'a combination of Italian feelings applied to a masterpiece of the classical English theatre which might prove, if successful, that times have changed in Europe and people of different backgrounds can easily work together for creating a new European conscience'.

This, he felt, was as much as political as a cultural gesture, in the context of a Europe that had three years previously taken its first steps towards economic integration with the signing of the Treaty of Rome, and one that was 'far more important to me than any diplomatic or political manoeuvres'.[3] The attempt to marry European visual style to English text failed, on the whole, to persuade critics. Kenneth Tynan in the *Observer* hailed the production as 'a revelation, even perhaps a revolution',[4] but elsewhere praise for Zeffirelli's stagecraft was tempered by censure for his handling of the verse; 'the poetry and the realism simply do not match. We are constantly in this production being brought up against this discrepancy'.[5] Posterity would vindicate Zeffirelli's approach, which proved to be more in tune with the decade that followed than that of his more cautious English colleagues, but not the *Othello* that he directed for the RSC the following year. With a miscast John Gielgud in the lead, the production was panned for its combination of highly elaborate decor, interminable scene changes and attempted psychological realism resulting in 'a typical piece of Italian decorative theatre in which the settings drowned the play'.[6]

Zeffirelli followed this debacle with a series of better-received opera and theatre productions, and in 1963 *Amleto* for the Proclemer-Albertazzi company (named after its leading actors, Anna Proclemer and Giorgio Albertazzi). Reporting from Italy early in 1964, the *Observer*'s Bamber Gascoigne challenged the attitudes behind the critical reaction to Zeffirelli's *Romeo and Juliet*. Gascoigne announced that 'the first thing that strikes one in Italy is the insularity of England', praised *Amleto* as a production which appeared to synthesize diverse European styles – 'classical, almost like a French production of Racine' in its grouping, Brecht-like in its use of visible lights 'beaming down on the heads of the players in a technique usually associated with "alienation"', yet also exhibiting the 'warm realism' of his Old Vic production – and offering in Albertazzi 'a more successful O'Toole; less violent in the public scenes, more genuinely thoughtful in the private ones'.[7] Gascoigne reported that it was hoped that the production would visit the Old Vic in September, and just over a week later a NT press release confirmed this and also stated that Zeffirelli would direct *Much Ado about Nothing* the following year.[8] Bearing in mind both the non-eventfulness of the NT's opening production of *Hamlet* and Zeffirrelli's uneven record in English-language Shakespeare, the double invitation was a bold move on Tynan and Olivier's part; it was also a sign of their institution's internationalist aspirations.

Amleto was the first non-Anglophone professional Shakespeare production to reach the London stage since the 1930s, which had briefly witnessed Alexander Moissi's German-language *Hamlet* at the Globe Theatre in 1930 and Jacques Copeau's staging of André Obey's *Le Viol de Lucrèce* (a version of *The Rape of Lucrece*) at the Arts in 1931. The Comédie-Française brought Molière and Racine four times between 1934 and 1948; Théâtre Renaud-Barrault visited in 1951 and 1956; as did both Marie Bell's and Roger Planchon's companies in 1960. From East Berlin, the Berliner Ensemble spent three weeks at the Palace Theatre in 1956; and the Moscow Art Theatre played at Sadler's Wells in 1957. Tynan was a passionate advocate of the German and Russian productions, praising the former's 'memorable and sculptural ruggedness' and 'blinding sincerity', and the latter's 'total acting': 'we act with our voices, they with their lives'.[9] Both residencies were arranged by the theatre impresario Peter Daubeny who, also in 1964, launched the first of the annual World Theatre Seasons at the Aldwych Theatre, which showcased the work of leading companies from across Europe, the United States and Japan. Although this was timed to mark the Shakespeare quatercentenary, Shakespeare was excluded from the seasons' remit which was to present 'the original in the original language'.[10] The NT's hosting of

Amleto thus heralded new, albeit limited, opportunities for the English Shakespearean stage to expand its horizons.

The production was received very favourably for the most part, with one critic going as far as to characterizing it as 'one of the most exciting evenings I have ever had in the theatre'.[11] The parochial obsession with Shakespeare's poetry which had shaped responses to *Romeo and Juliet* was nowhere in evidence, and the fact that *Amleto* was delivered in colloquial Italian prose without the aid of simultaneous translation was for most not an issue. There were some doubters: true to form Herbert Kretzmer, of the notoriously anti-European *Daily Express* (headline: 'A feast for the parliamo Italiano fans'), indulged his readers' prejudices by confessing that 'faced with a play produced in a language he does not understand', he experienced a 'very long night indeed'.[12] Others were more willing to engage. For B. A. Young, the finer points of Gerardo Guerrieri's translation provided a means of access to Albertazzi's characterization: 'As first rendered, [To be or not to be] ran "Essere o non essere, e tutto qui" – to be or not to be, that's all about it. What we heard last night was "Essere o non essere, questa è la problema", which is much less of a departure.' However, '"E tutto qui" ... would be characteristic of Albertazzi's Hamlet' who was 'not concerned with the spiritual aspect of anything'. As 'an Italian Hamlet ... his emotions blaze where we are accustomed to have them smoulder ... Why should an Italian Hamlet not weep when he says "But break my heart", and why should he not wipe the tears away openly with his hand ...?' Stereotypes of continental emotional incontinence aside, there was much to admire in a performance that 'stands out head and shoulders above anything else'.[13] Other reviewers concurred: Bernard Levin simply noted 'a vigorous and tormented Hamlet, deeply real in such scenes as the "rogue and peasant slave" soliloquy and in the rejection of Ophelia';[14] while *The Times* registered the 'intellectual ferocity' of a performance of 'spectacular details' that included Albertazzi's 'almost epileptic transformation' during his encounters with the (unseen) Ghost ('a projection of the Prince's super-ego'), which had him 'mouthing in sympathy with the whispered commands from the wings and speaking many of the Ghost's lines himself' (several reviewers also singled out Albertazzi's frenzied drumming at the climax of *The Mousetrap* as a highlight).[15]

As far as individual performances were concerned Albertazzi dominated the notices, but his co-star also drew praise; the closet scene, *The Times* reported, was played with an 'unbridled ferocity' that lent it 'an almost operatic quality, both as a stage picture and in Anna Proclemer's voluptuously penitent Gertrude'.[16] As Ophelia, 'a child whose chief need is for tangible physical protection',[17] Anna Maria Guarnieri's 'tempest of the mind' provided J. C. Trewin with 'the most moving mad scene I recall'.[18] Young paid the production the compliment of a second visit (not to have done so 'would have been mad'), and in a follow-up review he turned his attention to the supporting performances. Proclemer was 'outstanding' at first 'flaunting the classic beauty of her youth', but following the trauma of the closet scene her auburn hair 'turned completely grey, and the still lovely features are taut and lined. The Queen has lost her hold on life'. Guarnieri's business in her mad scene was 'about maternity, rocking the child, making its bed and so on, and this renders the sudden swift descents into coarse sexuality even more searing'. Alessandro Ninchi's Laertes was 'another character who grows up before our eyes': leaving for Paris, the 'golf-bag full of rapiers slung over his shoulder might have been the guitar of a student setting out to hitch-hike down to Cannes for the summer. But when he comes back he is a man – decisive, stern, controlled'.[19]

As these details suggest the costuming and general ambience were more-or-less contemporary, and *The Times* was taken with the vision of 'Hamlet as a modern man'.[20] Others may have been, as well: it is not known whether Peter Hall popped down from Stratford at some point during the run to take notes, but the *Hamlet* that he directed for the RSC the following year with 24-year-old David Warner in the lead shared some of this production's spirit. Ronald

Bryden, however, was not impressed, describing the Prince as 'offhand' and labelling the production 'an Italian equivalent of the notion that Mod-ish new audiences might be attracted to Shakespeare by casting, say, Albert Finney in a slang version of the play costumed by the avant-garde Carnaby Street'. If the production had a redeeming feature for this reviewer it was the set, a 'cosmic grey pavement sloped to a circular well from which [Albertazzi] dredged his soliloquies and rages as from some plughole of consciousness'.[21] Much remarked upon and admired, the set designed by Zeffirelli consisted of a steeply raked floor incorporating a downstage pit from which concentric circles radiated upstage; backed by a pair of traverse curtains and a blank cyclorama, this near-empty space was overhung with exposed lanterns ('like sinister sentinels', 'a cluster of suspended eyes') creating a 'daring chiaroscuro'.[22] Offering a clean break with the director's signature realism, the schematic setting created 'an image both of Hamlet's mind and of a blank universe in which man can rely on nothing but himself'.[23] Noticing that Albertazzi mapped his character in spatial terms, Young wrote that on 'O that this too too solid flesh ... he takes two or three deliberate paces inwards across the arcs, inward, that is, toward the centre of his personal problem'. Approaching 'Essere o non essere' he circled the pit, 'like a man with an unwelcome appointment', then descending 'a few steps into it, into the nadir of his existence'.[24] Levin thought the production placed a 'four-square insistence on Hamlet's Oedipal relation with his mother';[25] if so, the Freudian ramifications of Hamlet's journey around, into, and out of a deep hole seem to have been missed.

Harold Hobson, who in a lengthy review had only brief comments to make on the acting, was particularly attentive to the production's use of light and darkness. Grumbling that its depiction of 'a world in which daylight has no existence', a projection of a mind 'which, for the first three hours of the performance, has little in it but a troubled darkness', the production was 'hard on the eyes and the sensibilities of the audience', he nonetheless hailed an 'arresting' vision of the play. The 'deranged and gloomy' Elsinore of the first four acts prepares the ground for the 'great transformation' of the fifth, initiated (in a conflation of the end of 4.4 and 4.6) by Horatio raising a lantern aloft as he reads Hamlet's letter while the latter exits upstage: 'it lights the path of the retreating Prince. Hamlet ... is saved'. At the end of 5.1 'Hamlet and he turn on their heels in a single movement as a curtain rises behind them to reveal the Court, the King, the Queen, and Laertes. For the first time these are flooded with light, for Hamlet's mind is now lucent':

> For an infinitesimal space of time Hamlet and Horatio stand motionless with their backs to the audience, watching their enemies. Then with a firm tread they march into the Court, to the duel, to the poisoning and the slaughter. Zeffirelli has brought them to the point where they see everything and fear nothing. Mountains are rarely easy to climb, but the view from the top is tremendous.[26]

This language-transcending visual splendour, magnificently evoked here by Hobson, might have won over even Kretzmer of the *Express*. But the man who recommended that 'only those with some linguistic familiarity [should] make the journey to Waterloo Road' had already left after 'Polonius had just been killed and at least another hour of atmospheric gloom – augmented by electronic music – loomed ahead',[27] and as a consequence completely missed it. It served him right.

Young concluded his second review by urging his readers to 'Go without lunch for a day or two, do *anything* to fill up those empty seats for the last day', as it would be 'something to remember for a lifetime'.[28] Or, as he put it the day before (unable to resist a crack about Italians and railway timetables), 'It is worth missing any number of trains for, whether you speak Italian or not.'[29] His pleas went unheard. A few years later, Young recalled that audiences for the 'superb' production were 'pathetically small',[30] and his remembrance is confirmed by the NT's accounting. The Board minutes from 14 September

1964 note that *Amleto* had secured advance bookings totalling £1,424 for the two weeks, as compared to £3,771 for the one-week visit by the Bristol Old Vic company with *Love's Labour's Lost* and *Henry V*.[31] After the productions closed the box office returns confirmed that the NT was left with £1,281 from the Bristol Old Vic visit, and 'after deduction of the £2,000 per week guarantee to the Italian Company' a grand total of £53 from *Amleto*. As the Board minutes tartly noted, 'The visit of the companies had cost the National Theatre some £1,000 more than the cost of keeping the theatre closed.'[32]

If *Amleto*, to its sparse English audiences, purveyed its source-culture style as the quintessence of contemporary European cool then Zeffirelli's *Much Ado about Nothing*, which opened at the Old Vic five months later, was rooted in a version of Italian-ness that in many respects looked (and sounded) like its antithesis. Starting from the premise that, for English audiences, foreigners are loud, fantastical and intrinsically hilarious, Zeffirelli envisaged Messina as turn-of-the-twentieth-century small town Sicily, taking visual and generic cues from comic operetta and French farce: 'It will be a bit like Rossini, or the farces of Labiche', he promised the *Sunday Times*, 'like *The Italian Straw Hat*'. His interviewer continued: 'The clothes have been inspired by the puppet shows and sugar dolls peculiar to Sicily in the last century: fantastic shawls, thick black wigs ... gigantic hats trimmed with feathers and artificial fruit.'[33] Having 'more or less dispensed with a set' Zeffirelli used 'a series of differently coloured lighting states, playing onto hessian flats, to indicate changes of location, with the proscenium arch lit throughout by hundreds of fairy lights establishing the carnival atmosphere',[34] and filled the stage with multinational signifiers of the exotic: 'an air of Sicilian carnival, of Neapolitan fiesta ... extravagant costumes that might have come out of a South American revolution; noise, puppetry, greasy black hair, and melodrama villains' moustaches'.[35] A town band marched on and off, dignitaries bustled, Mafiosi lurked, women sported shawls and big hats, soldiers strutted in pillbox hats and red, yellow and blue uniforms, and the Watch were the local carabinieri, led by a Verges (Michael Rothwell) whose bicycle allowed ample opportunities for comic entanglement, and a Dogberry (Frank Finlay) prone to singing off-key snatches of Verdi. Robert Stephens's Benedick was 'a provincial Italian wide boy who soon exchanges his uniform for a variety of sharp suits',[36] and Maggie Smith's much-praised Beatrice combined a 'spirit and a pelting tongue'[37] with a rare vulnerability; 'faun-like', according to the *Spectator*, she blearily appeared on the morning of Hero's wedding (3.4) 'clad in an enormous eiderdown ... her arms part to reveal her clutching a cup of chocolate'.[38] Albert Finney's Don Pedro, a cigar-chomping 'parody of a Latin American dictator, executing peacock swivels on his pelvis',[39] was also much admired.

Although in many respects a fantasy world, this Messina contained a kernel of realism in that it was a plausible context for the play's masculine code of honour: within this Mediterranean milieu, Penelope Gilliatt observed, 'Hero becomes a wretchedly believable girl trapped in a perfectly recognizable Sicily where the same ferocious code of chastity endures to this day';[40] and Beatrice's 'Kill Claudio' (4.2.286) possessed 'a savage force that makes laughter unthinkable'.[41] Michael Coveney expands:

Zeffirelli had wanted her to play for another big laugh. Instead, she yelled, 'Kill Claudio' with a totally unexpected savagery. This outburst of towering, disinterested rage stunned the audience to silence and so petrified the scene that you felt the entire production might have to be abandoned, like an unruly football match suddenly blanketed in freezing fog. Robert held a very long pause and whispered, almost under his breath, 'Not for the world.'[42]

Emotional realism coexisted with broad physical comedy and outrageous slapstick, with 'a measure of mugging and gesticulating which makes the films of Gloria Swanson or the farces of Labiche look like tableaux vivants of unwinking decorum',[43] and a choreographed physicality that mimicked 'the stylized marionette movements of popular Sicilian players'.[44] The cast included a silent chorus of 'Inanimates', mime performers posing as statues, who acted as living scenery and at key moments came to life such as when the mermaids adorning a 'Bernini fountain' suddenly 'protest against Benedick's misogyny', sniggering in response to 'till all graces be in one woman, one woman shall not come in my grace' (2.3.26–8), 'to Benedick's astonishment'[45] (the promptbook notes '*Mermaids titter – Ben does double take*').[46] Another Inanimate introduced the entry of the Watch at the beginning of 3.3, as 'an actor armed as a conquistador climbed onto a pedestal to form a bronze statue'; at the end of the scene the arrest of Conrade and Borachio turned into a Western-saloon mass brawl and one of the Watch 'wrenched a sword from the grip of the "statue", replacing it with his umbrella which the "statue" raised to shelter from the rain'.[47] To stretch the comedy more broadly, various members of the cast affected comedy foreign accents: the locals 'mostly speak with a macaroni Italian accent', reported *Punch*, 'the Dons with some kind of paella Spanish';[48] *The Sun* caught 'Spanish, Italian and for some weird reason Welsh and Yiddish';[49] and the *Daily Express* 'Puerto Rican hoodlums in "West Side Story"';[50] the overall effect, wrote Bernard Levin, was of 'the kind of mock-Italian accents (adding an "a" at the end of words) that schoolboys think is [*sic*] funny'.[51] This prompted a response from Olivier, who defended 'the idea that the sound of the production should be Italianate, as well as the look, the feeling, and the atmosphere of it', and sidestepped the charge of ethnic stereotyping by suggesting that, rather than trying to 'get away with regional, Mummerset, or a vaguely "off" accent' it presented 'a strong atmosphere, redolence and impression of Sicilian character'.[52]

This cut no ice with Levin, who hated the production (the 'sheer breath-bereaving fatuity of what is going on in the Waterloo Road is the first thing to which attention must be drawn … one of the more excruciatingly tedious evenings at present available this side of Hell'),[53] and he was not alone. It divided its critics and its first-night audience, with boos from one side of the house competing with cheers from the other; Zeffirelli recalled that the first night audience 'laughed so much' that the *Observer* critic Penelope Gilliatt 'had to be rushed to hospital after the performance – she was pregnant and had been shaking so much she gave birth shortly after'.[54] Kretzmer buried his antipathy towards the director of *Amleto* to capture the populist mood; 'the show was applauded like a Broadway musical', and 'the result is a night of memorable visual impacts and galloping humours – the theatrical equivalent of a Saturday night spent eating candy floss on a merry-go-round at Battersea funfair'.[55] How very un-English this all was: as the *Times* critics diplomatically reflected, 'The international cross-fertilization of Shakespeare is still a relatively unfamiliar production technique, and we have yet to learn its rules.'[56]

Worse still, one of the rules of European Shakespeare that Zeffirelli adopted for this production was to use a partially translated (English to English) version of the play. This was the work of the poet and polymath Robert Graves, who initially proposed around three hundred emendations (some 140 were adopted) intended to clarify the text's obscurities. The idea was not Zeffirrelli's but Tynan's, who wrote to Graves in August 1964 with the idea of 'replacing dead similes, archaisms and words of changed meaning with *living* Elizabethan words and images', which would 'sweep away the dry cobwebs of text so that full understanding of the words isn't confined to academics'.[57] In a *Sunday Times* article, published before opening night, Graves stated that a 'representative of the National Theatre' had approached him to 'help them to produce a stage version ... which the ordinary intelligent audience member could follow without assistance',[58] and in a programme note he indicated that this putative spectator was not entirely speculative but a product of observation and market research: 'even the astuter part of a Shakespearean audience, which ought to lead the laughter and applause, often puzzles over difficult jokes and obsolete allusions, and gets left behind ... a survey of sixth-formers and undergraduates had shown that they tend to avoid Shakespearean plays for fear of not understanding them'.[59] Tynan himself had reported to the NT Board in October 1964 that 'a recent survey on adolescents and the theatre had shown that 85% did not go to see Shakespeare and other classical plays because they could not understand all the words';[60] and while this statistic sounds as made-up as his notorious estimate of the audience for Osborne's *Look Back in Anger* in 1956 ('roughly 6,733,000, which is the number of people in this country between the ages of twenty and thirty'),[61] it was presumably plausible enough to sanction Graves's enterprise.

Mindful that he was straying into an area of potential controversy, Graves emphasized that he was not modernizing the text but for the most part 'using Shakespeare's own vocabulary, and choosing another set of words that haven't gone completely out of use';[62] although he conceded that he had 'occasionally been forced to use words and phrases of which the first printed record occurs ten to twenty years after Shakespeare's death, though they may well have been current long previously'.[63] Defining the intervention as 'The simple method of re-Shakespeareanizing Shakespeare' he instances 1.3.54–6, which he quotes thus:

BORACHIO
> Being entertained for a perfumer, as I was smoking a musty room, comes me the Prince and Claudio in sad converse.

This was perhaps not the best example to cite, since Shakespeare's line is 'comes me the Prince and Claudio, hand in hand in sad conference', but Graves goes on to offer this reworking of the line:

> As I was employed in perfuming a musty room of the palace, along comes the Prince and Claudio in earnest conference.[64]

Graves's rationale is that 'Any scholar knows that he means "As I was busy fumigating a musty room of the Palace with a sweet-smelling fumigation, along comes the Prince and Claudio in earnest talk." But how many people in the average audience are scholars?'[65] This was one of Graves's more substantial interventions. The majority of textual changes are simple substitutions of vocabulary: 'darer' for 'squarer' (1.178), 'basket' for 'bottle' (1.1.242), 'daggers' for 'poniards' (2.1.233), 'whore' for 'stale' (2.2.24), weapons' for 'bills' (3.3.41) and so on. Some of the emendation is questionable, such as the correction of Dogberry's malapropism 'vigitant' (3.3.91) to 'vigilant', but this was not overall a process of one-way simplification: on a number of occasions Graves opted for more archaism rather than less, where the sense of the early modern term might be misconstrued: thus Beatrice's 'If the Prince be too important …' (2.1.64–5) became 'If the Prince be too importunate …'.

There was a small amount of rephrasing and explanatory expansion: Beatrice's snipe at the yet-to-enter Benedick, 'You had musty victual, and he hath holp to eat it' (1.1.48–9), became, more prosaically, 'The victuals had a musty taste, and he hath helped eat them'; and Claudio's comment on the love-struck Benedick, 'He is then a giant to an ape; but then is an ape a doctor to such a man' (5.1.197–8), was paraphrased in the style of an Arden Shakespeare footnote as 'An ape may take such a man for a giant, but an ape by comparison is a very doctor of philosophy.' Graves wanted to rework Beatrice's 'I had rather lie in the woollen' (2.1.27–8) but was persuaded by Maggie Smith that she could make the line work. 'I will even take sixpence in earnest of the bearward and lead his apes into hell', however, was translated as 'I will hire myself for sixpence a day, as the virgin in the proverb, and lead apes in hell.' That was what was recorded in the promptbook; in his *Sunday Times* article, Graves reflected at some length on the obscurity of this passage and proposed emending it 'in this sort of way': 'Therefore I will e'en go to the Bear Pit and hire myself to the Bearwarden for sixpence a day, as a notable spectacle of virginity, and lead his apes into hell.'[66] In this instance, Graves's 'improvement' created more difficulties of comprehension than it solved.

On the whole, Graves's emendations were such as would be apparent to listeners who knew the text very well indeed. To an extent he followed the example that had been set by John Barton and Peter Hall at the RSC in their adaptation of the *Henry VI* plays into *The Wars of the Roses* two years previously, by effecting a re-write that made better sense but still passed as authentically Shakespearean. Barton and Hall had the advantage of working with play texts that were largely unknown and little admired by theatregoers, and Hall was clear that mature Shakespeare should not be interfered with (as, indeed, was Graves, who insisted that he 'wouldn't touch a tragedy').[67] Barton's edits and pastiche blank verse were for the most part critically tolerated, even lauded; Graves's, which now seem routine and innocuous, divided opinion. Gilliatt thought that they were mostly 'not particularly illuminating, but certainly no heresy',[68] but Levin was incandescent: 'There is not one occasion ... on which the change is not wantonly unnecessary and, to boot, flat and dry beside the fresh and lively original.'[69] By openly admitting that even one for the most popular of Shakespeare's comedies was in need of remedial surgery, the production's creative team adopted a stance with potentially far-reaching implications for the National Theatre's approach to Shakespeare, and, had it been followed through, it might have set the company on a distinctly different (more populist, more accommodating, perhaps more European) path from the far more textually-fundamentalist RSC.

There is some evidence that public opinion was on its side; on 1 May 1965, Miss B. Crawter, London, wrote to George Rowbottom praising the production and urging him not to 'let the reactionaries put you off!'; Rowbottom wrote back stating that 'we are indeed conscious of the fact that such an approach to one of the Bard's works might well lead to controversy', but that this 'would never be regarded as a valid reason for the National Theatre being unwilling to mount such a production'.[70] In the event, *Much Ado* was the first and last time during the Old Vic period that a Shakespearean text was translated in this manner. Indeed, the production programme includes alongside Graves's note a passage that directly contradicts it, in the form of George Bernard Shaw's contrarian thoughts on *Much Ado*, with his rebuttal of 'The main pretension' that 'Benedick and Beatrice are exquisitely witty and amusing persons. They are, of course, nothing of the sort.' For Shaw, paraphrasing Shakespeare produces 'nothing more than the platitudes of proverbial philosophy ... Not until the Shakespearean music is added by replacing the paraphrase with the original lines does the enchantment begin'.[71]

Zeffirelli writes in his autobiography that he began rehearsals by telling his company that they were going to have 'fun'.[72] Robert Stephens's account of the production tells a different story. '*Much Ado* may have looked all right – in fact, it looked stunning – but it was misery to do, because it was so uncomfortable.'[73] The cast's discomfort notwithstanding, *Much Ado* turned out to be a minor hit, but unfortunately at a point in the 1964–5 season when it was too late to take advantage of it. Thirty-two performances were scheduled for a run that began on 16 February and ended on 19 June, fewer than Coward's *Hay Fever* (forty-five) and Miller's *The Crucible* (forty-one). The production eventually acquired a second lease of life, but it took a while to come about. The first period of the 1965–6 season, which opened on 12 October, consisted of two productions that had premiered in Chichester (John Arden's *Armstrong's Last Goodnight* and Pinero's nineteenth-century backstage comedy *Trelawny of the 'Wells'*), one new production (Congreve's *Love for Love*) and two carried over from 1964–5 (*Mother Courage* and *The Crucible*), none of which included any of *Much Ado*'s key players. Smith and Stephens were back with the company in the spring, the former in Peter Shaffer's *Black Comedy* and the latter leading *A Bond Honoured,* John Osborne's adaptation of Lope de Vega's *La Fianza Satisfacha.* With the repertoire completed by Jacques Charon of the Comédie-Française's production of what would prove to be one of the

NT's longest-running hits of the 1960s, Feydeau's *A Flea in Her Ear,* and Olivier's production of O'Casey's *Juno and the Paycock, Much Ado* had to wait until the start of the 1966–7 season to return to the Old Vic. Opening on 24 August, it became the most-performed play at the Old Vic of the 1966–7 season, occupying 58 of a total of 341 slots in a repertoire of eleven productions, among them the Olivier-led *The Dance of Death* and the premiere of *Rosencrantz and Guildenstern are Dead*.

Over the next fourteen months *Much Ado* went through a further four cast permutations, having by its closing night (1 December 1967) racked up more than one hundred performances (a total only exceeded, in the list of the productions considered in this book, by *Rosencrantz and Guildenstern*), and involved a total of seventy-three actors in its thirty-seven roles. Many of the cast changes were fairly routine (although it is worth recording that one of the Inanimates in the sixth and final cast was Sam Dastoor, the National's first British-Asian actor), others were more notable. Don Pedro, played to acclaim by Finney, passed to Derek Jacobi, whose own role as Don John went to rising star Ronald Pickup; Claudio, first played by Ian McKellen, went to Michael Byrne and then to Jeremy Brett; Verges was played in succession by Michael Rothwell, David Ryall, Graham Crowden and Charles Kay. Most importantly, Maggie Smith's departure from the NT at the start of February 1967 meant that Beatrice was taken by Joan Plowright. As Stephens recalled, she was 'desperately unhappy';[74] though *The Times*, taking the opportunity to revisit a production which it still regarded as 'an infuriating mixture of the laborious and the inspired', reported that while early on 'she seems oddly mirthless and too much the incipient shrew', this reading 'pays handsome dividends as we see her soften and mellow under the influence of Benedick's love'.[75] It may have been 'misery' to perform, but Stephens was in the end won over, confessing that 'when I saw it from the front, when I was re-directing it, I wept, it all looked so beautiful'.[76] Sometimes, actors just have to suffer a little.

A world elsewhere

The Sun announced the visit by presenting its readership with a conundrum: were there, it asked, '18,000 people in London who at the same time speak fluent German and have an interest in the classical theatre?' The unexpected answer, the report went on, was yes, since the Berliner Ensemble's residency at the Old Vic for three weeks in August 1965 was already almost sold out on the basis of pre-bookings, mostly for the company's productions of *Die Dreigroschenoper, Der aufhaltsame Aufstieg des Arturo Ui* and *Die Tage der Commune* (or, as their Anglophone audiences knew them, *The Threepenny Opera, The Resistible Rise of Arturo Ui* and *The Days of the Commune*). 'Curiously', however, the only show still taking bookings was Brecht's version of *Coriolanus*, which was attributed to the fact that it was 'Shakespeare's most tedious play, even before Brecht got at it.'[77] If both the arithmetic and the snap literary judgment are to debate, the jokey invocation of an extensive metropolitan constituency of German speakers seems even wider of the mark, since on this occasion the spoken word was probably the least marketable element of the forthcoming event. In *The Stage,* R. B. Marriott put the visit on a par with the Ensemble's London debut at the Palace Theatre nearly ten years earlier, when 'its work was so different from anything we had done': 'On the first night of *Mother Courage*, I remember people who very little or no German ... coming out of the Palace with tears in their eyes and in their imagination the tingling excitement of having witnessed, through feeling as much as intellectual impact, something of extraordinary originality and brilliance.'[78] The 1956 residency, which coincided with the start of the Angry Young Man era in English theatre, gave the lie to the notion that Brecht's theatre was dry, intellectual, emotionless; on the contrary, the work was perceived as passionate, committed, theatrically flamboyant and profoundly moving.

Nonetheless, its impact soon dissipated, and if the version of Brecht that followed generally received a poor press in Britain, it was in no small measure due to the efforts of his loyal-to-the-letter disciples; profiling the Ensemble's artistic director Helene Weigel just before the productions opened, Sean Day-Lewis took a sideways swipe at the 'English Brechtian cult, which has to some extent established her husband as a bore, and, what is worse, a naïve, political bore'.[79] One need look no further than the NT itself to see elements of the cult in action, even in the relatively well-received form of its own production of *Mother Courage*, directed by William Gaskill, which had opened three months previously. Gaskill thought that the Ensemble's staging of the play was 'the best I have ever seen of any play', and therefore his own was 'largely based on it'. He saw 'no reason', he claimed, 'to disregard the author's own detailed notes, not only on the placing of actors and scenery but on how these were arrived at'.[80] The results received a mixed response: *The Times* noted the 'devotedly Brechtian ... use of hard white lighting and spare realist properties' but thought that audiences 'will hardly miss its address to the emotions',[81] and Penelope Gilliatt that 'the play is achieved with ease and bareness',[82] while Harold Hobson found that 'The tedium of the National Theatre production ... is beyond description', so that a play that 'claims to be about the Thirty Years' War ... seemed more like the Hundred Years' War'.[83] In what was established early as the theme of British-theatre Brecht, the thread running through most of the reviews is that Brecht's theory is invariably contradicted by his practice, and that his theatricality can and should be disentangled from his (communist) ideology. Levin put this point with characteristic bluntness. Conceding that, for all Gaskill's 'Brechtian devotion', *Mother Courage* was still 'a great play' because, despite 'the author and his friends', 'the pitiful political rubbish he believed', and 'the drivel he talked and wrote', were 'contradicted by almost every scene he ever put on stage'.[84]

No doubt mindful of the widespread British perception that what Brecht needed was saving from himself, and that in the then-current Cold War environment the politics of Brecht's theatre might be best served by being soft-pedalled, the Ensemble's choice of productions to bring to London was both tactful and tactical. The political context was, to say the least, sensitive: the reasons why it had taken the best part of a decade for the company to make a return journey to the British Isles were embedded in the messy complexities of détente that included, amongst other things, the East German state's repressive treatment of its own citizens, the further travel restrictions placed on them both by the Western powers and by the DDR following the erection of the Berlin Wall in August 1961, and the efforts of successive British governments to balance their responsibilities to NATO with the need to be seen to be open to artistic and cultural exchange. Following the controversy over the Foreign Office's refusal to issue visas to members of the Ensemble to attend the 1963 Edinburgh Festival, travel restrictions were relaxed in March 1964 for 'teachers, artists, scientists and sportsmen'[85] enabling the company to accept the NT's invitation to visit the following year. It was the outcome of some fairly convoluted behind-the-scenes manoeuvring. In November 1963, the Board discussed a season that would have paired the Ensemble's *Coriolan* with the simultaneous hosting of Tyrone Guthrie's Nottingham Playhouse production of the play and of Zeffirelli's *Antony and Cleopatra*, 'the sort of experiment', Sir Kenneth Clark opined, 'that the National Theatre should undertake'.[86]

Two months later, when the 'political implications involved in the possible visits of the two German companies were discussed', it was thought more diplomatic to make overtures to West Berlin's Piscator Theatre:

> The Administrative Director said that he had discussed the matter with the Cultural Attache of the German Embassy and he thought the situation would be eased should the West Berlin company bring their production of *The Merchant of Venice* before the appearance of the Berliner Ensemble.[87]

A month on, Tynan was charged with the task of seeing the Bremen Theatre's *Henry V* (directed by Peter Zadek), with a view to issuing an invitation, since to 'bring over the Berliner Ensemble without also presenting a company from West Germany was considered inadvisable'.[88] Following the relaxation of travel restrictions, invitations were sent to the Bremen company and to the Ensemble to visit in August 1964, but by then it was too late, and the Ensemble's visit was postponed to the following year.[89] When it did take place, the plays they brought with them thus 'provided a number of major works from across Brecht's career while nonetheless still managing to avoid pieces that could give fuel to those who viewed the Ensemble as an organ of didacticism'.[90]

The season opened on Monday 9 August with *Arturo Ui*; *Coriolanus* followed on Tuesday, *The Threepenny Opera* on Wednesday and *The Days of the Commune* on Thursday. Overall, the productions were well received, irrespective of the political positioning of the reviewers' newspapers. It was no surprise that the liberal *Guardian* found *Arturo Ui* 'stunning', 'wildly funny' and 'wonderfully full of bark and bite';[91] less expected was Kretzmer's announcement in the right-wing *Daily Express* that the play 'rescues Brecht's reputation in London when it had reached its lowest ebb'.[92] *The Days of the Commune* showed the company 'versatile to a degree', according to the *Spectator*, as demonstrated in one scene 'wherein the workers celebrate quietly at a café', prompting the realization: 'how rarely "workers" are allowed to be quietly happy on stage'.[93] For Penelope Gilliatt, this production contained 'the best Stanislavskian acting west of the Moscow Arts', giving the lie to the 'crass myth' that 'the Berliner Ensemble has a rigid style'.[94] Alan Brien found an unexpected affinity between the Ensemble's acting and that of the NT's own artistic director: the 'collective style is at once heroic and self-critical so that they carry themselves with a relaxed tension that constantly summons up images from sport – a boxer about to deliver a knock-out, a diver as he splits the water. It is a combination found in only an occasional British actor, such as Sir Laurence Olivier or Albert Finney'.[95] *The Threepenny Opera* even managed to melt the heart of British Brecht's nemesis, Milton Shulman, who wrote that had its author 'continued to write musicals' like this 'the theatre world would not now be split into pro- and anti-Brecht factions. We'd be all for him'.[96]

In these shows the company was on home ground, and most viewers were happy to give them the benefit of the doubt. With *Coriolanus*, larger issues of cultural authority, ownership and appropriation, of perception and reception, were more obviously at stake. Reviewer and audience responses to a German-language presentation of a relatively unfamiliar play (on this occasion, Brecht-wise, doubly unfamiliar), and one that tends to provoke mixed feelings even in its own tongue, had to accommodate not only the challenges of seeing Shakespeare in words that were not his own but also the provocations of an adaptation that radically rethought the narrative, characterization and politics of the play. Brecht's *Coriolan*, which engaged him on and off from the early 1950s until his death, had a lengthy gestation. He first considered Shakespeare's play for adaptation as part of his repertoire planning for a theatre that was intended to act both as force for post-war consolidation and reconstruction and as a cultural exemplar in the new East German state. The reworking would thus have taken a place alongside three other adaptions of European canonical works: Lenz's largely-unknown 1774 drama *Der Hofmeister* (*The Tutor*), which premiered in 1950, Molière's *Don Juan* (1954) and Farquhar's *The Recruiting Officer*, which in 1955 became *Pauken und Trompeten* (*Trumpets and Drums* for when it came to London).

Already at least one stage removed from Shakespeare, Brecht started not with the English text but with Dorothea Tieck's early nineteenth-century translation. Brecht and his Ensemble collaborators treated Tieck's elevated, melodious idiom to what Ralph Manheim and John Willett call a process of 'roughening up',[97] and made structural and narrative changes, preserving some lines, rewriting others, cutting, condensing, and at key points adding completely new passages and scenes. A taste of the texts' roughness, which may have been lost on the production's London audiences, is offered by Brecht's version of Coriolanus's valedictory curse in 3.3, 'You common cry of curs! Whose breath I hate …' (3.3.120–35): 'I banish you! / And here remain with your uncertainty / Let very feeble rumour shake your hearts' (3.3.123–5). This becomes:

>   Ich verbanne euch!
> Und hier sollt ihr mir bleiben müssen, angst-
> Geschüttelt, euch bekackend, wenn ein Helmbusch
> Von ungwewohnter Farb im Tor auftaucht.[98]

Ralph Manheim translates:

>   I banish you!
> Stay here in Rome, shaking with fear, shitting
> In your pants whenever a plume of unfamiliar
> Color appears outside the gates.[99]

'There is a world elsewhere' (l. 135), which in Tieck is musically rendered as 'Noch anderswo gibt's eine Welt',[100] becomes in Brecht's version, the more terse, prosaic ''s gibt / Noch eine Welt woanders' ('There's / A world elsewhere').[101] Throughout, the harshening of the protagonist is counterpointed by the strengthening of the plebeians, who are allocated a degree of class-consciousness and political agency unimaginable in Shakespeare's text. Believing that Cauis Martius's individual tragedy is that his mistaken belief in his own indispensability, Brecht wrote that 'we have to get beyond a mere sense of empathy with the hero' and stressed that 'ultimately society pays, Rome pays also, and it too comes close to collapsing as a result'.[102]

Brecht paid close attention to the first scene, noting that its '*unity of opposites*' is 'the foundation on which the entire play rests',[103] and in 1953, having temporarily shelved the *Corolan* project, he wrote a lengthy dialogue on it, in which he pondered its dialectical content and structure. 'The play is written realistically', he observes, 'and includes sufficient material of a contradictory sort', and the scene offers a set of clear, very Brecht-like, lessons: 'lack of a solution can unite the oppressed class and arriving at a solution can divide it ... such a solution may be seen in a war'; 'the finest speeches cannot wipe away realities, but can hide them for a time'; 'the oppressors' class isn't wholly united either'.[104] In this dialogue-essay, Brecht weighs the options of amending the scene and of performing it as written, and his final thoughts on the play (in 1955) appear to show a change of heart, as he wonders 'if it would be possible to stage it without additions (made by me two years ago) or with very few, just by skilful production'.[105]

The first scene of *Coriolan*, however, revises both the portrayal of the mutinous citizens and the nature and outcome of their confrontations with Menenius and Martius. In its explosive opening lines, Shakespeare's text has the First Citizen moves immediately – and syllogistically – from protest to threat:

1 CITIZEN
> You are all resolved rather to die than to famish?

ALL
> Resolved, resolved.

1 CITIZEN
> First, you know that Caius Martius is chief enemy to the people.

ALL
> We know't, we know't.

1 CITIZEN
> Let us kill him, and we'll have corn at our own price. Is't a verdict?

(1.1.4–11)

Brecht moderates and rationalizes the First Citizen's position by shifting the demand to set the price of corn (in Brecht's text, bread and olives) to before, rather than after, the call to kill Martius:

ERSTER BÜRGER
> Ihr seid bereit, nicht eher unzukehren als bis der Senat zugestanden hat, daß den Brotpreis wir Bürger bestimmen?

BÜRGER
　Ja, Ja.
ERSTER BÜRGER
　Und den Preis für Oliven?
BÜRGER
　Ja.
ERSTER BÜRGER
　Caius Marcius wird un smit Waffengewalt entgegentreten. Werdet ihr davonlaufen oder werdet ihr kämpfen?
BÜRGER
　Wir werden ihn totschlagen.[106]
(FIRST CITIZEN
　Are you prepared to stand fast until the senate agrees that it's us citizens who decide the price of bread?
CITIZENS
　Yes, yes.
FIRST CITIZEN
　And the price of olives?
CITIZENS
　Yes.
FIRST CITIZEN
　Caius Martius will meet us with force of arms. Will you run away or will you fight?
CITIZENS
　We'll knock him dead.)[107]

At a stroke, the citizens' grievances become a set of coherent political demands, their antipathy to Martius a matter of rational calculation rather than mob anger. Realpolitik rules: they are not at all taken in by the parable of the belly, and, later in the scene, Menenius's sudden shift from the conciliatory to the confrontational is prompted by the early entry of Martius accompanied by armed men.

The inexorable movement of the action, according to Marxist dialectics, is towards a version of workers' democracy that has far more to do with the self-image of the DDR than with the politics of Shakespeare's Rome. At the end of Brecht's 3.3 (corresponding to Shakespeare's 4.6), for example, the citizens' doubts about Coriolanus's banishment ('When I said banish him, I said 'twas pity ... And so did I ... yet it was against our will' [4.6.140–6]) are abruptly dismissed:

ZWEITER BÜRGER
    Lieber zeigt ich
    Als Mut jetzt eine Waffe. War es klug
    Ihn zu verbannen?
SICINIUS
    Ja.
    Bürger langsam ab.
    Zum Kapitol![108]
(SECOND CITIZEN
    I'd rather have
    A sword to show than courage. Was it wise
    To banish him?
SICINIUS
    Yes.
    (*The citizens go out slowly*)
    To the Capitol!)[109]

Coriolanus's capitulation (5.3 in Shakespeare's text, 5.4 in Brecht's) is completely reworked, with Volumnia's appeals to her son cut (ll. 94–184), and the text rewritten for her to inform him first, that he is no longer indispensable, and second, that the people exercising their newly-acquired political power will certainly not surrender:

              Wenn du Rauch sehn wirst
Dann aus den Schmieden steigend, die jetzt Schwerter
Wider dich schmieden, der dem eignen Volk den
Fuß auf den Nacken setzen will und dafür
Sich seinem Feinde unterwirft.[110]

> (If you see smoke
> It will be rising from the smithies forging
> Weapons to fight you who, to subject your
> Own people, have submitted to your enemy.)[111]

Peter Holland states that Brecht's treatment was intended as anything but 'a Freudian study of Coriolanus' relationship with his mother',[112] and it is clear that Coriolanus surrenders to military, not maternal, power, directly contracting his claim, in Shakespeare, that 'All the swords / In Italy and he confederate arms / Could not have made this peace' (5.3.212–14). Nonetheless, there may be just a touch of the repressed in the penultimate scene: Brecht translates, 'boy of tears', the insulting epithet that Aufidius hurls at him in their final stand-off (5.6.101) as 'Muttersöhnchen', or Mummy's boy.[113]

His killing is brief, to the point and inglorious, and is followed by a terse and in its own quiet way even more brutal, additional scene, in which the Senate is seen getting on with its business. In place of Tullus Aufidius's duly respectful last words on his antagonist:

> Though in this city he hath widow'd and unchilded many a one,
> Which to the hour bewail the injury,
> Yet he shall have a noble memory.
> Assist.
>
> (5.6.150–4)

The Old Vic audiences heard this:

KONSUL
> Eine Frage:
> Die Marcier bitten, daß, nach der Verordnung
> Numa Pompilius' fur die Hinterbliebenen,
> Von Vätern, Söhnen, Brüdern, doch den Frauen,
> Erlaubt werd öffentliches Tragen
> Von Trauer für sehn Monde.

BRUTUS
  Abgeschlegen.[114]
(CONSUL
  Question:
  His family has petitioned that its women
  As stipulated in the law of Numa
  Pompilius concerning the survivors
  Of fathers, sons and brothers, be permitted
  To wear mourning in public for ten months.
BRUTUS
  Rejected.)[115]

This version's curt, bathetically anti-climactic final word sums up its view both of the protagonist, and of any lingering expectations that some kind of catharsis might be on offer (an offer that Shakespeare's tragedy also refuses to make).

Aware, perhaps, that these verbal and narrative subtleties (or, if you prefer, crudities) would be lost on the audiences for the London performances (with or without the *Sun*'s imagined 18,000 *Deutscher Sprecher*), the Ensemble produced for the occasion a hefty twenty-four-page programme which included a detailed scene-by-scene synopsis to help spectators follow the action and spot the divergences from Shakespeare, and a lengthy exposition by director Manfred Wekwerth and dramaturg Joachim Tenschert of Brecht's intentions. *Coriolan* (billed as *Coriolanus* at the Old Vic) was unfinished at the time of Brecht's death, mainly with respect to the battle scenes (1.4–1.10), which he had intended to redact into one scene, and which would be written in rehearsal 'because he thought it necessary to study the positions and movements of the actors'.[116] In lieu of this, the version published in Brecht's *Gesammelte Werke* in 1959 included these scenes from the Tieck translation, and this text was the basis for Wekwerth and Tenschert's production in 1964, when it was offered as East Berlin's contribution to the Shakespeare quatercentenary, and where it was seen and admired by Tynan. The pair were not satisfied with the adaptation as it stood, and in the programme they explained that 'The battle itself, with Coriolanus' victory over Corioli and his adversary Aufidius, is the great dramatic parenthesis which holds together the whole complex', and that 'the "duel" between Caius Martius and Tullus Aufidius – at the expense of the people – is the force that sets the story in motion. So that two great individuals can settle a personal feud, a war is made'.[117]

Although they don't say so here, according more prominence to Aufidius was the directors' way of sharpening, not diluting, the adaptation's dialectics, in that it helped 'to undermine Coriolan as a singular hero by framing his need for victories socially'; in a similar vein, the battle scenes 'show the savagery ... as ceremony, the chaos as order, that is only to be created by experts in warfare'.[118] The NT audience was presented with a somewhat blander account of the play as a 'presentation of rapidly shifting events, almost in the manner of a ballad, moving swiftly from victories to defeats, from the rise of heroes to their fall'.[119] Wekwerth and Tenschert were doubtless aware of the tension, in this context, between Brechtian and Shakespearean authority, and in the programme they exercised considerable ingenuity to justify their dramatist's bolder interventions. Regarding Volumnia's act of persuasion in 5.3, Brecht apparently 'felt that Shakespeare had worded it in a strangely uninspired way, giving Volumnia very weak arguments'. Brecht, they wrote,

> regarded Shakespeare far too highly to be satisfied with this explanation. He asked himself whether it was not possible that Shakespeare had made the speech deliberately weak in argument because he wished to suggest that there were, in fact, other reasons for Coriolanus's change of heart. His mother's speech might serve as the official explanation for it, but certainly it was not the only one.[120]

Wekwerth and Tenschert appeared to be arguing, on Brecht's behalf, that his rewrite actually recovered Shakespeare's real intentions, which for some reason or other he had been forced to camouflage.

Reviewers, in the main, tended to focus on the production rather than text. The brilliantly-orchestrated battle scenes, which were directed by dance-trained assistant director Ruth Berghaus, were particularly praised: 'as disciplined and quite as exciting as anything at the Royal Tournament at Earls Court', in the *Guardian*'s view, 'they have that almost slow-motion, trance-like choreography of those tumbling sword-fights which we first saw when the Pekin opera came to London'.[121] Spectacular in its stylized depiction of 'soldiers moving under shields like a single monstrous crab',[122] the fighting teemed with extraordinary detail: Penelope Gilliatt noticed how 'one of the generals suddenly leaps on to the crooked arm of the other and hangs there, like a basket',[123] and the *Spectator*'s man singled out the moment of the taking of Corioli:

> Two lines are formed, Volscians on the left, Romans on the right. The Romans reply in kind, producing a weird, unearthly effect, augmented perhaps electronically: the Romans reply in kind 'Cai-us Mar-ci-us' and very slowly the stage starts to revolve. The sound grows to a frenzy, the two lines meet and fight, shield pressed against shield, then separate, and, as they separate, here and there a dead man who has been held upright by the embrace crumples.[124]

The sound was indeed electronically augmented, with actors' voices and Paul Dessau's 'percussive and raucous' score relayed through the then-new technology of stereo speakers;[125] the effect, wrote Gilliatt, was of 'the human voice ... massed and notated almost as Schoenberg did it'.[126] The use of the revolve put physical acting work in precise alignment with staging and *mise en scène*: 'Against a plain white cyclorama, under a pitiless white light', the action took place 'before a vast arch, stone on one side for Rome, timber on the other for Corioli'.[127] Karl von Appen's designs were 'incomparably beautiful': 'all pale chalky greys and the browns of hide and wood ... The ironwork is exquisite – slender, stately chairs ... and an avenue of poles that two men decorate with the helmets of the vanquished, reaching up with staves like Victorian lamplighters'.[128]

This attentiveness to the small effects as much as to the large ones, and to the local and the particular, impressed the *Daily Worker*'s Bob Leeson, who recorded how in the first scene, as the plebeians attended to the First Citizen, 'the grey mass of the crowd breaks up and faces emerge, expressions form, like details of an old masterpiece, one rapt, one cynical, another doubtful ... As you leave the theatre, you can remember them all'.[129] Ronald Bryden noted a related moment where 'big' and 'little' history came into contact in what the programme identified as Scene 14 ('Two drunken Volscian officers curse this long period of peace and eulogize war', an episode that echoes the opening of *Mother Courage*):

> two drunken troopers stagger down a staircase, then retreat behind it to ease themselves with visible relief. Apparently this can count as alienation: the heroic mood is broken, we are reminded that men are but men, even demigods must piss. The fact that it's also a splendid naturalistic detail which instantly conjures all the riot and toping offstage, bolstering the play's rhetoric with a smell of reality rank as the base of an old bandstand, seems not to matter.[130]

At such moments, the language barrier seemed not to matter either.

Overall, the daring of the visual stagecraft and physical acting reconciled even the doubters: W. A. Darlington, who saw the production as a 'travesty' of Shakespeare's play, read Coriolanus's volte-face as a capitulation to 'a magnificent People's Army which will hit him for six if he doesn't go back where he came from pretty damn quick', but nonetheless conceded that the Ensemble's work displayed 'a Teutonic thoroughness which in some ways puts our own stage to shame', even if there was 'nothing spontaneous about this acting: you are conscious of all the calculation and practice and drill that has gone to its making'.[131] The *Daily Mail*'s Julian Holland, who had Brecht down as 'The man who made the Bard a bore', acknowledged that the 'writing failures' of this 'Marxist attempt to re-vamp the play', were more than compensated for by a production of 'outstanding and staggering force'.[132] The reviewer for *The Times* was also in two minds, writing that despite its efforts to 'wrench the drama into a Marxist pattern', the production was 'richly exciting', and he blamed Brecht's successors rather than the man himself for this, as, had he lived, 'his ironic and contradictory spirit would have saved it from the rigidly perverse treatment' it received here. This reviewer also admired Ekkehard Schall's Coriolanus (Figure 3.1), 'an unforgettable embodiment of the bullet-headed Junker – a loud-mouthed golden boy, his lips set in a fixed sneer, and his cat-like walk never far from violence'.[133] Like most of his colleagues, he evaluated Schall's performance in broadly physical terms; elsewhere, the actor was described as 'all proud muscle and swagger',[134] with 'a masculine presence and sheer weight and volume of delivery of a kind all too rare on our stage ... his sheer animal vigour goes a long way'.[135] The ever-observant Penelope Gilliatt was more precise, documenting a 'plump narcissist who smiles as he kills and has a frightening capacity to cut out when people are urgently communicating with him. When Menenius pleads or Aufidius curses, he looks away and goes deaf'. Gilliatt also noticed the 'very Brechtian trick' of having him play 'his discomforting electioneering scene' in 'a toga a foot too long for him', and his 'inglorious demise': 'hacked down in mid-chuckle by a ring of soldiers with their arms around each other like a rugger scrum'.[136]

Supporting performances received less attention, and the handful of reviewers that mentioned Helene Weigel's Volumnia expressed disappointment: the *Guardian* recorded that Weigel, 'in some trouble with her words, knocked her head on the ground thrice before Coriolanus, but the whole performance was in this respect unexpectedly flat. Intentionally, I shall be told, perhaps'.[137] *The Times* concurred: Volumnia was 'a remote, gentle-voiced figure who hardly seems connected with the action'. Moving 'exquisitely' she created 'an atmosphere of

FIGURE 3.1 *Wolf Kaiser, Ekkehard Schall and Helene Weigel in the Berliner Ensemble* Coriolanus, *1965. Photograph by Vera Tenschert, courtesy of the Bertolt Brecht Archive, Akademie der Künste.*

warm family charm in the first scenes', which was appealing but, the reviewer thought, 'foreign even to the Ensemble's view of Shakespeare'.[138] Perhaps Weigel was feeling her way into the part, which she had taken over from the widely-criticized Manja Behrens after the Berlin premiere; as it turned out, it was her 'last major new role', and would prove to be 'one for which she was much celebrated'; the production itself remained in the Ensemble's repertoire for fifteen years and was performed 276 times.[139] As a landmark early example of 'foreign' Shakespeare at the National Theatre, the Berliner Ensemble's *Coriolanus* appeared to negotiate the tricky circumstances of its reception as well as could be expected, but as only the second such venture to be hosted at the National during its Old Vic years it was also the last, and the organization had to wait more than two decades for another non-English Shakespeare (Ninagawa's *Macbeth* in the Lyttelton in 1987) to appear on any of its stages.

The visit had a postscript which would not have been welcomed by the Ensemble, and which serves as a stark reminder of the Cold War context in which its work continued to operate. On 30 August, the London press reported that two members of the company, 26-year-old actor Christian Weisbrod and the tailor Rolf Prieser, had the day before walked into the West German Embassy in London, intending to defect. According to an embassy official quoted in *The Times*, Prieser was already in West Berlin, and Weisbrod appeared to have gone to ground, while an Old Vic spokesman kept a tactful distance: 'If anyone defected from the company they certainly did not tell us ... They must have kept it very quiet.'[140] Prieser thereafter disappears from the record, but not Weisbrod, who on 15 September was reported to have returned to East Berlin, 'and asked to be permitted to play with the company again'.[141] Just over a month later, he was found dead in an East Berlin church, presumably but not certainly as a result of suicide. In an article on the incident in *Time* magazine the echoes of *Coriolanus* are heart-breaking: Weisbrod 'easily received a West German passport, a temporary home ... even a job offer'. But within a week he returned to East Berlin, torn, his brother suggested, 'between his loyalty to the company he loved and his desire to quit East Germany', to face a situation in which 'friends ... may have jeered at him as a fool for returning, or perhaps acidly criticized him for bringing the police around to question their possible duplicity'.[142] Perhaps Weisbrod had been subjected to 'severe covert pressure by agents of the GDR':[143] according to *The Times* he had been interrogated by the East German security police, and apparently told the Ensemble 'that he had made an "overhasty decision" which he regretted'. The article ended by noting that Weigel had posted her thanks on the company notice board, for 'that "exemplary attitude of deep humanity and political effectiveness" which, she says, caused *The Times* to say August 18 this was "one of the most persuasive advertisements yet for life on the other side" yet to be have been seen in Britain'.[144] There was a world elsewhere, but probably not for most members of the Berliner Ensemble – and certainly not for Christian Weisbrod.

If you have writ your annals true

It must have seemed like a good idea at the time. In September 1970 the National Theatre announced that it had acquired Paul Scofield (whom Olivier 'had been "wooing" for some time')[145] to play the leads in Carl Zuckmayer's *The Captain of Köpenick,* a new production of *Coriolanus* to be directed by Anthony Page, and a third play yet to be decided (in the event, it was Pirandello's *The Rules of the Game*). Appointed as an associate director, there was even talk that Scofield might be a plausible candidate for Olivier's successor as artistic director, and, following a lacklustre year, there was a general perception that the NT was in need of some heavyweight lead acting. *Köpenick* opened the following March to excellent reviews, but Scofield had in the meantime changed his mind about *Coriolanus*, and Page had withdrawn from the production. To fill the gap, Tynan suggested inviting Wekwerth and Tenschert over from Berlin as guest directors to repeat the success of five years earlier. Scofield was replaced by Christopher Plummer, and rehearsals began in the third week of March.

There are a number of versions of what happened next. Plummer traces the origins of the idea that he would play Coriolanus, and that Wekwerth and Tenschert would direct, to the encounter with Olivier that is recalled in Chapter 1. Plummer states that he approached John Dexter, who was too busy, and that he expected that Olivier would want to direct, but that the Germans 'will give it a different look, new and fresh, and because they are foreign their presence will smarten up the company'. Apprehensive that Olivier 'was much too close to the part' and 'would give me *his* business, give me *his* line readings', he turned him down, and 'went with the Germans instead'. Having worked on the part for several weeks he was, he claims, 'more than ready to go into battle'.[146] Things did not start well:

> It never occurred to me at the time, but turning up the first morning in the Rolls-Royce Corniche ... did not exactly endear me to the company. It was a stupid insensitive thing to do, but – damn it! – it was my only mode of transportation. I soon couldn't have cared less, for apart from three superb actors, Charles Kay, Ronald Pickup and Denis Quilley, most of the company were made up of a bunch of unwelcoming, humourless malcontents whose socialist leanings not only were far left of Lenin but made Harold Wilson look like King Farouk. Also, to my great disappointment, stroppiness had taken precedence over talent.[147]

Plummer was clearly living the part, though he had enough self-awareness to allow that 'my character's arrogance had clearly rubbed off on me', but he did not care, and at the end of the first aimless week of rehearsals, during which the directors 'seemed to be hugging the back wall of the rehearsal room showing little or no interest' while 'we were "blocking" the play by ourselves', things got a lot worse. Suddenly springing to life as, in Plummer's version, *Ve-haf-vays-of-making-you-tock* comedy Germans, the directors announced that 'Ve can begin. The new texts have arrived! You can srow all doze odder vuns away!' Aghast, Plummer read the title page of the typescript: '*Coriolanus* by Bertholt [sic] Brecht.'[148] With, as he saw it, his own role 'violently slashed to ribbons, reduced to a one-dimensional cardboard cutout' and 'the mob' now the heroes of the piece, Plummer tackled Olivier, then Tynan, both of whom professed their innocence, and, having persuaded the directors to restore some of the cuts, 'reluctantly went back to rehearsal'. But 'I was in the wrong play'; and following a meeting from which he was excluded, Olivier informed him that 'The bulk of the company voted you down.'[149]

Plummer might have left it there, but there was a score to settle with Tynan, who, he claimed, would 'turn the tables and change his story', maintaining that 'I was the difficult one, that it was I who caused dissension in the ranks. That is not true'.[150] Tynan's record of the incident is, unsurprisingly, at odds with Plummer's: the actor, he recorded, 'refuses to take direction, insists on doing it his way, and makes jokes about T. and W. in front of the company'. The dilemma for Olivier was whether to sack Plummer or the directors, and Tynan reported with satisfaction that he opted for the former. 'Faced with a choice', Tynan wrote, 'between the values of two ex-leaders of the Berliner Ensemble and the values of the star of *The Sound of Music*, which do we choose'. The whole episode, he concluded, was 'a splendid vindication of the new collective leadership at the NT'.[151]

Plummer walked, and his part was taken by Anthony Hopkins. Three weeks later, *The Times* picked up the story: Wekwerth and Tenschert, it gleefully reported, thought they were to direct Brecht's version (in which 'a near-psychotic Coriolanus is presented, not as the defender of Rome but as a vicious parasite who instigates private wars for his own glory') and had to be taken aside for a quiet word with the NT directorate for it to be 'discreetly explained to them what was required'. The directors nonetheless apparently persisted with the Brechtian line, prompting Plummer's departure, although the script was reportedly revised: 'and to avoid confusion, each one has been given a different coloured cover – red for the original, purplish-pink for the second and gold for the one now in use'.[152]

Denis Quilley, cast in his NT debut role as Aufidius, remembered it differently. On the very first day of rehearsal, 'in strolls Olivier, with that shoulder-swinging gait of his, looking gloomy. "Bit of a cock-up, chaps ... let's just read through the Shakespeare so that the boys can hear your voices, then we'll have a bit of a chat"'. Nonplussed, the cast did the read-through, broke for lunch, and returned for the 'cock-up' to be explained. 'Eventually a compromise is reached: the Boys will direct Shakespeare's play, but they will "adapt" it first':

> So we spend the first week rehearsing in piecemeal fashion while the script is cut, rearranged and reshaped, to get it into a Brechtian form ... [5.3] somehow became a scene in which Coriolanus hears the citizens arming, and decides that he cannot march against 'The workers'. When Olivier saw this scene in rehearsal, he said, 'Funny – I always thought it was something to do with his mother.' Chris Plummer saw the writing on the wall (and also saw that the design for his costume was a little unflattering), and promptly pulled out and hot-footed it back to Hollywood ... We brought it off rather better than one might have expected.[153]

Here, then, are four accounts of the circumstances that meant that this *Coriolanus* was probably doomed from the outset.

The question of which version to trust is possibly less important than that of whose interests the competing stories ('which might have come', Ronald Bryden remarked, 'from an Evelyn Waugh novel')[154] served, and in this respect they illuminate the context in which the production took place. In Plummer's and *The Times*'s accounts, Wekwerth and Tenschert conform to national and political stereotype, coming across as pair of humourless, doctrinaire and not-particularly-bright apparatchiks at odds with their English hosts, strangers in the house for Shakespeare. The rumours persisted up to and beyond the opening night. In his *Guardian* review, Philip Hope-Wallace reiterated the claim that the company 'had a terrible time' rehearsing 'one of the poorest accounts of the play that I can recall',[155] and Irving Wardle went further, wishing for a 'rehearsal case-book' to be published 'charting the internal conflicts that led up to this singularly incoherent production'. When the directors attempted to impose their will, Wardle, presumably choosing his words with care, suggested that they had 'run into British resistance' resulting in 'an uneasy compromise'.[156] Not one of these critics appeared to have read the interview that Wekwerth and Tenschert had given to the *Morning Star* on 4 May, where they stated that they never expected to direct Brecht's version, and that the playwright himself believed that it would eventually be 'possible to convey [his] interpretation using Shakespeare's original text'. This, they affirmed, was 'the starting-point for our production of the Shakespearean version at the National Theatre'. Seeing themselves as cultural ambassadors working to promote mutual understanding, they stated that 'we found a real "Coriolanus" ensemble. The actors have reacted wholeheartedly to what is for them very unusual working methods. It has been an intensive and productive co-operation where suggestions have been taken up, used and developed collectively'.[157]

Wardle's assertions provoked a strong response from the cast and stage management team, who, led by Constance Cummings (playing Volumnia), signed a joint letter to *The Times*, which, quoting the 'British resistance' allegation, stated their 'wish to refute categorically Mr. Irving Wardle's presumptuous inference'. On the contrary,

> we found their ideas stimulating and thought provoking, and we accepted them whole-heartedly. The rehearsals were conducted in an atmosphere of mutual respect and enjoyment, and were wonderfully exciting. We all hope that we can have a further opportunity of working with them in the not too distant future.[158]

In hindsight, Quilley offered a slightly more guarded endorsement ('we all worked with a will to bring this strange hybrid creature to life'), but conceded that Wekwerth and Tenschert, 'despite their daft conviction that they could turn Shakespeare into something he wasn't, were canny and experienced theatre men'.[159] Nonetheless, the narrative of plucky Brit actors battling against their Teutonic overlords held considerable appeal, tapping as it did both into the long-standing mistrust of authoritarian foreign directors and, implicitly, into a deep vein of English anti-German sentiment that was being mined with particular vigour during the period. 'It made me almost curse', declared the *Daily Mail*'s Peter Lewis, 'to see such powerful acting thrown away and to see Shakespeare hammered out into two dimensions';[160] Bryden, who was relatively positive about the production and Brecht's reworking of the play, felt that the company had been 'strait-jacketed' into 'an alien hand-me-down'.[161] Inevitably, allusions to the Third Reich crept into some of the reviews, with Hopkins being described as 'a cross between a fisherman and an SS-man'[162] and Cummings as having 'more than a hint of the Nazi girls' corps about her'.[163]

In truth, everyone at the NT was aware that this was, to use the term employed in the minutes of the Board meeting of 5 October 1971, a 'ready-made German production',[164] which involved recreating Karl von Appen's sets, and some of the blocking, for the Berliner Ensemble production still in repertory in Berlin. Hard white light beat down on the stage, and much use was made of the revolve and of the huge double-sided gateway-arch, with its brick façade for Rome, rotated to reveal crude Volscian timbers. Its texture, as Holland points out, was however subtly different: whereas the rough stone of the Ensemble's arch suggested 'the effective parity of the two nations', the NT's 'neat brickwork' seemed to indicate 'a more achieved, perhaps even more civilized Rome than its neighbour'.[165] This was not a radical shift of political emphasis, but it brought the production closer to the mainstream British traditions of staging the play. Less welcome, for almost all the reviewers, was the signature half-curtain (a 'maddening echt-Brechtian shower bath')[166] that traversed the stage between scenes. The problem was that the device was not just misconceived, but also ineptly executed: 'the failure to weight the flimsy curtains which swish irritatingly across the stage' meant that 'they billow out to reveal the harassed scene shifters at work'.[167] For Quilley the half-curtain played havoc with the rhythm of the play, and of his performance, generating all too many 'moments when I, for one, was waiting in the wings with every nerve in my body urging me to go on and pick up where Tony Hopkins was leaving off, only to have to wait while that bloody curtain came across'.[168]

It was, nonetheless, in accordance the directors' treatment of the text which presented the action as a Brechtian sequence of episodes, and was less drastic than some of the accounts alleged. Their alterations, which were in tune with long-established European modes of dramaturgic practice in which the boundary between translation and adaptation is customarily flexible, consisted of cutting, transposing and re-ordering material rather than rewriting. Unsurprisingly, there were deep cuts to much of the material critical of the citizens and tribunes, including Martius's diatribes in his first big speech ('Your virtue is / To make him worthy whose offence subdues him ... And hews down oaks with rushes' [1.1.173–80]), the dialogue of the looters who appear at the start of 1.5 ('This will I carry to Rome ... I took this for silver' [l. 1; l. 3]), Menenius's derisive characterization of the tribunes ('You are ambitious for poor knaves' caps and legs ... All the peace you make in their cause is calling both the parties knaves' [2.1.68–79]), and the citizens' self-incrimination of the 'many-headed multitude' (2.3.16–17), so that the Second and Third Citizens' humorous elaboration of how their wits 'would fly east, west, north, south ... at once to all points o'th' compass' (2.3.18–37) disappeared, along with their self-deprecation:

5TH CITIZEN
   For once when we stood up about the corn, he himself stuck not to call us the many-headed multitude.

14TH CITIZEN
> We have been called so of many; I say, if he would incline to the people, there was never a worthier man.
>> (Enter CORIOLANUS in a gown of humility and MENENIUS)[169]

The aim might have been to adjust the play's representation of the commons to the ideological requirements of the DDR, but it could backfire; the *Evening News* critic saw in the treatment a depiction of actually-existing Communism in 'an austere, lavatory-tiled Rome in which the plebs are the grey, grim-faced people whom you can see in the streets behind the Berlin wall'. Seated on 'prison benches', they stared 'with hollow eyes as Coriolanus explains why they should vote him consul. There is Marxist fervour in their political cry of "What is the city but the people?"'[170] The *Sunday Telegraph* concurred: 'only the faces of the plebeians remain sullen and long-suffering: it is they who have to foot the bill'.[171]

There were significant cuts to the scene of Coriolanus's final confrontation with Volumnia (5.3; the production's Scene Twenty-Four) that, without introducing Brecht's additions, sought to perform their work of ascribing his capitulation to Rome's political strength rather than to conflicted personal loyalties. Coriolanus's exchange with Virgilia, in which, inter alia, he kneels before Volumnia and longingly invokes 'a kiss / Long as my exile, sweet as my revenge' (5.3.37–56), was cut, as were with his idealization of Valeria as 'chaste as the icicle / That's curdied by the frost from purest snow / And hangs on Dian's temple' (5.3.66–8), and Volumnia's personalization of the the women's entreaty: 'Even he, your wife, this lady, and myself / Are suitors to you'; 'Yet we will ask; / That if you fail in our request, the blame may hang on your hardness' (5.3.77–8; 5.3.89–91). In a scene in which much hinges upon what is unsaid, the directors' orchestration of silence was notable. On 'To his surname Coriolanus longs more pride / Than pity to our prayers. Down!' (5.3.172–3), the promptbook records: '*All 3 ladies kneel. Virg Val still CS Vol URC at tent ent. kneels and rests forehead on ground at Cor's feet. Long pause.*' Rising *'slowly'*, Volumina moved downstage left, *'almost falls, Val & Virg just rising, save her fall.'* On 'Come, let us go' (5.3.179), *'They move DL stop turn to Cor'*; Coriolanus followed, stopped, *'looking after them. Pause.'*[172] In this version, Coriolanus did not hold Volumnia *'by the hand silent'* (l. 185 SD); the women exited, 'leaving him to speak the line "O mother, [mother!] [W]hat have you done?" in soliloquy'.[173] Wekwerth and Tenschert cut his lines admitting to Aufidius that 'it is no little thing to make / Mine eyes to sweat compassion', his cry of 'O mother! wife!', and his admission that 'All the swords / In Italy and her confederate arms / Could not have made this peace' (ll.199–203; ll. 207–14). The scene thus ended with the sharp pragmatism of Aufidius's aside, 'I am glad thou hast set thy mercy and thy honour / At difference in thee. Out of that I'll work / Myself a former fortune' (ll. 204–6).

Elsewhere Wekwerth and Tenschert trimmed, tidied and streamlined, particularly from 4.5 (Scene Eighteen) onwards, with various minor roles conflated to create the double act of Spurius and Calvus, Volscian Everymen who made their first entrance in place of the First and Second Servingman encountered by Coriolanus on his arrival at Aufidius's house, reappeared as the Watchmen who challenge Menenius in 5.2, and served as Aufidius's lead conspirators in 5.6. More adventurously, the directors radically transformed the female and domestic interlude of 1.3 (which, in Shakespeare, begins as Volumnia and Valeria *'set them down on two low stools and sew'* [1.3.0 SD]) by splitting the scene in two, with 1.4, the first battle scene, in the middle. In the first half (Scene Three) Martius, rather than acting as the absent subject of Volumnia's eulogy, was present centre stage, and the scene began with him delivering her (slightly reworded) first line, 'I pray you, Virgilia, sing, or express yourself in a more comfortable sort', and Virgilia's interpolated sung response, taken from one of the wedding poems of Catullus ('Quid datur a divis felici optatius hora …' [What can Gods give more welcome than the happy hour?]).[174] Borrowing from *Antony and Cleopatra*, 4.4, in what may also have been a reference to the Pope-robing sequence in Scene Twelve of Brecht's *Life of Galileo*,[175] Volumnia's eulogy was delivered as she dressed Martius for battle, transforming the son and husband into an inhuman fighting machine as she spoke, so that her wish for multiple sons to 'die nobly for their country' (1.3.25–6) was uttered to his face. Craftily, Wekwerth and Tenschert rounded off the scene with a combination of text transposed from 4.1 and lines interpolated from *Antony and Cleopatra*:

MARCIUS
> O love,
> That thou couldst see my wars today, and knew'st
> The royal occupation! Thou shouldst see
> A workman in't.

Enter a CAPTAIN *armed*

CAPTAIN
> Good morrow, general.

MARCIUS
> To business that we love we rise betime
> And go to't with delight.

CAPTAIN
> The morn is fair.

MARCIUS
> Come, my sweet wife, my dearest mother, and
> My friends of noble touch; when I am forth
> Bid me farewell, and smile. I pray you, come.[176]

The scene ended with '*War music*' and a taped chant: '*Let war begin; let war begin; let war begin.*'

As we have seen, the directors in 1965 had elaborated an ingenious rationale on Brecht's behalf for the Berliner Ensemble production; for the 1971 production, they likewise set out their thinking about the play and their handling of it in a lengthy programme note. Their view of the anti-hero's place in the scheme of the drama had not shifted at all: approaching the play 'dialectically', they state that 'what gives the fable its impetus' is that 'the two great heroes must have their duel, even if the earth is forfeit', but that 'the things which hold no interest for the two heroes, bent on their duel, hold interest for us: who foots the bill? whose backs are they fighting on? who are the real losers?' These emphases suggest that their directorial approach was akin to Brecht's final musings on the first scene in which, having weighed up the validity of rewriting Shakespeare's text, he cautiously opted for thoughtful staging rather than rewriting, and the editorial work discussed above largely confirms this. But the note goes further, focusing at length on the question 'Why does Coriolanus change his mind?' As in 1965, the individualist-psychological-mother-domination solution was deemed insufficient; the answer, apparently, was a quasi-Brechtian one that is already inherent in the text:

> We ask ourselves: what is it that moves Coriolanus so profoundly, apart from the fact it is his mother who is speaking? Not the words in themselves. What then? Perhaps it is what she *does not say*. What he hopes she will say. And what she refrains from saying ... all the people who come to visit Coriolanus in the Volscian camp ... beg him merely to *turn back and spare the city*. At no point does any of them suggest that Coriolanus *should come back to Rome*. But that is precisely what Coriolanus – in our opinion – wants to hear ... The fact that no one begs Coriolanus to return to Rome leads us to the implicit conclusion: that anyone who believes himself to be indispensable will be destroyed by that belief [emphases in the original].[177]

Plebeian resistance, in other words, is operative in the very absence of its articulation; a case, to adapt Brecht's famous dictum, of having one's pudding and the proof of eating it.

In the lead role, Hopkins was praised by reviewers for making the best of a bad situation. The supporting cast received some attention, though Wardle, in keeping with his view that the whole show had been forced on its cast, saw only 'glaringly implausible acting ... a phalanx of unconvinced, externally imposed performances at variance with the company's regular style'.[178] Bryden, in his way, agreed: Cummings 'gives a remarkable performance, but it's not her own',[179] though her rendering of her 'great plea' was 'very decently done',[180] according to the *Guardian*. Quilley's Aufidius also earned plaudits, with Young referring to his 'indolent pride which is most effective' and Lambert reporting that his 'magnificent' playing 'held the house with effortless power'.[181] But it was Hopkins that commanded the reviews. Many registered a dangerous, animal physicality that was reminiscent of Schall: as 'a sort of Roman General Patton', he prowled the stage 'lowering his head like a dominant gorilla, smiling his contempt and swaying on his feet like a boxer waiting for a bell';[182] 'thick-necked, bullet-headed, staring ... a human fighting machine'.[183] Hopkins was 'all clenching of fists and complacent, oddly sly smirks, all slouch, swagger and wary, hopeful rocking from foot to foot' for Benedict Nightingale; this was impressive but utterly reductive, a depiction of Coriolanus as a 'sweaty thug'.[184] The *Spectator*'s Kenneth Hurren, who really hated the production ('abysmal ... untenable in its premises, an unspeakable bore in performance, and in point of the most elementary details ... a disgrace to reputable professionalism'), agreed: Hopkins's Coriolanus was, simply, 'an arrogant, war-drunk bully'.[185]

Others, however, detected more nuance and some surprisingly delicate detail, such as 'the way his tongue explores his lips and teeth like a prize-fighter's, the only hint of nervousness, as he braces himself on the balls of his feet to face an adversary or hostile crowd'.[186] For Wardle, ironically, this was 'the most sympathetic' Coriolanus he had seen, 'Modest and almost winsome, delivering his first insults to the crowd with offhand gentleness, and resolutely refusing to drop into infantility in the scenes with Constance Cummings's Volumnia.'[187] Robert Cushman in *Plays and Players* also appreciated Hopkins's 'warmth' and spoke for many when he stated that 'The National Theatre have needed a young tiger for a long time and I hope they can hold onto this one.'[188] In

Hopkins, the critics sensed, was some of the Olivier-esque star power that appeared to have deserted the Old Vic, and herein lay the production's greatest irony: its efforts to cut Coriolanus down to size ultimately produced a display of rather old-fashioned heroic acting.

Coriolanus was the second poorly-received production by international guests that year, following Argentine Victor Garcia's critically-savaged production of Fernando Arrabal's *The Architect and the Emperor of Assyria* in January. Just as the earlier *Coriolanus* appeared to put paid to foreign Shakespeare on the NT stage for decades, this was the last time that alien interlopers were allowed into the Old Vic's rehearsal rooms, and it was not until 1977 that the National, now installed on the South Bank, risked extending an invitation to another foreign guest director: the result was Swiss actor Maximillian Schell's 'brilliantly organized and physically exciting'[189] production of Horváth's *Tales from the Vienna Woods*. There would be six more Shakespeare productions at the NT before it left the Old Vic, two of them directed by Olivier's successor, Peter Hall. They, and he, are the subject of the next chapter.

4

Hall

This island

Peter Hall began his second full week as director of the National Theatre with a Monday morning planning meeting for *The Tempest*. He had the idea of commissioning some contemporary popular musicians to write the score, and squeezed around the table in his office in Aquinas Street were the four members of progressive rock outfit Gryphon, described by Hall as 'a talented pop group who specialize in medieval and renaissance music'. The meeting, Hall is sorry to report, 'got off to a bad start': 'one of the group was walking on this cold November day in bare feet. And I planted my boots firmly on them as I sat down'.[1] Hall does not labour the ironies of this painful collision between the values of his own suited-and-booted establishment milieu and the dreamy other-worldliness of the counter-culture, but in the weeks to come he had good reason to wonder whether the invitation had been such a good idea. When the NT's musical director, Marc Wilkinson, made the initial approach to the group's management company in September 1973, conveying Hall's 'thoughts regarding the style of the music' ('"Monteverdi = Pop", very lyrical and imaginative'), he indicated that with rehearsals scheduled to begin 'on or about January 1', the songs would need to be ready by then.[2] On 3 January 1974, Hall noted that Gryphon had to date 'delivered one dirty folded manuscript paper with a rather conventional-looking setting of "Come unto these yellow sands" scribbled on it in pencil ... It doesn't sound as if we are going to get much of their attention'.[3]

The band were in the Cotswolds, recording their second album, whose title, *Midnight Mushrumps*, trippily cross-references Prospero's necromantic invocation in the final scene (5.1.39) with the prog-rockers' naturally-occurring hallucinogen of choice, but the group did manage to deliver a serviceable recorded score for the first night of *The Tempest* on 5 March, which was augmented by three NT in-house musicians. In the production programme, a note by jazz critic Derek Jewell explained that the group had been described as 'the 13th century Slade', but this seems pretty wide of the mark. Slade, a Black Country four-piece kicking around the grimier reaches of glam rock, had by 1974 notched up six top ten hits with a combination of piledriver rhythms, powerchords, leeringly misspelt song titles ('Look wot you Dun', 'Mama Weer All Crazee Now', 'Cum on Feel the Noize') and an air of bovver-boy menace. Gryphon were led by two alumni of the Royal College of Music, who, according to Jewell, 'play a blend of medieval and modern music – medieval rock, if you like', and who had 'rediscovered the crumhorn ... and with guitars, mandolins, drums, recorders, harpsichord and sundry other sounds create rare and inventive music'. Emphasizing the band's broad-based appeal, Jewell reassured the NT audience that as well as performing 'folk songs, Elizabethan jigs, Tudor court ballads, that kind of thing', Gryphon rocked, occasionally daring 'to throw in a reinterpretation of the Beatles or *Ain't She Sweet* or an original song'.[4] Gryphon's contribution occasioned little comment, though Robert Speaight referred in passing to the 'dreary modern music',[5] and Irving Wardle reported that the score 'mingles medieval dance (with growling reed instruments) and Indian pop', which was 'very stately' and (the phrasing is cryptic) 'discreetly turned on'.[6] Derived from the incidental music for the production, the twenty-minute title track of *Midnight Mushrumps* was subsequently blessed with a concert performance by Gryphon at the Old Vic on 14 July; three months after the album was released. This is, to date, the only rock concert ever to have been hosted either by the Old Vic or by the National Theatre; whether it stands as a crossover event yet to be equalled, or as an experiment best not repeated, is for history to determine.

During the same month, Hall took the press on their first tour of the in-progress South Bank complex (4 July), learned that he was so overdrawn he needed to earn more than twice as much from freelance work outside the NT than he had budgeted for, was informed by Harold Pinter that he 'might be pregnant' (Hall: 'A play is on the way') and warned by John Dexter that 'the company were deeply unhappy, lost, unled, and there was a degree of disloyalty up and down the corridors which he had never met in the theatre in his life'.[7] This was, by now, all in a day's work for Hall; when he met with Gryphon in November, he was already used to treading on people's toes. One of the first and foremost perceived victims of his footwork was Laurence Olivier himself. Olivier surrendered the directorship reluctantly, and for a long time nursed a deep sense of grievance that the NT Board had appointed Hall behind his back. In his memoirs, Hall reveals that the jockeying for position dated back more than a decade; while he was directing Olivier in *Coriolanus* in Stratford in 1959, the actor invited Hall 'to be his number two at the National Theatre. I was flattered but said that I would sooner be my own number one'.[8] Hall was initially approached in 1971 by Lord Goodman, Chair of the Arts Council, when Olivier's ill-health was making it increasingly difficult for him to lead the National in trying times; Hall told him that he was reluctant to step into Olivier's shoes against his will as 'I had no wish to be cast in the role of the usurper.'[9] The situation drifted on for the next nine months, with Olivier, according to Hall, 'saying he was going one day and thinking of staying the next';[10] while the actor, by his own account, 'gave up': 'I opted out, I allowed myself to be cut adrift from my will.'[11] Still lobbying hard for Michael Blakemore as his successor, Olivier states that he was told to stay out of it and then on 24 March 1972 informed by Max Rayne, Chair of the National Theatre Board, that 'he was at that moment (1500 hours) giving me six months' formal notice' and that 'my place would be taken by Peter Hall'.[12] The rancour is palpable; Hall, on the other hand, records that when Rayne reported this conversation to him, Olivier's response 'could not have been more generous', though Hall 'suspected it was rather a bitter pill for him to swallow'.[13]

Olivier blandly asserts that the six-month notice period (which, in the event, stretched to nineteen months, as he did not formally end his reign until 31 October 1973) worked out amicably enough, with Hall and Olivier acting as co-directors from April, but Hall indicates otherwise. Olivier, according to Hall, was infuriatingly prone to vacillation and histrionics. On 22 January 1972 he pictured Olivier 'in a devilish mood ... changing ground on everything', on 26 February referred to his 'Machiavellian love of intrigue. He loves being naughty' and on 6 March let rip about 'an appalling press release for next week about his going': 'it is exactly like the great actor-manager saying farewell to his public – with the proviso that if they insist he will be appearing again next week'.[14] Olivier was an irritant during the painful, protracted (and ultimately fruitless) negotiations between Hall and his RSC protégé and opposite number Trevor Nunn over a proposed merger between the two organizations, discussions that absorbed a great deal of time and energy during 1972 and 1973. At a joint meeting held on 15 April 1972, where there 'were tears in everyone's eyes', it was agreed that the RSC, which was continuing to struggle with a massive deficit, 'could not go on as it was' and that amalgamation with the NT would be in the interests of both: 'All our problems seemed solved.'[15] As discussions continued, mistrust developed on both sides, and at the start of 1973 Hall wrote in exasperation that 'on the one hand we have an RSC chairman [George Farmer] who is convinced the RSC is being taken over by the National, and on the other hand, we have Larry who is convinced that the National is being taken over by the RSC'. 'I wish', he sighs, 'they could see they are both wrong'.[16] By the end of March, Hall was 'getting more and more worried' by the prospect of a merger, not least because 'now I am getting to grips with the needs of the South Bank, I am appalled by the size of that operation alone'.[17] Olivier had his own view, and on 18 April *The Times* published a letter from him which attempted to downplay talk of a takeover, and which set out his belief that 'the National will content itself with the South Bank, and the RSC with Stratford on Avon and the Barbican'.[18] Hall notes that he had agreed a draft of the letter that included the point that 'a main reason for the proposal to join us together was that it would be cheaper' and that the 'paragraph was not, though, in *The Times*. Larry had cut it out'.[19] Olivier was, of course, proved right: on 23 October 1973 it was announced that the proposed merger was off, and, despite some vague warm words from Farmer ('There may be ways in which we may collaborate'),[20] that was it. In his autobiography, Hall looks back on the period with bemusement: with hindsight, the amalgamation 'never really made sense'.[21]

We can only guess at the form a merged RSC–NT, spread across some configuration of Stratford, the Aldwych and the South Bank, might have taken, but it seems more than possible that it would have been rooted in the priorities that Hall had established for the RSC in 1960, which remained its raison d'etre. Callow writes that Olivier's reign 'was the glorious end of an era rather than the beginning of a new one' and that Hall's regime saw a shift to 'theatre as a serious, responsible enterprise, run on sound business principles, properly endowed, systematically engaging with the drama of the past and the present, and taking its place among the great institutions of this great nation';[22] this was the founding agenda of the RSC, and for some, Tynan among them, it was all too redolent of that company's 'Roundhead' culture. Having worked hard to keep Olivier on board, Hall treated others still loyal to the old order differently. He was ruthless with Tynan: having made it a condition of his appointment that Olivier's chief courtier was to leave, he found himself 'fed up with everyone pussy-footing around the subject'[23] of his behind-the-scenes briefing and manoeuvring, and on 5 July 1972 he called a meeting with Tynan to sack him. 'Before I could deliver my blow', he writes, 'he told me ... the time had come to move on'. Responding to Hall's complaint that he was sick of reading about their alleged rivalry, Tynan had the wit to riposte that 'he had planted so many stories in the press himself, he no longer believed anything he read'.[24]

Seeking to govern in an ostensibly more open and democratic manner, Hall established a group of associate directors initially consisting of Olivier, Blakemore, Jonathan Miller, John Schlesinger and Harold Pinter. The *Diaries* document repeated skirmishes with those that Hall labels in his autobiography 'the enemies within',[25] Miller and Blakemore (who subsequently sought to settle the score with Hall in his own account of the period).[26] In February 1974, possibly wishing to repeat the success of Williams's *As You Like It*, Miller proposed an all-male production of *The Importance of Being Earnest* to the associates' group. Pinter was emphatically opposed, on the grounds that 'an author has certain clear intentions' and that this clearly contradicted them.[27] Pinter may have had other motives about which he stayed silent; a year earlier, in correspondence with Hall, he ventured that he would 'one day like to direct *The Importance of Being Earnest*', and also 'in about two or three years the only Shakespeare I would feel even remotely confident of handling: *Othello*'.[28] In his autobiography, Hall goes further: 'Pinter asked him beadily what he was trying to prove. Was it, he enquired, that Wilde had actually wished that he could write a homosexual play about the pairing off of men?'[29] Things were never the same with Miller again, and a year later, to Hall's great relief, he resigned.

Readers and reviewers of the *Diaries* have not been slow to identify the Shakespearean (and other) resonances of much of its action, some of which seem to have been deliberately cultivated. Olivier is, alternately, Lear-like in his determination to both abdicate and retain the appurtenances of power and Hamlet-like in his apparent indecisiveness. Interrogating Miller in the wake of the *Earnest* row, Hall asked him 'why he had been behaving in a Coriolanus-like way, booking himself up outside the NT ... yet going around saying he was resigning as he was fed up with not being used'.[30] But it is Hall's own surrogations that are of most interest, and he is too much of a writer not to be conscious of the interplay between life and art that, whether or not he recognized it at the time, is evident in the subsequently edited and published text (in one meta-entry, reading Lord Reith's published diaries, he sees a 'record of egomania and paranoia. He hated everybody. He used his diary as a means of letting off steam. I wonder if I'm doing the same').[31] Reviewing the *Diaries* for the *Observer*, Hilary Spurling detected 'a grasping, oppressive, reactionary empire-builder, voracious as Tamburlaine, power-mad like Richard III', cited Hall's account of being awarded an honorary degree when he 'distracted himself with what turned out to be – as in *Macbeth* – a grim forecast of things to come by imagining himself undergoing the ceremony in reverse: "The graduate stands there while all his failures, vices and betrayals are read out, and people nod approvingly"' and concluded that 'it would take a hard heart not to marvel at the touch of Tamburlaine – or Bajazeth beating his brains out against the bars – in this bold, rash, frank, fascinating book'.[32]

Spurling is well-disposed towards the *Diaries*; not so Blakemore, who saw his first opportunity to get even in the form of a parody version, published in the *Observer* the following Sunday, *The Claudius Diaries*, which includes Claudius sharing a 'sandwich lunch' with Hamlet ('I explained that I had only his best interests at heart ... He's going to be impossible to work with'), and enjoying a boozy dinner with Polonius: 'Over the third bottle he leant towards me, full of fun, and whispered, "To thine own self be true ... and bugger the rest!" In these troubled times, with the envious yapping at my heels, that's sound advice I mean to follow.'[33] This is all good knockabout, but it also signals towards a vital truth: the point is not that the various layers of fiction, role-playing and myth-making obscure or distort a historical reality that can be correctly accessed through retrieval of the 'facts', but that, for this chapter, these acts of fiction *are* the facts. Making use of the *Diaries* in the preceding and following pages to make sense of the events they claim to document, what I tell is less the story of those events than a story about the stories that have been spun around them. For a chapter that deals primarily with *The Tempest* and *Hamlet*, this seems entirely apt.

The first mention of *The Tempest* in the *Diaries* is in the entry for 4 July 1972. Hall told Olivier that it is 'the one play I wanted to do' and that he saw him as an against-the-grain Prospero, 'a man of power, of intelligence, as shrewd and cunning and egocentric as Churchill'. Olivier seemed interested, though Hall suspected that he would not play Prospero, but would open the South Bank complex with Lear, 'directed by Michael Blakemore'.[34] The nature of Hall's personal investment in the play was no doubt evident to himself, and throughout the period that *The Tempest* was conceived, planned and executed, there was a hint of embattled self-identification with Shakespeare's magus, beset by plotters and opponents on all sides (colleagues, the press, the Arts Council, builders, unions, the Caliban-fringe), determined to conjure magic through an art that would be so potent if circumstances would allow it. Six weeks later (24 August), the subject arose again, with Hall now discussing with Olivier 'the possibility of me doing *Lear* with him', while maintaining his preference for *The Tempest*', which 'I do want to do.'[35] Three weeks before he began his term as co-director with Olivier, following the first meeting on 8 March 1973 of the NT associate directors, Hall was 'very neurotic about my first play for the National', still wanting it to be *The Tempest*: 'But can I do it without Larry?'[36] Evidently he could: on 3 May he records that Alec Guinness had turned down his invitation to play Prospero, and that, feeling he 'must persevere', he had decided to approach John Gielgud, whom he regarded as 'perhaps too gentle and nice' but amenable to being pushed 'into a harsher area of reality'.[37]

Once Gielgud agreed, Hall (7 July) had 'wonderful thoughts' about the play and a vision of an opening tableau:

Gielgud aloft, head some sixteen feet high. From his shoulders a vast cloak which surrounds the stage. In his hands a huge staff. He dreams. He places the staff in the centre of the stage and it begins to sway from side to side. It becomes the mast of a ship. Within his cloak are shapes, spirits, children. They sing. All the music is vocal.[38]

Even though Hall probably did not have Gryphon and their ilk in mind at this point, it sounds like a prog-rock dream (compare and contrast the album cover art of that group's 1974 release, *Red Queen to Gryphon Three*);[39] the director's first thoughts on a production score referred only to worries about the suitability of 'Modern music', which he saw as diametrically opposed to Shakespeare's, which 'deals with its harmony, its order, its symmetry, its powers of resolution'. Commissioning a contemporary composer, Hall reflected, 'would be like asking Jackson Pollock to design Prospero's magic island'.[40] A month later (12 August), having asked designer John Bury to sketch his vision of the opening scene, Hall scrapped it: 'it is too potent and too mechanical'.[41] By now he was wedded to the idea of the play as masque, 'Inigo Jones, a piece of early Baroque theatre',[42] and he spent a 'marvellous' day off (Saturday 29 September) reading Roy Strong and Stephen Orgel's just-published 843-page two-volume study of Jones: 'theatre scholarship at its best ... Just facts, facts, facts'.[43]

It's a pity that Hall was unable to access the argument that Orgel subsequently developed from his collaboration with Strong, to the effect that the Court masque was an absolutist art-form, wherein the 'most complete expression of the royal will' was manifested 'in Inigo Jones's ability to do the impossible',[44] for it would have provided a perspective, of sorts, upon the 'terror' he confessed about 'such a difficult play to do' and upon his utopian dream of being free to 'work for a month with the actors before designing it'.[45] More recently, James Shapiro has imagined Shakespeare in the first decade of the seventeenth century at an evening at Whitehall, 'measuring the chasm between the self-congratulatory political fantasy enacted in the masque and the troubled mood outside the grounds of James's palace';[46] looking around during one of the ugliest decades of the twentieth century, registering the fuel crisis, the three-day week, escalating terrorism in Northern Ireland, strikes, spiralling inflation, bad music and awful haircuts, Hall would have known how he felt. 'What worries me', he confided on 13 December, 'is that out of the chaos we are getting into, some simple and extremist group of the far right or the far left may very well break up our society and take over'.[47]

Neither Hall's apocalyptic fears nor his rehearsal fantasy were realized, and on 3 December he presented Gielgud with the set design, only to become embroiled in a four-hour argument about Prospero's costume, ignited by the actor's observation that 'he was a boring man, it was a boring part, and he didn't want to look boring'. By the end, Gielgud agreed to a beard, a 'scholar's coat' and a 'scholar's hat', while apologetically declaring himself 'a romantic who loves the old-fashioned theatre'.[48] Following the awkward meeting with Gryphon on 12 November, Hall had in the meantime spent an evening at the rock venue the Rainbow in Finsbury, watching the major-league progressives Yes perform tracks from their 1972 release *Close to the Edge* as well as their soon-to-be-released double-album magnum opus *Tales from Topographic Oceans*; though it was 'too long', it was 'extremely sophisticated musically, and rewarding'. 'Five awesome young men make a thunderous noise which would completely eradicate the London Symphony Orchestra.'[49] The classically-inclined, opera-directing Hall was not alone in this judgment; six years after the broadsheet press had comprehensively ignored the Beatles' landmark, Robert Shelton in *The Times* hailed 'an historic concert of, to coin a word, "rockophonic" music', declared that 'this is not just a step past "Sergeant Pepper", but rather the threshold toward the ultimate bridging of the gap between the music of the academy and the tunes of the discotheque' and offered a hostage to fortune by predicting that the 'third movement alone ... will be studied 25 years hence as a significant turning point in modern music'.[50]

Tony Palmer, for the *Observer*, was less impressed, describing the concert as 'an endurance test' and the album ('pop music from first to last, though the music contains much that might be loosely described as jazz, electronic music and Bach-like organ toccatas') as 'a four-movement work of Wagnerian pretension', and concluding 'No amount of frenzied presentation, spectacular though it was at the Rainbow, could hide the paucity of musical invention.'[51] Palmer's then-minority view was a straw in the wind; within a few years, the music of Yes and their fellow men (and the makers and fans of this music were, overwhelmingly, young and male) would be routinely derided as addled, turgid and pretentious, as symptomatic of the worst excesses of hippie culture. Still, as a musical genre that sought to purvey pastoral fantasies through front-rank technology and baroque visuals, prog-rock suited the masque very well. The music was only part of the picture: Palmer's reference to the 'spectacular' presentation alludes to the group's characteristically prog-rock penchant for large-scale theatrics, with a stage 'composed of ambiguous shapes that were meant to be transformed by the lighting ... so that sometimes they appeared like flowers, sometimes like animals, or machines, or an inanimate landscape'.[52] Perhaps this appealed to Hall; like Shelton, he might also have noticed the 'vital work' of Rick Wakeman, 'a sequined Dr Faustus pacing about his keyboard laboratory'.[53]

It is easy to laugh, but there was more to Hall's wooing of the prog-rockers than a meeting of interests between an establishment aching to be seen as hip and a middle- and upper-middle class counter culture equally desperate to acquire an aura of musical respectability. For their part, the likes of Gryphon and Yes were, as Edward Macan puts it, exploring 'an idiom' that 'can be understood as a forum in which the musicians attempt to forge a dialectical relationship between the high culture of their parents and the popular culture that they grew up in';[54] underpinning Hall's efforts to make *The Tempest* historical-yet-contemporary, high cultural and popular, was the same dynamic as had been expressed in more forthright terms during his 1960s RSC heyday. In 1963, Hall told the company that he felt that they should reject the perception that they were a 'square, institutional, conservative' theatre 'supported by middle-class expense accounts' and embrace 'people who have never been to the theatre', which meant 'particularly the young'. Two years later, he wrote that this demographic did not 'think of the theatre as a high-brow, intellectual and difficult institution', and was 'an audience that is growing and growing fast – as fast as our new universities, as fast as the large sales of LP records and paper-back books'.[55]

This was the audience, as we saw in Chapter 2, for *As You Like It* and *Rosencrantz and Guildenstern are Dead*. In both of these shows, as in the RSC work that referenced 'Beckett, Genet, Arden, Pinter and many of our younger writers'[56] through Shakespeare and vice-versa, we can see what Alan Sinfield has labelled 'Shakespeare-plus-relevance' or 'the combination of traditional authority and urgent contemporaneity which proved so effective'.[57] As Stuart Hampton-Reeves elegantly summarizes, Hall's task was to trace 'the contours of the present through a representation of the past'.[58] For Hall, that dynamic was activated within a theatrical apparatus that by 1973 was increasingly seen not as the solution but as part of the problem. Hall's most adventurous forays into contemporary Shakespeare during the previous decade (*The Wars of the Roses*, *Hamlet*) were works of the proscenium stage, productions that were comfortable within its architectural, institutional and cultural constraints; so too was *The Tempest*. Hall witnessed the RSC's Shakespeare-plus-relevance model tested to the limit in July 1973 when he travelled to Stratford to see Buzz Goodbody's pop-rock, modern-dress *As You Like It*, a production he described as 'modish and awful': 'I have rarely been so upset in the theatre I regard as my home.'[59] Goodbody, who had a background in fringe theatre, saw a more fundamental problem with the Stratford stage, and between 1973 and 1974 she was instrumental in setting up the RSC's first permanent studio theatre, The Other Place, a 200-seat converted tin hut that opened on 10 April 1974 with her cut-down version of

King Lear. Keith Hack's *The Tempest* followed in October, and the contrast with Hall's NT production could not have been greater: 'The rough wooden plank of the stage is the island', Hack stated, 'There are no props, no gauzes and no palm trees.'[60]

When rehearsals for the NT *Tempest* began on Thursday, 2 January 1974, this lay in the future; for the time being, Hall was more preoccupied with the lingering presence of the NT's past, in the form of reminders that the island was not quite yet his. Olivier, as was his custom, invited himself along to the first rehearsal, making Gielgud uneasy and ensuring that 'the poor new members of the company (and especially the young ones) had the hideous experience of reading with Sir L's beetle brows watching them'.[61] Among that company were Michael Feast as Ariel, Denis Quilley as Caliban, the 21-year-old Jenny Agutter as Miranda, then best known for her film roles in *The Railway Children* (1970) and Nicolas Roeg's grim outback survival drama *Walkabout* (1971), and Arthur Lowe as Stephano. In the diary entry, Hall records that Lowe 'was just naturally funny as soon as he opens his mouth' and that it was 'a joy to have a clown as a clown. No artificial work is required'.[62] Lowe, who proudly styled himself an actor (albeit a permanently jobbing one), might have bristled at this description, but there was no question that this was astute casting. Lowe had a very well-established screen persona and public profile; since 1968 (the year in which he briefly appeared in the NT's Somerset Maugham revival, *Home and Beauty*), he had starred as the put-upon, socially-aspirational Captain Mainwaring in the much-loved BBC television sitcom *Dad's Army*; he had merely to raise an eyebrow at the right moment to earn a big laugh. Little survives in the critical record of the details of Lowe's performance, though Irving Wardle described him as 'a dangerous buffoon with powerful sense of his own dignity',[63] and Benedict Nightingale as 'inordinately pleased with himself';[64] both make his Stephano sound rather like Mainwaring.

Gielgud was another matter; after a week of rehearsals Hall admitted that the actor 'worries me', while (self-)

characterizing Prospero as 'a man who is contained and careful', who 'does not reveal himself to the audience', who 'can hardly reveal himself to himself', is 'controlled' and 'not emotional but puritanical'.[65] Ten days later, the production was 'pointing the right way';[66] another ten days, and Hall dashed from rehearsals to a public lecture by Frances Yates on *The Tempest* and its debts to 'the Rosicrucian doctrine and to the Hermetic tradition', and from there ('if you had not read her books you wouldn't have had the least idea of what she was talking about') to dinner with Peter and Natasha Brook, where he was told of the work of Robert Wilson ('a painter/ dancer / director who makes expensive shows which are like slow-motion Magritte pictures') and interrogated about his production; Brook was 'unimpressed'.[67] Another two weeks, ten days before the first preview on 26 February, and there was an elegiac, slightly fatalistic sense of acceptance, of endings meeting beginnings: Hall had a conversation with Gielgud in which the actor remembered 'in his youth how wonderfully immediate Baliol Holloway and Dorothy Green had been', yet 'by the end of their lives, even they seemed to him rhetorical old hams'. Because he felt 'he was the same', Hall records, 'he wanted to do *The Tempest* the way I wanted'.[68] Close to the first night, Hall was interviewed by *The Times*, where it was pointed out that this was his first Shakespeare in eight (it was actually seven) years, and where he revealed more of his emotional investment in the play: 'who could not be stimulated by the fact that this is the final statement of a man who could do everything, and has done everything?' *The Tempest* is 'a play about art and imagination, and ultimately about the futility of it all'. For Hall, it was 'totally unblinking, and the ending brings no resolution'.[69]

On 5 March, the day on which the once staunchly Labour-voting Hall woke to the news, ambivalently received, that Harold Wilson had been returned as Prime Minister of a minority Labour government, the show had its first night. It was 'the best we have so far given. The production *just* floated … there were the beginnings of a lightness and ease'.[70] Hall knew that this was the start of this *Tempest*'s journey but also that, for the press, it was its end; first-night euphoria gave way to the adrenalin rush of reading the next-day notices, which were 'what is known as mixed'.[71] Predictably, the *Guardian*'s Michael Billington did not buy into Hall's scheme; he praised Gielgud's 'exquisitely spoken and musically phrased' performance and set it at odds with a 'lethargic, vulgarly spectacular, masque-like production' that submerged the play and its lead 'in opulent excess' and in which 'ideas emphatically take second place to spectacle';[72] Wardle, conceding that the 'spectacle is generally splendid', also thought it 'hollow'.[73] Wardle was one of a number of reviewers to plant a wedge between the production and Gielgud: 'on John Bury's stage – a raised disc with an upstage promontory, and descending to floor level for the entrance to the cell – Prospero can control and view the action from outside, keeping his own tempos and long-studied inflexions in isolation from the shows he conjures up'. On 10 March, Hall scanned the Sundays: the *Sunday Times* is 'awful', the *Observer* 'wonderful' and *Sunday Telegraph* 'dismissive'.[74] For Frank Marcus of the *Telegraph*, the production 'bears witness to a love affair with Inigo Jones' and was only redeemed by Gielgud, who 'stands aloof and remote', with 'the austere and erect bearing of a Bellini Doge, and it is his mellifluous cadences which enchant';[75] and Harold Hobson's review in the *Sunday Times* was overshadowed by the lengthy notice he gave to David Hare's new play, *Knuckle* (directed, as it happened, by Blakemore), which opened at the Comedy Theatre the same week. Suggesting that 'the less said about *The Tempest* the better', he admired 'the calm flow of Gielgud's musical delivery, which floats on like the majestic Oxus, untouched by frosty starlight, or Polar star' but was dismayed by Hall's use of the grotesque elements of antimasque, 'the horrible malformed figures who provide the feast' for the disrupted banquet (3.3.17), 'with babies growing out of the backs of women and protruding through their chests', and by the staging of the masque: 'There is a Juno [Dana Gillespie] whose breasts are so enormous that whilst they are on stage they absorb the attention to the exclusion of all else in fascinated horror.'[76] A week later, Nightingale dismissed Hobson's 'appalled fascination' with Gillespie's breasts but found other grounds to object: 'confronted with waiters with breasts growing from their heads, heads from their breasts, legs from their backs and babies from their stomachs, one is surely permitted to register rather more than a gentlemanly surprise'. After all, 'Even Emily Post could not feel too guilty for spilling her soup if it was served by a grey-foam salamander with a gigantic penis.'[77]

Gillespie was an example of what Robert Cushman in the *Observer* termed the production's 'trendy' casting.[78] Making her debut as a teen pop artist in the mid-1960s, she was the first Mary Magdalene in the 1972 London premiere of *Jesus Christ Superstar*, sang backing vocals on David Bowie's breakthrough album, *Ziggy Stardust*, the same year and went on to a hugely successful solo career as a blues singer. Beside her, as Iris in a sung-through staging of the masque, was Julie Covington, who had appeared in the West End's other Jesus-themed rock opera *Godspell* in 1971 and who had a hit with her soundtrack recording of 'Day by Day'. Trendy or not, it worked for Cushman, and Hall's description of his review as 'wonderful' is spot on, not only in the self-interested sense that he dedicated three quarters of the 1,500 words of his *Observer* column to a production for which there was 'only one word ... fabulous' but also, more importantly, because it is model of detailed, thoughtful and authentically critical theatre journalism – and as such, therefore, worthy of a closer look. Delivering his verdict in the first paragraph, Cushman dives straight into the first scene, 'a thoroughly convincing storm, the hard-working sailors beset by a bunch of troublesome courtiers scrambling up from a cabin below decks', and from there via the ingenious segue to the second: 'At the close of the scene the roof of their cabin slams shut; standing on it, the first of a series of inspired transformations, is Prospero.' Here Cushman presents the lineaments of a refutation of Billington's charge that the production's use of spectacle was meretricious and empty;

and his review is alert throughout to charged visual doublings and juxtapositions: 'the appearance of Ariel as a water-nymph when we expect the lumbering entrance of Caliban (I know the play by heart and this moment still took me by surprise, so cunningly is it staged), and the arrival of Ferdinand on the spot where Caliban had stood only a second before'; the costuming of Prospero as 'a dead ringer for his usurping brother Antonio [Cyril Cusack], who emerges, far more than Caliban, as the play's negative pole', so that 'One glance between the brothers at the end establishes them as eternally unreconcilable'; and the appearance of Lowe's Stephano ('as funny as you would expect and more than twice as mean') at the end, where 'his function in the play is brilliantly illuminated in his stolen robes, to be greeted by Prospero's wry "You'd be king of the isle, sirrah?" Suddenly the stage appears thronged with monarchs, true and false; not for nothing do mirrors feature heavily in Mr Bury's set.' Cushman notes the 'mobility' of the sliding scenery, 'a theatrical delight, to be relished as such', the 'two set pieces' of 'the vanishing banquet, borne by "strange shapes" like a bad baroque dream of fertility corrupted', and 'the show of goddesses, sung throughout (which I found excessive, but pardonable), with Iris perched aloft, somewhere under a rainbow' (Figure 4.1); the inverted echo of Judy Garland's signature tune in *The Wizard of Oz* is odd, but resonant.

Cushman finds space to praise Feast's Ariel, who 'apparently *lives* in the sky ... whence he regularly descends by pulley'; 'by his constant changes of shape' he 'comes as close to incorporeality as can be asked' and 'sings both tenor and counter-tenor, rendering in the latter the lovely original setting of "Full fathom five"' (Gryphon, offstage, take a bow). Quilley's Caliban, 'a Hiawatha who has gone berserk with a tomahawk and scalped himself', is also admired: 'His roar of "freedom" has amazing force (in every performance of Mr Quilley's there is one moment that makes me think him the most exciting actor in the world and this is it).'

Gielgud, of course, receives the most focused attention: from the conjuring of the storm at the beginning, he is far

FIGURE 4.1 *The set for the masque in* The Tempest, *directed by Peter Hall, 1974, with stage-hands sitting in for Juno and Ceres. Photographer unknown, courtesy of the National Theatre Archive.*

from 'serene or untroubled', for 'magic on this scale requires of him an enormous effort of concentration; his magician's robe wears him down and it is a relief to him to shed it'. For Cushman, Gielgud's Prospero 'is engaged in a race against time and this awareness colours the whole of his dispute with Ariel, whose demand for liberty "before the time be out" endangers the whole scheme'. Gielgud was also prepared to work against the grain of his own tradition: '"Our revels now are ended" is savage rather than lyrical', and his 'renunciation of revenge is tremendous'. Delivering the epilogue, Gielgud 'sets his seal on the role forever'. Not everything worked: Ferdinand (Rupert Frazer) and Miranda are 'conventional', Agutter, 'in virtually her first stage role, does little more than obey orders', and the courtiers are 'pallid'; overall, 'the remarkable performances are outnumbered (not outweighed) by the mediocre ones'.

Cushman is better-disposed towards the production than most but less optimistic about the NT's future than many of his colleagues. He ends by lamenting the NT's expected imminent departure from the Old Vic, 'a perfect theatre', for the South Bank, a prospect he finds 'increasingly depressing'. Across the reviews, there is a sense that it is not just the effectiveness of Hall's treatment of the play that is being tested but also its legitimacy; and this, inexorably, leads to questions about the National Theatre, its mission and its practice. In a follow-up to his review, Billington renewed the charge that *The Tempest* was 'old-style scenic Shakespeare', while reassuring himself that Hall's innate theatrical good sense meant that he had 'no real fears that the National Theatre will become a temple of scenic extravagance',[79] as if the evidence of one production demonstrated anything about the risk that it might. For all their shared interest in the politics of theatre, neither Billington nor Hall engaged with the most potent of parallels between the production and the Stuart masque: both were occasions of deliberate, conspicuous and unsustainable profligacy. Having read Orgel and Strong, Hall could have noted their observation that the political significance of 'Inigo Jones's ability to do the impossible' was indicated by 'exchequer records' that 'testify to the extent of the crown's investment in such assertions'.[80] For James I, lavishing huge sums of money on the masque was more than a means of delivering the statement of royal power; it was the core of the statement. Defiantly conceived in a context in which funding pressures threatened to put the move to the South Bank (a driver of Hall's appointment) in jeopardy, Hall's *Tempest* made a not dissimilar assertion: whereas the RSC responded to the increasingly severe economic conditions of the mid-1970s by moving, in the Grotowskian terms offered by Peter Thomson reviewing their 1975 season, 'Towards a Poor Shakespeare',[81] Hall's NT set sail in the opposite direction.

As *The Tempest* proved, it was a course fraught with risks. Shifting our perspective from the production's captain to the below-decks team that were responsible for the day-to-day implementation of its voyage, we discover a work that, because of its resource-rich, tech-heavy nature, was more than usually prone to gaffes, mishaps and mechanical failures. The stage manager was Jackie Harvey, and the production history documented by her show reports reveal that barely a performance passed without damaging incident (and also that, despite her not-infrequent outbursts of exasperation, she was well-versed in the gallows humour that is her profession's stock-in-trade). The trouble began at the second preview, when the mechanized table that effected the trick of the vanishing banquet malfunctioned, and this '*quaint device*' (3.3.52 SD) was a recurrent source of problems throughout the run: for the tenth performance there was 'No smoke from the banquet table' and the 'Blind did not close';[82] this happened again at the twelfth, thirteenth, seventeenth and eighteenth performances, after which Harvey pleaded, 'could this long break be taken advantage of in thoroughly overhauling this devise'.[83] Hall was present at the tenth performance and noted that 'Over the 5 performances that I have seen, the table has so far worked once' and also that the 'transition to the trees being revealed [at the start of 2.1], which should be magic, got a laugh last night. The trees were revealed before they were in place (the screens and the trees were clearly not co-ordinating). And they juddered and shuddered'.[84] After the forty-seventh performance, Harvey finally snapped: 'The banquet table blind only closed ¾ of the way; if ever there was an example of a complicated prop which should not have been made up as a home-made string / chewing gum / elastic band effort held together only by determination and a little bit of luck …'[85]

The table was but one of Harvey's headaches: the extensive use of trucked and flown scenery put the actors, set and stage crew constantly at odds, and the introduction of a new wireless loop cueing system compounded the mayhem: 'Upstage truck operator didn't hear his cue until end of 1st comics scene & therefore his move was delayed until the next scene change';[86] 'My cue-ing over the loop came out over the stalls during the masque (Sound Dept. believe there must be a connection between that & the fact that at the same time the stage mics. were on').[87] Just before the loop system was installed, stage management team member Douglas Cornelissen wrote to his colleague Tom Pate to warn him that 'in some instances members of the public who use deaf aids might be able to receive the same messages and instructions over their personal instruments' and, mindful of a potential 'public relations problem', asked him to ensure that they were not tempted to 'suddenly leap about trying to pull ropes or striking props!'[88] Part of the challenge was that the scenic 'magic', as Hall termed it, was precariously reliant upon the variously-skilled labours of a stage crew of no fewer than twenty-seven (seventeen day men, four show men, five casuals and one prop man, according to the records), to hand-operate the flying and truck machinery; following the debacle of the prematurely revealed tree, stage technician Jason Barnes wrote to Harvey stating that he was 'concerned about the fact that we rely on casual labour to make up the numbers for these performances'.[89] Errors of timing and co-ordination were frequent and, on at least one occasion, lethally hazardous: 'Scene change into 1st Lords scene [2.1] taken at 100 m.p.h. by the flymen; trapping Mr Fraser [Rupert Frazer, Ferdinand] between the two crossing wings.'[90] During the final performance, Harvey recorded another incident: 'Only one tree (P.S.) set for 2nd comics scene. The operator in the O.P. flys says "I turned the handle and nothing 'appened." It was O.K. for subsequent use.'[91] It is a small detail, but the irritation that seeps through the scrupulous, ever-so-slightly pointed transcription of the dropped 'h' speaks volumes about the nature of backstage labour (and class) relations at the Old Vic at this moment. With the move to the South Bank, they would get much worse.

Harvey reported on 23 April that 'Sir John' was 'very worried about reflexions of actors in metal strips on upstage section of assembly flats (result of letter from member of audience)'.[92] The 'letter' referred to here was from a Miss Mary Walker of Hull, who wrote to Hall, Bury and Gielgud on 18 April to offer her thoughts on the production. Having secured a seat in the side section of the stalls (E.6), she found that her 'favoured diagonal view',

> ALAS! It had a grave disadvantage – I all too often perceived a characteristic of the material used for set, that members of the audience sitting in the centre block would not be aware of.
>
> The material -? part actually GLASS? – REFLECTS!!![93]

Fretting through Gielgud's first scene, Walker spotted what 'seemed to be a STAGE-HAND sitting just above / behind (stage right)'; distracted by persistent coughers and by the noisy late arrival of 'a WHOLE PARTY' twenty minutes in, it was only after 'some unhappy and bewildering many, many moments (I think)' that she decided 'that it was in fact a stage reflection – IT WAS "PROSPERO" – and I had thus been worried for Sir John quite needlessly'. Mary was partially mollified, though: 'Due to the coughs and reflection combined I feel I would love just to have a performance of Prospero's speeches – no-one / nothing else – in order truly to revel in Sir John's performances', and, conceding that since 'Sir John received me in his dressing room for a moment my journey from HULL was not without its satisfactions', concluded: 'It occurs to me that you may care to know how much this DEVOTEE appreciated the GIELGUD section of the Tempest programme. Thank you Mr. Hall. THANK YOU SO MUCH MR. TREWIN. I loved it – a lovely, lovely gesture I presume to think.' It is not hard to see why this would have caused Gielgud to worry, as it reveals what seems to be a fundamental flaw in Bury's design, and the letter prompted an internal memo from Fran Marsh, assistant to the acting general manager, which noted that, while the actors' reflections were (as Cushman had observed) part of the scheme, the 'stagehand' was a member of the stage management team 'sitting in the flange', and thus visible to 'approximately the first four rows of the Stalls, and similarly in the Dress Circle'; 'This remains a drawback of the present Old Vic stage.'[94]

At Stratford, the RSC gestured towards simplicity and directness by experimenting with scenic austerity and in small-scale non-proscenium spaces; at the Old Vic, Hall's *Tempest* offered itself as a prototype of the kind of spectacle that the new NT complex would more comfortably accommodate. In the *Times* interview, Hall indicated that he expected the production to transfer to the Lyttelton (at that point, expected to open in 1975) and that 'the concepts' explored in the show 'can be developed on our new stage, when it is ready'. At the Old Vic, he suggested, 'we're putting *The Tempest* into a pint pot. When we move it will look different'.[95] The idea that the solution to the problems inherent in thinking big was to think even bigger is characteristic. In the *Diaries* Hall repeatedly berates the myopic, parsimonious attitudes of the funders, noting for example an emergency meeting with the Arts Council in 1975 where there was the 'usual' debate: '"We quite see you want an extra £900,000 but surely you can do something with £600,000. It's a lot of money." But I know if we go into the new building under-subsidised ... we shall be criticised for being the most expensive inadequate theatre in the kingdom.'[96] But Hall was equally aware that his was a situation of unique privilege, as was exposed when he convened a meeting of fringe companies at the unfinished South Bank complex in May 1974, ten weeks into the run of *The Tempest*. Knowing that the entire National Theatre project was regarded with resentment on the alternative scene, he recognized that 'it is impossible for them to *like* an institution swallowing millions of pounds, when a few hundred can mean the life or death of their own enterprises. I would be the same'.[97]

For Hall, 'the production does not have the physical grace and clarity that I would have liked', and 'I have taxed myself and the organisation far too early.'[98] And that, as far as the *Diaries* are concerned, is almost that, but for the entries for 13 April, which documents 'John's surprise seventieth birthday celebration' at the end of the show, for 10 June, narrating a 'jolly evening' on tour in Bristol, and, finally, for 29 June, the last performance, which concluded with an 'obviously very moved' Gielgud saying that 'for forty years he had been playing at the Old Vic, and this was probably his last performance there'.[99]

It wasn't, quite. The National Theatre's last night at the Old Vic, nearly two years later, was on 28 February 1976, when

Gielgud, Ralph Richardson and Peggy Ashcroft led a revival of Val May's show *Tribute to the Lady*, created to honour the theatre's founder, Lilian Baylis. Gielgud, according to Callow,

> tore into 'O what a rogue and peasant slave am I' with astonishing velocity and perfect coherence, providing a moment in which form and content were so perfectly wedded that he seemed to deliver the essence of the play, and the essence of the central tradition of playing Shakespeare, within the three minutes that it took him to speak the speech.[100]

A while before this, there had been some degree of continuity between the end of the *The Tempest* and what Gielgud did next. In Hall's staging, the epilogue became a moment when Gielgud (or Prospero, or both) 'takes on the appearance of Shakespeare himself just before the curtain comes down': 'It was something which happened at one of the earliest rehearsals. John suddenly took off his hat and there was that noble brow and Shakespeare. If we'd strived for it then possibly it would have looked awful; but it just came by chance and it was too good to lose.'[101] Nightingale wondered 'what better picture could we take away' than 'that of Sir John ... the dome of his head bared in tacit homage to the Droeshout engraving, his face pinched but serene, as if to record a history of pain endured and overcome?'[102] For Speaight, at odds with most of the reviewers in thinking this production of the play 'by a long way the best I have seen', this was 'more magical than any magic he had wrought', as Gielgud reappeared 'in the everyday attire of a Shakespeare who had retired to Stratford ... with the epilogue as his last word, he wandered off into immortality'.[103]

Just over a month after *The Tempest* closed, the identification of Gielgud with Shakespeare became even more literal; on 14 August, he opened at the Royal Court in the lead role in *Bingo*, Edward Bond's biographical drama (subtitled *Scenes of Money and Death*), depicting Shakespeare at the end of his life. In the play, Bond's Shakespeare confronts the cruel and oppressive reality of early modern England, reflects upon his failure to meaningfully oppose it and takes the (for Bond) entirely logical step of committing suicide. Arthur Lowe, in the cast playing Ben Jonson, described it as 'a sequel to *The Tempest*' and, irrepressibly getting hold of the wrong end of the stick, declared that 'Clearly some kind of melancholia had set in to Shakespeare by then and that's the mood of the man in Bond's play. I suppose if he were living nowadays they'd give him some happy pills and that would be that ...'[104] Hall went to see the production on 20 August and was impressed by a portrayal of Shakespeare as 'a man who sold out to the bourgeoisie and no longer stood up for the progressive currents of his time'. The entry continues: 'Today I was handed one sheet of paper outlining a television commercial for an insurance company's pension fund which I could do. £1000 for two days' directing work Ridiculous ...'[105] As Hall appears to acknowledge, no further words are necessary.

Although he doesn't mention it in the *Diaries*, Hall's interest in *Bingo* neither started nor ended there. At the beginning of April 1973, he wrote to Bond inviting him 'to write a play for the National – big, small, long short – whatever you wish'; the playwright politely demurred and stated his preference to continue offering his work to the Royal Court.[106] *Bingo*, however, premiered in November not at the Court but at the University of Exeter's Northcott Theatre; in October, Bond wrote to his publisher observing that 'The RSC, the National and the Court all want to do it'.[107] In December, Hall wrote to John Russell Brown, who had been appointed as associate director and head of the Script Department in June, reporting a conversation with Gielgud, in which he expressed an interest in Bond's play; Brown agreed to acquire a copy of the script forthwith, whilst cautioning that he 'would not be very happy about JG as Shakespeare'.[108] Brown, who had stepped into the role vacated by Tynan, was one of Hall's more significant appointments and one that signalled the difference between the composition of Olivier's cabinet government and Hall's. In contrast to the journalist-poacher turned dramaturg-gatekeeper

Tynan, Brown was a Shakespearean critic and theatre scholar, at the time Professor of English at the University of Sussex, previously head of Drama and Theatre Arts at the University of Birmingham, and Fellow of the Shakespeare Institute. He was also the author of numerous books on Shakespeare and modern drama, and editor of the Arden second series *The Merchant of Venice*.[109] If Tynan's penchant for playing the dandy served as a useful foil to Olivier the showman, Brown's impeccable scholarly credentials appealed to Hall's Roundhead instincts, though he could sometimes also require diplomatic handling; in April 1974, Hall had to warn him that he was 'getting a certain amount of feed-back about him as an over-rigorous academic' and to 'just exercise great care and tact'. Fortunately, Brown 'took it very well'.[110]

The day after *Bingo* opened at the Royal Court, Hall offered the theatre's artistic director, Oscar Lewenstein, a National Theatre co-production of the play, which would play in repertory with *The Tempest* the following spring.[111] The next day, Bond responded: he liked the 'idea of one of my plays at the National theatre', and, not one to downplay the significance of his own work, speculated that 'the combination of Prospero + Bingo ought to go very well – the sort of confrontation that helps a theatre to define itself – perhaps?'[112] A week later, having seen the production, Hall wrote to his associate directors stating that he had hoped to secure the play for the NT when he read it the previous year, that Bond had 'understandably' offered it to the Royal Court and that 'we could present substantially the present production at the Lyttelton next spring'.[113] He wrote to Bond again, praising the play as 'magnificent'[114] and the same day sent a memo to director Bill Bryden urging that 'we must do everything we possibly can to present the play'.[115] Within a week, the NT's General Administrator Peter Stevens made Lewenstein a formal offer, which included a £5,000 advance and a number of points to 'bear in mind', which included 'the specialist appeal of the script and production which will be enhanced by its nursing in the context of a National Theatre repertoire', 'conversely, its vulnerability as a straight commercial presentation in a West End theatre, should one be offered' and '(not being pompous) the appropriateness of a National Theatre presentation during its first season of a fine play by a major author of our time'.[116] Lewenstein passed the negotiations over to the impresario Eddie Kulukundis, who, having managed to raise the advance to £7,000, agreed the terms.[117] Still unsure of the next season's scheduling, Stevens wrote back offering to pay the production's storage costs until the South Bank transfer was confirmed.[118] The plan was based on the assumption that the transfer would take place in the spring, and when it became apparent this was not to be the case, Stevens wrote again, apologizing that, in view of the 'dire' scheduling situation, 'it may be that John Gielgud would agree to do BINGO at the Old Vic next year, but it may not be possible for us to twin it with THE TEMPEST'.[119]

Twelve days later, the entire project was dead in the water. Operating the Old Vic cost-effectively, Stevens wrote, could only be managed by 'doing fewer productions of our own and running them for longer. This means that we have not been able to go ahead with certain of our own productions and under these circumstances it would be wrong to bring in an outside production'.[120] The next day Hall offered Bond profuse apologies for 'the very intolerable and surprising delays' that had been 'sprung' upon him and conceded that he could not 'try to hang on to the play, much as I loved it'. 'I can only hope', he forlornly concluded, 'that when we are installed on the South Bank, the possibility will be there of reviving it'.[121] That possibility was never realized, and thus the *Bingo–Tempest* pairing joined the ranks of the National's counterfactuals, a juxtaposition of Shakespeare and a contemporary play, led by a great actor, that might have been, at the very least, intriguing and provocative.

It was not the only Gielgud might-have-been of that period. For some months, Brown had been pressing the case for Kyd's *The Spanish Tragedy*, a play which, he urged the Board, exerted 'an enormous influence on Shakespeare', had a 'tellingly and intensely realised' central role in the part of Hieronimo and 'by its rhetoric and poetry has a unique blend of drama and musical excitement'.[122] A week into *Tempest* rehearsals, Hall wrote to Brown encouraging him 'to talk to John Gielgud' about the play, as he was 'back on the idea of melodrama';[123] and at the end of January he wrote again instructing him to 'follow through': 'we *have* to find another part for JG. I don't believe he will return in THE TEMPEST unless there is something else to do'.[124] Three days later, Brown replied: 'THE SPANISH TRAGEDY is going to JG, Wednesday.'[125] And that, as far as the records are concerned, was that; whatever Gielgud made of Kyd's play, he kept it to himself, and the production never happened.

Very like a whale

If Hall's *Tempest* was a labour of love, a play that, as he repeatedly asserted, he very much wanted to direct, his *Hamlet* originated in another, very different place. The first mention of *Hamlet* in the *Diaries* is in the entry for 2 July 1974, three days after the last night of *The Tempest*, which records an 'excellent' meeting with Albert Finney, who declared himself 'ready to take on the big parts', to 'try to examine a rougher, more instinctive form of classical acting', including Hamlet and Tamburlaine. Hall thought that Finney (aged thirty-eight) was 'five years too late for Hamlet' but that he should try, as it 'must assuredly be interesting'.[126] 'Interesting' is hardly a word to set the stage on fire, and the next time the topic comes up (14 May 1975), Hall, having secured Finney's agreement, admits that 'I can't say I have an overwhelming passion to do *Hamlet* again … but I would like to see Albie play the part.'[127] In the interim, following Finney's suggestion, Hall had made repeated attempts to engage the world-leading Italian director Giorgio Strehler, first writing to him on 22 July 1974, when he stated that Finney would be 'very excited at the prospect' of his involvement.[128] Receiving no reply, Hall wrote again a month later, plaintively enquiring whether Strehler had 'any feelings about the project', and yet again, passive-aggressively, two weeks later: 'It may be that that the idea does not interest you at all. It this is so, a brief line saying no would be most helpful.'[129] This prompted a telegram response from Strehler's General Manager ('GRATEFUL KIND OFFER STREHLER ANYHOW FULLY BOOKED UNTIL END DECEMBER 1975') and a follow-up letter the next day:

> Important is the choice of the first piece to take up in your theatre. Giorgio isn't yet mastering your language, which he likes and is busy with. Therefore Hamlet would not have been the right work for a first production in your house. Such masterpiece of the classical English and world literature needs a complete mastering of the language and may lie in the future.[130]

A Strehler-directed *Hamlet* at the National Theatre might have been a marvel to behold, but it was not to be. The task was now Hall's, and towards the end of July 1975 he confessed: 'I took on *Hamlet* as a gesture of trust to Albert. I didn't much want to direct it', and practically the only thing sustaining his interest was the possibility of doing the play 'as I want to, full-length'.[131]

The spectacle of Hall, torn between duty and desire, unsure whether he wants to direct *Hamlet* or not, serves the purposes of literary irony, but it does not augur well for the production; and perhaps he had reason to doubt his own motivation. On 14 June, Hall went to Stratford to see Buzz Goodbody's stripped-down studio production of *Hamlet* at The Other Place, which was 'amazing ... one of the best I have ever seen', and directed with 'complete certainty and clarity'. 'Because this was Shakespeare in a room, it could be quick, intimate and flexible.'[132] Maybe Hall saw in Goodbody's work something of the urgency and sense of purpose that had fuelled his own production of the play for the RSC in 1965, which had starred a 24-year-old David Warner in an intensely political rendering that, as Peter Holland puts it, 'connected Hamlet himself more firmly with a young audience than had been the case for centuries'.[133] Unlike both of Hall's productions of the play, Goodbody's *Hamlet* was in modern dress, a subject on which he had formed firm views. Two year previously, a week before he saw Yes at the Rainbow, he attended Jonathan Miller's NT Mobile touring production of *Measure for Measure*. Located in the Vienna of Sigmund Freud, 'conceived on a shoestring, with a deliberately drab set', the small-cast production presented a stark alternative to the prog-baroque splendours of *The Tempest*, invoking 'a society governed by bureaucratic rule and petty-bourgeois professionalism', according to Peter Ansorge, and making an 'immediate modern sense' that 'takes us into deeper moral waters than most directors care to navigate'.[134] Hall considered it 'the best production of Miller's that I have seen' and was impressed by the small-scale proxemics that allowed the actors to use 'conversational tone', enabling verse-speaking that was 'rapid and human, with none of the gloss of rhetoric or the inflation of emotion'. But it lacked 'true music', and the setting worked to 'merely illuminate some things and obscure others': 'Shouldn't we now, if we want to do Shakespeare out of period, re-write it? It would be absurd, but at least it's logical.'[135]

Hall was having none of that, and by the end of July he had come to believe that though 'we have come some distance in the last twenty-five years in understanding the rhythm of a Shakespeare play ... we still cut like barbarians'. Resolving that 'my future direction in Shakespeare must be to reveal the total object as well as possible', Hall declared: 'I feel in my blood that I know how' (4.4.65–6: 'from this time forth / My thoughts be bloody or be nothing worth').[136] There are traces here of the operatic approach that would later harden into the position that Hall would identify as a kind of 'fundamentalism', whereby Shakespeare's text is seen as 'a piece of writing containing its voicing and staging in precise rhythms through precise codes'.[137] Meanwhile, the commitment to completeness was generating logistical headaches, not least with respect to that crucial but overlooked aspect of theatregoing experience, the placement of the production's intervals. Towards the end of August, Michael Hallifax wrote to Hall setting out the options. The first involved a start of 6.00 pm, a first act of one hour, followed by a twenty-minute break, a second act of an hour and a quarter, a second fifteen-minute interval, and a third act of two hours. The second scenario moved the production onto the terrain of opera performance, positing a fifteen-minute interval after a one-hour first act, a Glyndebourne-style dinner break of an hour after another hour and a quarter, and a third act of two hours.[138] A few days later, Hallifax wrote again, suggesting a 6.30 pm start, a mini-interval of two minutes after an hour, a half-hour interval after a further hour and a quarter, and a final act of an hour and a quarter, with a mini-interval of two minutes halfway through 'for coughing etc (Houselights to half)'. Hallifax had evidently cooled on the prospect of picnics in the Waterloo Road, and for interval refreshment now suggested 'Sandwiches or Kedgeree or chicken wallop – order in advance.'[139] This would have resulted in a running time in excess of four and a half hours, which, even for Hall, was stretching it, and in the event the show started at 7.00 pm, ran for two and half hours before one interval only of twenty minutes, and ended just before 11.00 pm. For many reviewers, this was punishing enough.

Completing his work on the text around the same time, 'comparing Quartos and Folio', Hall 'managed to fillet it … of practically all its punctuation except what is essential to sense'.[140] He was assisted by Brown, to whom he declared that, as a result, he was 'getting closer to the proper delivery of a Shakespeare text … than I ever have done in the past'.[141] Rehearsals for *Hamlet* commenced on 22 September, the day that Hall moved to his new office in the still-uncompleted South Bank complex. When Hall first discussed Hamlet and Tamburlaine with Finney, they had expected to be settled in the new building well before this date; it was now expected that it would become operational by the following spring. So work started in rehearsal rooms on the South Bank for a production that would preview at the Old Vic from 4 December, transfer to the Lyttelton on 16 March 1976, and close on 15 January 1977, after a total of seventy performances. Things started well enough. Champagne was shared on the terrace before the first rehearsal, and Finney arrived (twenty minutes late, Hall notes) looking 'wonderful with his beard: a powerful, passionate, sexy Hamlet, glowering with resentment'; the read-through demonstrated that 'if you play on the line and keep going, think forward, the full-length play is neither too long nor too complex'; and the rehearsal room was 'quiet, has good daylight, height, and is warmed'.[142]

Within a week, 'when Albert walked on to the stage and launched into the current problem of Hamlet – was he to be or not to be? – it was electric and urgent'.[143] The gravediggers' scene was rehearsed 'with a real skull', and the 'actuality of the scene was immediately apparent; actors, stage management, everybody aware of a dead man's skull among us'.[144] This was the kind of immediacy sought by Goodbody, rarely encountered in either rehearsal or performance; and the rehearsal was followed by a chat with Ralph Richardson, who told Hall that Finney should treat the part 'like the most amazing train' and that all he had to do is 'get on it and rush along through cuttings, through stations, through tunnels until he finally reached his desination'.[145] By mid-October, things were more precarious: Hall had 'a sense that I am hanging on by my fingernails' and Finney, though 'very funny ... we'd just reached base camp and were now ready for the ascent', started to question whether 'we really need all those pack animals, all that food, all those medical supplies, oxygen; what was oxygen doing? Where were we going anyway?'[146] It is difficult to work out what Finney, or Hall, mean by this, unless it is a reference to the inevitable accumulation and elaboration of the machinery of production around the raw work of rehearsal; when the time came to run the first half, Hall worried 'I am losing my grip', because, paradoxically, it was all progressing *too* smoothly: reflecting that rehearsals 'have been so organised, so organic, so creative', he admits to his 'deep-seated desire to have things go wrong so that I can heroically make them right at the last minute' ('O cursed spite ...' [1.5.196]).[147] From this point on, give and take technical setbacks, Hall was increasingly convinced that 'there is something wonderful in this production if only I can bring it home', and by the time of the first preview (4 December), everything 'is now becoming *Hamlet*: the outside world is receding'.[148]

This was probably just as well, as the outside world was that of the tail-end of a year that had seen non-stop industrial disputes, a mainland bombing campaign by the IRA, price inflation hitting a historic peak of nearly 25 per cent; and, to cap it all, Queen's six-minute prog-rock monstrosity 'Bohemian Rhapsody' in the third of its nine weeks at the top of the singles chart. The first preview was an 'undoubted success', but the second half was 'not right', and, four days later, 'the first alarming preview that there's been – alarming because I confronted for the first time the possibility of failure... I thought it was going to be a break-through. After tonight I am not so sure'.[149] The emotional vacillation is to some extent a product of the innate rhythms of any rehearsal and preview cycle, and to some degree a reflection of Hall's personality, but the doubts are real enough and, as the divided critical response to the production proved, not without foundation. On opening night, Hall, 'reasonably calm', dictated one of the lengthiest, and most introspective, of all his diary entries, generating a passage that, for want of a better word, I will call a soliloquy:

> This is the closest I have reached to the heart of a Shakespeare play in my own estimation; it is the production which over the last fifteen years has the least gap between my hopes and the facts on stage. It is also pure and clear. On my instinct I have discovered a great deal about Shakespeare which I have always known in my head: the way scene must follow scene; the way lines are written for coming on and going off; the way every scene has a thematic line five or six lines in, to catch the audience's attention so that they know what the scene is about. And the production is the closest I've ever got to a unified style of verse speaking which is right. I feel

now I know how the verse should be treated. In Stratford days what I did was intellectual. Now I have found a way of doing it which is based on feeling and passion. It has been a very satisfying experience.[150]

As someone said in a not unrelated situation (*Hamlet,* 5.2.221), 'The readiness is all.'

The next day, some of the critics were 'wonderful', and some 'dreadful'.[151] In the 'wonderful' camp were the *Daily Mirror*'s Bill Hagerty, and Billington, Kretzmer and Cushman; in the 'dreadful', Wardle, Tinker, Hurren and Hobson. Hagerty was excited by 'your rough, rugged, two-fisted Hamlet. Your working-class Hamlet, if you like';[152] Billington had 'never seen such a totally satisfying blend of actor and concept': the production had 'the merit of speed, fluency and clarity', Finney made the soliloquies 'an attempt to isolate the audience in his dilemma', he had 'never felt more personally threatened by "To be or not to be" where Finney rushes on at speed, procures a dagger from behind his back and scans the front stalls', there was contemporary resonance in the play's world of 'insecurity, fear and an almost Nixonian delight in eavesdropping', and, in conclusion, this was 'the finest production of *Hamlet* I have yet seen and one that will invite discussion, argument and microscopic examination for a long time to come'.[153] For Kretzmer, Finney 'continues the contemporary line of rebellious Danes who mirror the savage absurdities of our age' and 'reflects the dilemma of modern man adrift in the continuing terrors of our own disjointed century'; 'it is a performance that defies any semblance of romantic sympathy, and winds up all the stronger for its sparseness and austerity'.[154] Cushman had less to say about Finney, recording that his performance, 'though short on explicit characterisation, is compounded of raw irony and intelligence; and for once the soliloquies are as enjoyable as the banter' but hailed the production itself as 'in a double sense, revolutionary', in that, by repudiating the 'highly detailed style, thick with props and intellectual concepts' that Hall himself had perfected, it returned to the full-text, bare-stage treatment that had not been seen at the Old Vic since the 1930s.[155]

John Bury's design was, indeed, austere: a black, marble-effect floor overlaid with a painted white circle from which radiated diagonal lines, backed by a grey wall with a single arched doorway at the centre, 'the most unassuming and self-effacing production of Shakespeare I've seen for ages',[156] according to Benedict Nightingale. Neither the 'wonderful' nor the 'dreadful' notices found much to object to in this setting, but for the latter this was probably only because there was no space to do so. Tinker welcomed the opportunity offered by the uncut text to 'swim with the tides of the narrative and discover how each wave takes us to the next', but Hall 'seems determined that we shall swim in leaded boots ... he has gone on to give us all and nothing at all'; the style was 'that time-honoured school of English acting which Hall did so much to slay during his stay at Stratford', the 'sort of direct declamation to the audience' that 'might kindly have been described as operatic if any except Denis Quilley's Claudius could bring a hint of music to the text'; and Finney's 'forte for rugged passion is largely wasted'. The frontal delivery of 'To be or not to be' which so impressed Billington 'makes us feel like casting directors at an audition where the hall is being rented by the half-hour, and reminds us that if this Hamlet is studying at Wittenburg it must surely be on a post-graduate course'.[157]

Wardle indicated what he thought of Finney's Hamlet by deferring discussion of it until the penultimate paragraph of his review (the 'voice rasps as monotonous as a buzz saw ... Finney has the energy and presence to carry the part physically; but he casts no light on it') and instead contrasted Hall's RSC version with the current one, the one driven by an 'urgent need to re-examine the text' that meant that 'the tragedy swung round and confronted us like a great dark mirror', where 'You knew from personal experience who David Warner's Hamlet was', the other 'a ponderous cultural event which will attract the star-following public and gratify spectators of the "Shakespearian intentions" school'. Supporting performances were little better:

Quilley 'communicates little beyond fear masked behind an ingratiating smile', Roland Culver's Polonius 'races through the part with a speed and monotony that kills the sense' and Angela Lansbury's Gertrude was 'an anonymous performance consisting of an embattled appearance and a poetry voice'.[158]

Most withering of all was the *Spectator*'s Hurren, who took stock of critical opinion and declared that 'my confrères, I'm afraid, have been far too civil with it'. Hurren had an axe to grind when it came to the National and Shakespeare: he savaged its *Coriolanus* in 1971, and dismissed its 'messily elaborated'[159] *Tempest* in a sentence, but even by his standards the review is excoriating. Suspecting that the choice of play was intended to pair the inauguration of the South Bank with that of the Old Vic twelve years previously, he wrote that it was a 'tediously inadequate production' that was 'unworthy of the occasion', 'in total a sorry and tragic business, funereal of aspect, carelessly organised, often antic in its casting and in important respects indifferently performed'. Finney was 'as dreadful as might be imagined of an actor of his unquestionably superior talents': 'for a man who has the crust to speak of the dapper Claudius as "a king of shreds and patches" his dress is remarkably slovenly and tatterdemalion, He is also too old'. Vocally '(unless I was mistaken about a couple of lapses into a Scottish accent), he seems halfway to playing Macbeth, and in his appearance he seems halfway to playing Lear'. Not just too old but too solid too: alluding to Finney's much-publicised fitness regime, Hurren waspishly observes that for 'all those dedicated hours in the gym', 'his agility seems less the mark of youth than of surprisingly spry middle age'. The 'antic' casting included Susan Fleetwood's Ophelia; watched by a silent chorus of 'grey old men, generally standing about in attitudes of shock', she was in her mad scene 'considerably more tiresome than touching', and Hurren suspected that 'most of them were wishing she would just go jump in the brook', and that 'quite a few ... would have been pleased to give her a push'. Considering the 'general loquaciousness' of the 'odd but lovely couple' of J. G. Devlin and Stephen Rea's Irish gravediggers, he concluded, 'it is a good-sized hole they excavate, conveniently big enough not only for Ophelia ... but for the whole show, which should there be interred forthwith'.[160]

Hall professed bewilderment in his diary: 'Why are they, the bad ones, so angry? I suppose because this is a different kind of Shakespeare, undecorated, and in some sense uncomfortable.'[161] With reactions this polarized, one wonders whether there was more at stake than the merits of the production itself. Hurren's passing reference to Finney's 'aggressive, regional rasp' suggests that there might have been some class politics in play, but for all his early credentials as a horny-handed Northern son of the British New Wave in the 1960s (notably in Karel Reisz's *Saturday Night and Sunday Morning* [1960]), the idea that Finney was some kind of working class hero was long buried. More pertinently, Hurren's critical perspective was shaped by ideological antipathy to the entire National Theatre project, which as a state-supported, overmanned branch of the culture industry, deserved to be bracketed with what the *Spectator* thought of as the bloated, sclerotic and irresponsibly-indulged other components of the public sector (for which Finney's performing body stands as proxy). By now, reviewers of almost every NT production were used to treating them as tests of institutional policy and achievement; as with *The Tempest*, Hall's *Hamlet* was subjected to sceptical scrutiny, to the demand that the work should self-evidently justify the organization's financial advantages and institutional privileges. It hardly helped that the NT was making its transition to the new building at the moment that the other large-scale nationalized industries (notably car and steel manufacture) seemed to be heading towards a stage of terminal crisis.

Hobson's *Sunday Times* review offers a more complex, and more conflicted, response. The production was 'a resounding success', Hobson sarcastically announced, with Finney perfectly cast for 'an age that puts only a low value on grace, style, and subtlety': the 'voice is monotonously rasping, his mind does not respond to the text, and his way of taking curtain-calls suggests insufferable conceit'. Its importance was 'political, so political in fact that Mr Hall startles us into realising that, though we may on previous occasions have seen Hamlet, we have never before seen "Hamlet"'. The combination of inadequate central performances and complete text provoked a radical rethink of priorities: 'all through the play Denmark is in dire peril, and the crucial scene becomes not the famous soliloquies, which Mr Finney speaks with memorable insensitivity to their changing moods, but that it which Claudius instantly agrees to let Fortinbras's army march through his country'. Hall's 'great achievement' is to show 'that "Hamlet" is a play about a country on the brink of ruin, and incapable of pulling itself together'.[162] The allegory, as far as 'relevance' is concerned, is obvious: Hall's *Hamlet* had become a state-of-the-nation play. The extent to which Hobson is being ironic is unclear, but his against-the-grain reading corresponds surprisingly closely to Brecht's – this from a critic who was staunchly anti-Brecht from first to last. As it happened, Brecht is quoted at length in the production programme (alongside twentieth-century commentators ranging from Freud to Kott), with reference to 'the bloody and dark period in which I am writing, a period where reason is misused and more and more distrusted'. For Brecht's Hamlet, 'In the feudal enterprises to which he has returned, reason is at cross-purposes with him. Practice is unreasonable; his reason is unpractical. He falls: a tragic victim of the contradiction between such reason and such actions'.[163] There is, however, no suggestion that this is the key to Hall's production; the programme makes as much of the play's early modern context, with nods towards the Elizabethan World Picture and the Senecan and world-as-stage traditions, and features a pantheon of Hamlets, from Thomas Betterton to David Warner. Finney's bearded face, twinned with Burbage's, visually dominates: whether the reviewers liked it or not, the show was his.

Audiences clearly did like it. In box office terms, the critical commentary, good or bad, made no difference at all; as the *Guardian*'s Michael White remarked in the paper's diary column in December, the 'prestigious and divisive' production was 'packing them in' regardless of the reviews; apart from 'the 100 or so tickets sold each morning', the show had been 'sold out since November 18 – three weeks before the critics saw it'.[164] But the extended life cycle of this *Hamlet* meant that its conversation with the print media continued long after its first night. Early in the new year, Hall had lunch with Peggy Ashcroft and was upset that she didn't like the production at all. Grumbling that it is 'not usual for her to misunderstand what I'm up to', in the same entry he observes (of Blakemore's imminent production of the Ben Travers farce *Plunder*) that 'Michael gets stuck in a dogmatic theory about the way to do a play and doesn't seem to realise it could be wrong – or needs development'.[165] The pot-kettle irony of this remark evidently escaped him, and on 16 March *Hamlet* became the second of the Old Vic's last-season productions to transfer intact to the Lyttelton for its opening week. Prior to this, on 28 February, Finney stood in for Olivier (who, pleading illness, had tactfully bowed out) to compère the Old Vic farewell performance of *Tribute to the Lady*, in which, as noted above, Gielgud showed what his Hamlet lacked (Hall: 'Gielgud began Hamlet's "O what a rogue" speech at such a high pitch that I feared he would go into orbit; he did').[166]

The evening of 16 March, with Princess Margaret in attendance, was a royal gala performance, an establishment event slightly overshadowed by the shock announcement, made earlier that day, that Harold Wilson had resigned as prime minister. Hall reports with satisfaction that the queue for day seats (150 at £1.00) started at 5.00 am; the box office 'opened at half past eight and by quarter to nine all the seats were gone'.[167] Had he been reading the letters page of *The Times*, he would have known that many members of the NT audience were far from happy with this situation. On 6 February, it published a letter from one Peter Holland of Trinity Hall, Cambridge, who, speaking for the 'large numbers of people who regularly attend the Old Vic', pointed out that the new ticket system would prevent them 'from seeing productions at the new theatre'. Whereas the Old Vic's ticket pricing structure and day seat system had benefited theatregoers unwilling or unable to pay top-range prices, 'particularly students, who have always made up the largest proportion of the Gallery audience', the new flat rate of £2.35 for all advance seats effectively put the NT's work beyond the reach of some of its most loyal supporters. It was, Holland wrote, 'difficult enough for us to arrive at the theatre in time for the performance, let alone find time to spend queuing in the morning or two hours before the curtain goes up'; and he crossly signed off, 'This National Theatre no longer seems to want the nation to visit it'.[168]

There was plenty more of this to come. In the meantime, newspaper reviewers took the opportunity of the transfer to re-evaluate Hall's production in its new setting. Hobson was pleasantly surprised, finding that Finney, 'perhaps inspired by the new theatre, plays Hamlet with a fire and intensity I failed to observe when the production was given at the Old Vic'.[169] Cushman confirmed his positive account of the Old Vic premiere, feeling that the production fitted the space much better, as 'the lines of John Bury's set (dowdy at the Vic, magnificent here) were completed by those of the auditorium. The stage-floor was patterned like a target, and soliloquies were delivered with magnetic effect from the bull's eye'. It was, Cushman, concluded, 'the peak of the week'.[170] Wardle was less persuaded that the stage, '20ft wider and deeper than that of the Vic', worked to the show's advantage, as 'the recurring impression arises of a physical proscenium haunted by the spectre of the open stage', and the design 'throws tremendous emphasis on the central stage position'. Used well, 'it can produce moments as thrilling as the silvery apparition of Denis Quilley's Ghost at the climax of the closet scene', but 'As Finney uses it, all too often it means simply that we get a battering.'[171]

The most considered evaluation of the production appeared over a year after it closed. In the course of writing what proved to be one of the most vivid and insightful records of English Shakespeare performance in the first half of the 1970s, *Shakespeare in the Theatre* (1978), Richard David paid repeated visits to productions in Stratford and London, and Hall's *Hamlet* was one of them. In a chapter entitled 'The problem of Hamlet', David pairs the production with Goodbody's, which transferred from Stratford for a run at London's Roundhouse from January to March 1976, as a study in contrasts. He does his best to be even-handed, but it is clear that he much preferred the Goodbody version, which he found 'intensely gripping and emotionally convincing' and characterized by 'crispness and pointedness' and 'singleminded drive'.[172] Lacking the latter, the NT *Hamlet* was 'a thing of shreds and patches' that 'confirmed that the set pieces that are restored were not mere decorations but served specific ends in Shakespeare's plan' but failed to 'compensate for this lack, as it might have been expected to do, by an added richness and sonority derived from its uncut text'.[173] David notices in particular the strong design feature that had become apparent to Cushman when the production transferred, which he describes as 'a pattern of chalk-pale lines radiating from a point under the portal in ever-widening tracks to the front of the stage and, when the space behind the portal was lit, repeating the pattern in a mirror image on the far side'. The lines 'intersected and passed through a circle immediately in front of the portal, some six yards in diameter and occupying perhaps a third of the playing space'.[174]

The detail provides the grounding for David's identification of a formalization, and a conceptualized use of space, that are nowhere evident in Hall's account, which maps the rehearsal journey as a voyage of spontaneous discovery, a quest for immediacy and truth. David's suspicion that at least some production choices were pre-emptively shaped by its architectonic design is confirmed by rehearsal photographs (Figure 4.2), which indicate that, from the beginning, the circle both defined the space of this *Hamlet* and determined its choreography. At its most schematic, the stage geometry suggested 'that the personages of the drama were to be seen as pawns in Fate's game of chess', or, perhaps, as creatures caught in a web; as the action unfolded, other patterns, of varying degrees of subtlety, emerged. Thus 'the Ghost, on its first two

FIGURE 4.2 *Simon Ward, Albert Finney and fight director William Hobbs in rehearsal for* Hamlet, *directed by Peter Hall, 1975. Photograph by Antony Crickmay, courtesy of the V & A Theatre and Performance Collections.*

appearances, could not, it seemed, penetrate the charmed circle that protected its interlocutors', but when Hamlet confronted it, 'it was the Ghost that took possession of the circle, a possession confirmed in a blaze of light from above, while Hamlet hovered in the shadow at its edge until, at the Ghost's pronouncement "I am thy father's spirit", he bowed himself to the ground within the circle'. Later, Rosencrantz and Guildenstern (Oliver Cotton and Gareth Hunt), 'under wary interrogation by Hamlet, were circumscribed and prisoned within the circle', and 'Claudius's plotting with Laertes [Simon Ward] saw the former initially sustaining 'a constant movement within and across the circle as he paraded his smooth, insinuating arguments before a Laertes motionless and suspicious on its circumference'. Laertes signalled his capitulation when he 'stepped briskly inside the circle and with "I bought an unction from a mountebank" overtly committed himself to the party of evil'. For David, these carefully-plotted moments were 'not ineffective', but they were extraneous, 'decorations' that had 'a strong air of artificiality' when compared to the 'strikingly direct and natural dispositions at the Roundhouse'.[175]

My point is not that the benefit of repeated observation and time for reflection afforded David an authority that the first-night reviewers lacked, nor that seeing it from the outside (rather than, as for Hall, the inside) rendered his account more reliable because more objective. It is that, more than is usually the case, commentators seemed to have witnessed very different versions of the same event. Milton Shulman even articulated these differences in a single review, predicting 'audiences divided between those entranced by the fluid, simple line of action and those fighting off sleep', and, at the end of a long list of faults, concluding that 'it is still an evening that from time to time can make the spirit soar and the mind reel with wonder'.[176] Like the possibly imaginary cloud that Hamlet invites Polonius to inspect, Hall's *Hamlet* is at one moment almost in the shape of a camel, the next backed like a weasel, and then like a whale – very like a whale (3.2.379–84). I know no means of resolving this indeterminacy, which is endemic to the practice of performance history itself; and in this respect this *Hamlet* exemplifies the elusive and ultimately disappearing subject of this book, a disparate body of theatre work that mattered in very different ways to those who participated in it. My task has been that of a scholar-Horatio, assigned 'to speak to th'yet unknowing world / How these things came about' (5.2.386–7), weaving together these strands of perception, opinion and speculation, to generate the story of the stories that 'these things' have generated. Writ large, this is also, finally, the story of the unique period in the National Theatre's history when Shakespeare, for those involved in the making of it, really, centrally mattered.

Conclusion

'Thus Peggy and Sam Beckett, two people I loved dearly, inaugurated the whole building.'[1] This is how Hall remembered the move to the South Bank, and the contrast with the opening of the Old Vic thirteen years earlier could not be more marked. Whereas Olivier had launched his operation with a prestigious, action-driven, large-scale production with a cast of fifty, Beckett's *Happy Days*, which opened on 8 March, was not really even a two-hander but largely a solo piece for Peggy Ashcroft, quietly supported by Harry Lomax's Willie; already a contemporary classic, the play announced the NT's new, forward-looking mission. Yet Shakespeare was still the occasion for the 'official' opening show at the Lyttelton; the first performances of *Happy Days* were previews, and it was *Hamlet* on 16 March that provided the royal gala performance. Hall had already made sure that Shakespeare's words were the first to be spoken in the new building some months earlier, when he took a rehearsal of the first scene on the Lyttelton stage; a report in the *Evening Standard* (19 December 1975) depicted Daniel Thorndike (nephew of Dame Sybil) in role as Barnardo and revealed that the 55-year-old actor had begun his career at the Old Vic in the 1930s.[2] *Hamlet* was one of seven productions to transfer from the Old Vic, and it remained repertoire until the beginning of 1977. In this respect, at least, it served as a link between the NT present and its past.

When it came to the opening of the Olivier auditorium it was not, as Archer and Barker had anticipated, with the Second Tetralogy but with the two parts of Marlowe's *Tamburlaine*, with Finney again in the lead, and the shift away from Shakespeare seemed even more pronounced. During the thirteen years that followed with Hall as director of the National, fifteen Shakespeare productions were mounted across its three auditoriums; a total which was numerically greater than the dozen or so of the Old Vic period but in the context of a total of over two hundred productions, proportionally much less. They included John Dexter's opportunity to finally direct *As You Like It* in 1979, Michael Rudman's *Measure for Measure* with an almost exclusively Afro-Caribbean cast in 1981, the 1986 Mobile *Hamlet*, the first Shakespeare at the National to be directed by a woman (Cicely Berry) and Hall's season of late plays in the Cottesloe in 1988, which served as a farewell to the NT stage while enabling him, with *The Tempest*, to end his tenure as he had begun. Little, if any, of this work made anything like the impression generated by the productions of the 1960s, but the NT had become a different kind of enterprise, with Shakespeare now one not-particularly privileged component among many.

Looking back at the thirteen years of National Theatre Shakespeare productions at the Old Vic, one registers widely diverse practices and mixed achievements but little sense of a coherent pattern or sense of purpose. To a certain extent, this was a consequence of the bifurcation of national theatre ideal into two companies in Stratford and London, which meant that the RSC assumed the formerly primary role of custodian of the canon, with the NT struggling to define the nature of its relationship to Shakespeare in the meantime. Key RSC productions of the period were statements as well as achievements, among them *The Wars of the Roses* in 1963, *The Romans* cycle in 1972, Peter Hall's epochal *Hamlet* in 1965 and Peter Brook's *A Midsummer Night's Dream* in 1970. The National's output contained moments of individual brilliance (Olivier's and Smith's performances in *Othello*, Olivier's Shylock, Gielgud's Prospero) and, in *As You Like It* and *Rosencrantz and Guildenstern are Dead*, two productions that exactly caught the contemporary mood; it also saw some adventurous forays in to more European territory by accommodating Zeffirelli, Wekwerth and Tenschert. In this sense, Shakespeare at the National Theatre at the Old Vic matched Tynan's definition of the work as Cavalier: flamboyant, individualistic and, one way or another, defiantly out of time. Arguably, the more significant work of the Old Vic period lay in the area of the non-Shakespearean classics and contemporary drama: in William Gaskill's revivals of Farquhar (*The Recruiting Officer* in 1963 and *The Beaux' Stratagem* in 1970), Olivier's *Three Sisters* (1967) and Hall's *John Gabriel Borkman* (1975); and in the premieres of Shaffer's *The Royal Hunt of the Sun* (1964) and *Equus* (1973), Nichols's *The National Health* (1969) and Pinter's *No Man's Land* (1975). These, and other, productions were as central to the National's mission as its Shakespearean interventions; they defined the context in which these took place and provided the yardstick against which their achievements could be measured.

In time, the National would restore the prominence, though not the centrality, of Shakespeare, notably when Nicholas Hytner assumed the reins in 2003 with a state-of-the-nation *Henry V*, the first production in the UK to cast a black actor (Adrian Lester) in the title role. That story however, lies beyond the scope of this book.[3] My aim has been to reconsider the achievements of the National Theatre during the period in which, more than at any other point in its history, it could be genuinely regarded as a house for Shakespeare.

APPENDIX

Cecil Day-Lewis's prologue for the Gala Performance of *As You Like It* on 14 May 1968:

> Curtain up on this dear, honoured scene
> A South Bank Cinderella wears the crown tonight
> Of all our country's theatres. The stage
> Which Kean enthralled, and Baylis wove
> Dazzling tradition on a shoestring
> Makes good the vision of a hundred and fifty years.
> Old Vic, your roof held generations
> In a magic spell, and we have known
> So many incandescent nights flash past, and flown away.
> No wonder, where the young dream their dreams
> And learn their trade; stars come back
> To celebrate their nursery's renown.
> Here every man once bought, for a small price, audience
> For Shakespeare. And still gleans not self-knowledge
> From the hero's fall, but heroine's love's sacrifice.
> This stage is all the world; in all our hearts
> Rosalind smiles, Lear howls, Malvolio preens.
> Old cockney Vic, with what strange art
> You bring us strollers into one family,
> That learned, through discipline, patience,
> Tears, and gaiety: the play's the thing.
> You show world theatre, old and new today,
> Man's heights and depths, and what he may yet crave,
> Yet come to be.

NOTES

Introduction

1. Daniel Rosenthal, *The National Theatre Story* (London: Oberon, 2013), 3–4.
2. 'La Comédie Française at the Gaiety', *The Times*, 3 June 1879.
3. Geoffrey Whitworth, *The Making of a National Theatre* (London: Faber and Faber, 1951), 36.
4. Ibid., 31–2.
5. William Archer and H. Granville Barker, *A National Theatre: Schemes and Estimates* (London: Duckworth and Co., 1907), 39.
6. Ibid., 162, 165.
7. Richard Findlater, 'The Winding Road to King's Reach', in *The National: The Theatre and its Work 1963–1997*, ed. Simon Callow (London: Nick Hern, 1997), 81.
8. Callow, *The National*, 6.
9. *Parliamentary Debates: House of Commons (Hansard), 1948–9* (London: HMSO, 1949), 484.
10. Findlater, 'The Winding Road to King's Reach', 82.
11. Rosenthal, *National Theatre Story*. For accounts of the Shakespearean careers of the protagonists, see Abigail Rokison, 'Laurence Olivier', in *Great Shakespeareans, Volume XVI: Gielgud, Olivier, Ashcroft*, ed. Russell Jackson (London: Bloomsbury Arden Shakespeare, 2013), 61–109; Stuart Hampton-Reeves, 'Peter Hall', in *Great Shakespeareans, Volume XVIII: Brook, Hall, Ninagawa, Lepage*, ed. Peter Holland (London: Bloomsbury Arden Shakespeare, 2013), 47–78.
12. John McEnery played Hamlet for the premiere; he was succeeded by Ronald Pickup and Barrie. Pickup went on to play Guildenstern in the production's twelfth cast, which must be a unique instance of this trajectory counting as a promotion. Caroline John was the first Ophelia, followed by Louise Purnell, Helen Bourne and Maxwell-Muller.

Chapter 1

1. 'A National Refresher', *Observer*, 20 October 1963.
2. 'Desperate Calm of First Night', *Guardian*, 23 October 1963.
3. J. C. Trewin, 'First Night', *Illustrated London News*, 2 November 1963.
4. Harold Hobson, 'A Hand Upon the Royalty', *Sunday Times*, 27 October 1963.
5. 'A Hamlet to Cheer', *Daily Sketch*, 23 October 1963.
6. Eric Gillett, 'Exciting "Hamlet" by O'Toole', *Yorkshire Post*, 23 October 1963.
7. B. A. Young, 'At the Play', *Punch*, 30 October 1963.
8. Bamber Gascoigne, 'Extrovert at Elsinore (S.E.)', *Observer*, 27 October 1963.
9. Bernard Levin, 'After a Wait of 100 Years, this will do for a Start', *Daily Mail*, 23 October 1963.
10. Hobson, 'A Hand Upon the Royalty'.
11. Roger Gellert, 'Without the Prince' *New Statesman*, 1 November 1963.
12. J. C. Trewin, 'First Night'.
13. John Gardner, 'The Plain Man's Guide to Hamlet', *Stratford-upon-Avon Herald*, 25 October 1963.
14. Trewin, 'First Night'.
15. Our Dramatic Critic, 'Routine Performance of Hamlet', *The Times*, 23 October 1963.
16. Laurence Olivier, *Confessions of an Actor* (London: Weidenfeld and Nicholson, 1982), 204.
17. Levin, 'After a Wait'.
18. Gascoigne, 'Extrovert at Elsinore (S. E.)'.
19. Philip Hope-Wallace, 'Ghosts Afoot at the Old Vic', *Guardian*, 23 October 1963.
20. Our Dramatic Critic, 'Routine Performance of Hamlet'.
21. Gellert, 'Without the Prince'.
22. Alan Brien, 'Moody Prince Charming', *Sunday Telegraph*, 27 October 1963.
23. T. C. Worsley, 'Hamlet', *Financial Times*, 24 October 1963.
24. Barry Norman, 'O'Toole's Hamlet', *Daily Mail*, 22 October 1963.
25. Samantha Ellis, 'Hamlet, National Theatre, October 1963', *Guardian*, 12 March 2003.

26 Robert Stephens, *Knight Errant: Memoirs of a Vagabond Actor* (London: Sceptre, 1996), 62–3.
27 'Women for "Hamlet" – But not for Speeches', *Daily Telegraph*, 18 November 1963.
28 Ellis, 'Hamlet, National Theatre, October 1963'.
29 Trewin, 'First Night'.
30 Richard Anthony Baker, 'Dan Meaden, Stage, Film and Television Actor', *The Stage*, 10 January 2012.
31 Callow, *The National*, 14.
32 John Dexter, Memo to Michael Birkitt, 1 December 1975.
33 Rosenthal, *National Theatre Story*, 79.
34 Kenneth Tynan, *Letters*, ed. Kathleen Tynan (London: Weidenfeld and Nicholson, 1994), 458.
35 Our New York Dramatic Critic, 'Kazan Defeated by the Changeling', *The Times*, 23 December 1964.
36 Our Dramatic Critic, 'Routine Performance of Hamlet'.
37 Gascoigne, 'Extrovert at Elsinore (S. E.)'.
38 Young, 'At the Play'.
39 Trewin, 'First Night'.
40 David Pryce-Jones, 'Son et Lumière', *Spectator*, 1 November 1963.
41 Gellert, 'Without the Prince'.
42 Robert Speaight, 'Shakespeare in Britain', *Shakespeare Quarterly*, 15, no. 4 (1964), 377–89: 378.
43 Dominic Sandbrook, *Never Had It So Good: A History of Britain from Suez to the Beatles* (London: Abacus, 2006), 720–1.
44 Barbara Hodgdon, 'Race-ing *Othello*, Re-engendering White-Out', in *Shakespeare, The Movie: Popularizing the Plays on Film, TV, and Video*, ed. Lynda E. Boose and Richard Burt (London and New York: Routledge, 1997), 26.
45 Barry Norman, 'Olivier's Challenge', *Daily Mail*, 14 April 1964.
46 W.A. Darlington, 'Black, but Comely', *Daily Telegraph*, 18 May 1964.
47 J.C. Trewin, 'Olivier's Othello', *Illustrated London News*, 2 May 1964.
48 Bernard Levin, 'And Now Othello Falls to Sir Laurence', *Daily Mail*, 22 April 1964.
49 David Pryce-Jones, 'Olivier', *Spectator*, 1 May 1964.
50 Our Dramatic Critic, 'The Moor Built Up at Iago's Expense', *The Times*, 22 April 1964.

51 Philip Hope-Wallace, '*Othello* at the National Theatre', *Guardian*, 22 April 1964.
52 Bamber Gascoigne, 'A Moor for All Time', *Observer*, 26 April 1964.
53 Ronald Bryden, 'Olivier's Moor', *New Statesman*, 1 May 1964.
54 Levin, 'And Now Othello Falls to Sir Laurence'.
55 Bryden, 'Olivier's Moor'.
56 Our London Drama Critic, 'Sir Laurence Olivier a Superb Othello', *Glasgow Herald*, 23 April 1964.
57 Herbert Kretzmer, 'I Shall Dream of this Othello for Years', *Daily Express*, 22 April 1964.
58 Pat Wallace, 'That Old Black Magic', *Tatler*, 13 May 1964.
59 B. A. Young, 'Othello', *Financial Times*, 23 July 1964.
60 Kretzmer, 'I Shall Dream of this Othello for Years'.
61 John Solomos, *Race and Racism in Britain*, 3rd edn (Basingstoke: Palgrave Macmillan, 2003), 80.
62 Olivier, *Confessions*, 209.
63 Laurence Olivier, *On Acting* (London: Sceptre, 1987), 101–2.
64 Hodgdon, 'Race-ing *Othello*', 26.
65 Olivier, *On Acting*, 99.
66 Ibid., 101.
67 Ibid.
68 Ibid., 96–7.
69 Ibid., 102.
70 Kenneth Tynan, in *Olivier at Work: The National Years*, ed. Lyn Haill (London: Nick Hern Books, 1989), 75.
71 F.R. Leavis, 'Diabolic Intellect and the Noble Hero: or The Sentimentalist's *Othello*', in *The Common Pursuit* (Harmondsworth: Penguin, 1962), 136–59. Tynan in *Olivier at Work*, 76.
72 Ibid., 76–8.
73 Ibid., 79, 80.
74 John Gardner, 'Othello's Olivier', *Stratford-upon-Avon Herald*, 1 May 1964.
75 Fergus Cashin, 'Olivier – But with a Look of Jolson', *Daily Sketch*, 22 April 1964.
76 Milton Shulman, 'Olivier Sniffs a Rose, and so Begins a Landmark of Acting', *Evening Standard*, 22 July 1964.
77 Alan Brien, 'Scenes from Olivier', *Sunday Telegraph*, 26 April 1964.

78 Christopher Plummer, *In Spite of Myself: A Memoir* (New York: Alfred A. Knopf, 2008), 520.
79 Brien, 'Scenes from Olivier'.
80 Olivier, *On Acting*, 100–1.
81 Ibid., 97.
82 Susan Leigh Foster, *Choreographing Empathy: Kinesthesia in Performance* (London and New York: Routledge, 2011), 1.
83 Peter Evans, 'An Historic Performance', *Southern Evening News*, 24 July 1964.
84 'Olivier as Superb Othello', *Yorkshire Evening Post*, 23 April 1964.
85 J. C. Trewin, 'Standing Ovation for Olivier', *Birmingham Post*, 22 April 1964.
86 Trewin, 'Olivier's Othello'.
87 'The Moor of Waterloo Road', *The Times*, 28 April 1966.
88 Bosley Crowther, 'Minstrel Show "Othello"; Radical Makeup Marks Olivier's Interpretation', *New York Times*, 2 February 1966.
89 Richard Klein, *Cigarettes are Sublime* (Durham and London: Duke University Press, 1993), 2.
90 Ibid., 117.
91 Maggie Smith, in *Olivier at Work*, 26. The image of Smith and Olivier smoking is reproduced on the facing page.
92 Levin, 'And Now Othello falls to Sir Laurence'.
93 'What's on in Town', *Yorkshire Evening Post*, 22 April 1964.
94 Alan Dent, 'The Olivier Othello', *Financial Times*, 23 April 1964.
95 Young, 'Othello'.
96 Our Dramatic Critic, 'The Moor Built Up at Iago's Expense'.
97 Gascoigne, 'A Moor for All Time'.
98 Jacob Suskind, 'Olivier's Othello a Masterpiece', *Montreal Star*, 5 May 1964.
99 Billie Whitelaw, *... Who He?* (London: Hodder and Stoughton, 1995), 74.
100 Ibid., 90–1.
101 Plummer, *In Spite of Myself*, 518.
102 Whitelaw, *... Who He?*, 94.
103 Ibid., 94.
104 Paul Menzer, *Anecdotal Shakespeare: A New Performance History* (London: Bloomsbury Arden Shakespeare, 2015), 71–2.

105 Whitelaw, ... *Who He?*, 94.
106 NT Board Minutes, 13 January 1964.
107 For the first cast of *The Royal Hunt of the Sun*, the women's roles were taken by Louise Purnell and Jeanette Landis, and the Peruvians Indians were all male; subsequent casts included a few women in the ranks of the latter. The first cast of *Rosencrantz and Guildenstern* featured Caroline John as Ophelia and Mary Griffiths as Gertrude, roles subsequently taken, respectively, by Louise Purnell, Helen Bourne and Jo Maxwell-Muller, and by Jane Wenham. There were seventeen Courtiers and Attendants, among them Petronella Barker, Margo Cunningham, Kay Gallie and Maggie Riley. During the course of the production's lifetime a total of thirteen women were seen in these walk-on roles, alongside forty-one men.
108 Irving Wardle, 'National Theatre Avoids the Pitfall of Privilege', *The Times*, 11 March 1967.
109 NT Board Minutes, 11 May 1970. The minute also suggested that this, or 'another "serious" Shakespeare play' would open, 'it was hoped, around the date of Shakespeare's birthday – a pattern which might be repeated annually'.
110 Joan Plowright, *And That's Not All* (London: Weidenfeld and Nicholson, 2001), 143.
111 Harold Hobson, 'Paths of Dalliance', *Sunday Times*, 22 December 1968.
112 Irving Wardle, 'Gentle Enchantment of Olivier Production', *The Times*, 20 December 1968.
113 B. A. Young, 'Love's Labour's Lost', *Financial Times*, 20 December 1968.
114 Jeremy Kingston, 'At the Theatre', *Punch*, 1 January 1969.
115 R. B. Marriott, 'Imaginative, Witty and Tender "Love's Labour's Lost"', *Stage and Television Today*, 24 December 1968.
116 Hilary Spurling, 'Sugar is Sweet', *Spectator*, 27 December 1968.
117 Isabella Beeton, *Mrs Beeton's Book of Household Management: A Guide to Cookery in all Branches* (London: Ward Lock, 1861), 1.
118 Spurling, 'Sugar is Sweet'.
119 Hobson, 'Paths of Dalliance'.
120 Ibid.
121 B. A. Young, 'The Merchant of Venice', *Financial Times*, 29 April 1970.

122 Olivier, *On Acting*, 109.
123 Jonathan Miller, *Subsequent Performances* (London: Faber and Faber, 1986), 107.
124 Ibid., 104–8.
125 John Goodwin (ed.), *Peter Hall's Diaries: The Story of a Dramatic Battle* (London: Hamish Hamilton, 1983), 14.
126 Olivier, *On Acting*, 112.
127 Irving Wardle, 'Merchants all', *The Times,* 29 April 1970.
128 Ronald Bryden, 'The Jew Among the Gentleman', *Observer*, 3 May 1970.
129 Young, 'The Merchant of Venice'.
130 Wardle, 'Merchants all'.
131 J. C. Trewin, 'Sir Laurence as the Jew of Venice', *Illustrated London News*, 9 May 1970.
132 Olivier, *On Acting*, 110.
133 Ibid., 111.
134 Michael Billington, *The Modern Actor* (London: Hamish Hamilton, 1973), 83.
135 Miller, *Subsequent Performances*, 108.
136 Hilary Spurling, 'Strangers in Belmont', *Spectator*, 9 May 1970.
137 Miller, *Subsequent Performances*, 108.
138 Billington, *The Modern Actor*, 88–9.
139 Olivier, *On Acting*, 118.
140 James C. Bulman, *Shakespeare in Performance: The Merchant of Venice* (Manchester: Manchester University Press, 1991), 78.
141 Wardle, 'Merchants all'.
142 Spurling, 'Strangers in Belmont'.
143 This is the legendary oldest-surviving café in the world, still in business on the Piazza San Marco.
144 *The Merchant of Venice*, dir. Jonathan Miller (National Theatre at the Old Vic, 1970), Untitled list.
145 Young, 'The Merchant of Venice'.
146 Miller, *Subsequent Performances*, 107.
147 Bryden, 'The Jew Among the Gentlemen'.
148 Benedict Nightingale, 'Tribal Behaviour', *New Statesman*, 8 May 1970.
149 Plowright, *And That's Not All,* 150–4.
150 In a cast of thirty, Sylvestre and Beaton were two of five black actors, alongside Valerie Murray, Elizabeth Adaré and Derek Woodward. The play's author alleged that Olivier was against

this, claiming that he proposed that 'the regular girls in the company should black up', and suggesting Plowright for the lead. See Alec Patton, 'How *The National Health* Improved the National's Health: Peter Nichols, Michael Blakemore, and the National Theatre Company', *Theatre Journal*, 61, no. 3 (2009), 447. Prior to this, the Trinidadian actress, Pearl Prescod played Tituba in the 1965 production of *The Crucible*.
151 Young, 'The Merchant of Venice'.
152 Wardle, 'Merchants all'.
153 Jeremy Kingston, 'Theatre', *Punch*, 6 May 1970.
154 Olivier, *Confessions*, 218.
155 Ibid., 222.
156 Nicholas Ridout, *Stage Fright, Animals, and Other Theatrical Problems* (Cambridge: Cambridge University Press, 2006), 40, 47.
157 The NT Board Minutes of 24 April 1967 record a debt of gratitude to Olivier reporting that 'the year-end position would be within the Budget ... this result would not have been achieved without the extra performances of OTHELLO which the Director had unselfishly given'.
158 Olivier, *On Acting*, 113.
159 Ibid., 114, 116.
160 Ibid., 116–17.
161 Ibid., 117.
162 Ibid., 118.
163 In 1971, he gave one of his greatest stage performances as James Tyrone in Eugene O'Neill's *Long Day's Journey into Night* at the New Theatre. He followed this with Antonio in Eduardo de Filippo's *Saturday, Sunday, Monday,* and John Tagg in Trevor Griffiths's *The Party* in 1973. The last two were really cameos: the grandfather in the one, always stealing hats and falling asleep on stage for much of Act 2, and Tagg, the Glaswegian Trotskyist, who is really only there for the sake of one long, extraordinary speech, enabling Olivier to be at his most scene-stealingly virtuosic.

Chapter 2

1 Ira Nadel, *Double Act: A Life of Tom Stoppard* (London: Methuen, 2002), 193.

2   'Helping Playwrights Get Ideas', *The Times*, 11 September 1964.
3   Nadel, *Double Act*, 150.
4   Sheridan Morley, 'New Challenge for Non-Stop Trevor Nunn', *The Times*, 28 June 1977.
5   Nadel, *Double Act*, 166.
6   Harold Hobson, 'Educating Edinburgh', *Sunday Times*, 4 September 1966.
7   Keith Harper, 'The Devious Route to Waterloo Road', *Guardian*, 12 April 1967.
8   Ibid.
9   Nadel, *Double Act*, 113–18.
10 Tom Stoppard, *Rosencrantz and Guildenstern are Dead* (London: Faber, 1968), 9.
11 Ibid.
12 NT Board Minutes, 12 December 1966.
13 *Rosencrantz and Guildenstern are Dead*, dir. Derek Goldby (National Theatre at the Old Vic, 1967), Promptbook, 26.
14 Michael Coveney, 'Graham Crowden Obituary', *Guardian*, 22 October 2010.
15 Hilary Spurling, 'Prints of the Japanese Buskin', *Spectator*, 21 April 1967.
16 *Rosencrantz and Guildenstern are Dead*, dir. Derek Goldby (National Theatre at the Old Vic, 1967), Costume Plot.
17 Nadel, *Double Act*, 180.
18 John Russell Taylor, 'Rosencrantz and Guildenstern are Dead', *Plays and Players*, June 1967.
19 Nadel, *Double Act*, 181.
20 Ibid., 554.
21 Stoppard, *Rosencrantz and Guildenstern are Dead*, 96.
22 Cyril Dunn, 'Briefing: Footnote to the Bard', *Observer*, 9 April 1967.
23 'The London Charivari; Theatre', *Punch*, 12 April 1967.
24 John Lahr (ed.), *The Orton Diaries* (London: Methuen, 1987), 135. When the reviews of *Rosencrantz and Guildenstern* appeared, hailing 'a major theatrical debut', Orton drew a snarky comparison with the less than fulsome response to his first stage play, *Entertaining Mr. Sloane* (1964): 'it's the second play that's the test ... We'll see what happens to Tom Stoppard over the next few years' (137). Orton, unfortunately, would

not, as he was murdered by his lover Kenneth Halliwell on 9 August.

25 W. A. Darlington, 'Two Characters in a Dreadful Limbo', *Daily Telegraph*, 12 April 1967.

26 Irving Wardle, 'Drama Unearthed from Elsinore's Depths', *The Times*, 12 April 1967.

27 Peter Lewis, 'Faces in the Crowd are Lords at Last', *Daily Mail*, 12 April 1967.

28 Wardle, 'Drama Unearthed'.

29 Lewis, 'Faces'.

30 B. A. Young, 'Rosencrantz and Guildenstern Are Dead', *Financial Times*, 12 April 1967.

31 Lewis, 'Faces'.

32 Ronald Bryden, 'Out of Their World', *Observer*, 16 April 1967.

33 Harold Hobson, 'A Fearful Summons', *Sunday Times*, 16 April 1967.

34 Lewis, 'Faces'.

35 Hobson, 'A Fearful Summons'.

36 *Rosencrantz and Guildenstern are Dead*, Programme.

37 Bryden, 'Out of Their World'.

38 Young, 'Rosencrantz and Guildenstern'.

39 Jeremy Kingston, 'Theatre', *Punch*, 19 April 1967.

40 'The London Charivari: Theatre', *Punch*, 26 April 1967.

41 Spurling, 'Prints'. Spurling later had the grace to admit that she was 'the most dreadful, scathing, whingeing, destructive critic, a battlaxe' (Paul Laity, 'A Life in Writing: Hilary Spurling', *Guardian*, 17 April 2010).

42 D. A. N. Jones, 'Spear-carriers', *New Statesman*, 21 April 1967.

43 D. A. N. Jones, 'Safe Play', *New Statesman*, 5 May 1967.

44 Ibid.

45 Kenneth Tynan, *Tynan on Theatre* (Harmondsworth: Penguin, 1964), 42.

46 The diary column for 12 June 1967 reported on the looped run-out groove at the end of Side 2, which mixed banter between the band members with a 15 kilohertz tone, 'a whistle inaudible to the human ear, and outside the range of modest record-players, but on high fidelity equipment a loud and clear call to all dogs'. In a separate item, the column also reported that Stoppard was 'hard at work in his cottage in the Chilterns to meet a deadline next Wednesday on a new play for Mchael

Codron' (P. H. S., 'The Times Diary', *The Times*, 12 June 1967). Unbeknown to the diary-writer, there was a canine connection: the play was *The Real Inspector Hound*, which opened at the Criterion Theatre on 17 June 1968.
47 Wilfred Mellers, 'Pop Mod', *New Statesman*, 9 June 1967.
48 Charles Reid, 'Sir William's Bear', *Spectator*, 9 June 1967.
49 Gerald Larner, 'David Jordan and the RMCM Orchestra at the Free Trade Hall', George Odam, 'The Aeolian Quartet at the Bath Festival', Ian Breach, 'Carmell Jones at Club 43, Manchester', *Guardian*, 9 June 1967.
50 Benny Green, 'Hushing up the Audience', *Observer*, 11 June 1967.
51 John Russell Taylor, 'Rosencrantz and Guildenstern are Dead'.
52 Ibid.
53 John Russell Taylor, *Anger and After: A Guide to the New British Drama* (Harmondsworth: Penguin, 1963), 324–5.
54 *Rosencrantz and Guildenstern are Dead*, Show Report No. 11, 9 May.
55 *Rosencrantz and Guildenstern are Dead*, Show Report No. 47, 25 January.
56 Frank Dunlop, Letter to George Rowbottom, 7 June 1967.
57 G. A. Haw, Letter to Rowbottom, 1 August 1967.
58 Diana Franklin, Letter to G. A. Haw, 7 August 1967.
59 Matt Trueman, 'A Princess and a Lackey: The Actors' Guide to Rosalind in *As You Like It*', *Guardian*, 13 July 2015. For an account of the production that places it in the context of the stage history of the play, see Robert Shaughnessy, *Shakespeare in Performance: As You Like It* (Manchester: Manchester University Press, 2018), 129–42.
60 NT Board Minutes, 20 June 1966.
61 Rosenthal, *National Theatre Story*, 131. See Jan Kott, *Shakespeare our Contemporary*, trans. Boleslaw Taborski (London: Methuen, 1965).
62 'All-Male Cast for *As You Like It*', *The Times*, 24 August 1967.
63 'National Theatre's "Fringe" Play', *The Times*, 14 December 1967.
64 Tynan, *Letters*, 365. The songs Tynan had in mind were 'Eleanor Rigby', 'For No One' and 'Here, There and Everywhere.' The 39-year-old Tynan attempted to ingratiate himself further by informing McCartney that

'Tomorrow Never Knows' is 'the best musical evocation of L.S.D. that I have ever heard'. In reply, McCartney joked, 'Maybe I could write the National Theatre stomp sometime? Or the ballad of Larry O'.

65 'Dexter Dispute Over "As You Like It"', *The Times*, 23 March 1967.
66 John Dexter, *The Honourable Beast: A Posthumous Autobiography* (London: Nick Hern Books, 1993), 19.
67 'The Old Way with Shakespeare', *The Times*, 7 August 1967.
68 'Britten Opera Strikingly Produced', *The Times*, 24 February 1967.
69 William Mann, 'Opera Restored for Berlioz Celebrations', *The Times*, 21 May 1969.
70 Kenneth Pearson, 'The Man Who Plays Rosalind', *Sunday Times*, 1 October 1967.
71 Paine Knickerbocker, '"As You Like It" Was Not to Be a Female Impersonation', *San Francisco Sunday Examiner and Chronicle*, 21 July 1974.
72 Pamela Howard, 'A Distinctive Vision', in *Ralph Koltai: Designer for the Stage*, 3rd edn, ed. Sylvia Backemayer (London: Nick Hern, 2003), 104.
73 Frank Marcus, 'Modern Arcadia', *Plays and Players*, October 1967.
74 Pearson, 'The Man Who Plays Rosalind'.
75 Backemayer, *Ralph Koltai*, 17.
76 Pearson, 'The Man Who Plays Rosalind'.
77 Mrs Kay, incidentally, was the actress Venetia Maxwell, best known for her work in the long-running television soap opera series *Crossroads*.
78 Pearson, 'The Man Who Plays Rosalind'.
79 Trueman, 'A Princess and a Saucy Lackey'. Koltai's costume sketches are in Backemayer, *Ralph Koltai*, 18–21. The proposed costume for Touchstone reflects the ubiquitous Beatles influence, with its wearer sporting a classic moptop and wearing that looks more like an Afghan coat than the striped tailcoat with epaulettes that Derek Jacobi wore in performance.
80 *As You Like It*, dir. Clifford Williams (National Theatre at the Old Vic, 1967), Costume Plot.
81 Pearson, 'The Man Who Plays Rosalind'.
82 Trueman, 'A Princess and a Saucy Lackey'.

83 Pearson, 'The Man Who Plays Rosalind'.
84 'The London Charivari: Theatre', *Punch*, 4 October 1967.
85 Ronald Bryden, 'The Wrong Kind of Achievement', *Observer*, 8 October 1967.
86 Knickerbocker, '"As You Like It" Was Not to Be a Female Impersonation'.
87 Milton Shulman, 'Delicious – But I Still Prefer Vanessa', *Evening Standard*, 4 October 1967.
88 Bryden, 'The Wrong Kind of Achievement'.
89 Philip Hope-Wallace, 'As You Like It at the Old Vic', *Guardian*, 4 October 1967.
90 Bryden, 'The Wrong Kind of Achievement'.
91 Irving Wardle, 'Comic Result When Men Take Over From Actresses', *The Times*, 4 October 1967.
92 Clifford Williams, 'Production Note', *As You Like It*, Programme.
93 Knickerbocker, '"As You Like It" Was Not to Be a Female Impersonation'.
94 Spurling's review ('Dan Dare's Arden', *Spectator*, 13 October 1967) was mixed: on the one hand, she regretted the 'strain of boisterous vulgarity, at once cheap and overdressed, which we have learnt to associate with visiting productions from Eastern Europe', and thought that the 'men dressed as girls, far from adding new and subtle tensions, have considerably simplified the text'; on the other, she found Kay's Celia 'perhaps the richest, most delicately humorous and study of this lady', and that the production had 'an uncommon delicacy'.
95 David Nathan, 'Success for the Boys', *The Sun*, 4 October 1967.
96 Herbert Kretzmer, 'A Triumph for the National Theatre', *Daily Express*, 4 October 1967.
97 Shulman, 'Delicious'.
98 Hope-Wallace, 'As You Like It'.
99 Marcus, 'Modern Arcadia'.
100 Peter Lewis, 'Taking a Dream Trip with the Bard', *Daily Mail*, 4 October 1967.
101 Lewis, 'Taking a Dream Trip'.
102 Shulman, 'Delicious'.
103 Wardle, 'Comic Result'.
104 Martin Esslin, 'Theater in London: "As You Like It", or Boy Meets Boy', *New York Times*, 15 October 1967.

105 D. A. N. Jones, 'Disguises', *Listener*, 9 November 1967.
106 Shulman, 'Delicious'.
107 Jeremy Kingston, 'Theatre', *Punch*, 11 October 1967.
108 Harold Hobson, 'Absorbed in Sweet Propriety', *Sunday Times*, 8 October 1967.
109 Wardle, 'Comic Result'.
110 Bryden, 'The Wrong Kind of Achievement'.
111 W. A. Darlington, 'Experiment Comes off Brilliantly', *Daily Telegraph*, 4 October 1967.
112 Trueman, 'A Princess and a Saucy Lackey'.
113 Esslin, 'Theater in London'.
114 Dana Adams Schmidt, 'Male Cast Opens in "As You Like It": Londoners Applaud Old Vic Version in Modern Spirit', *New York Times*, 6 October 1967.
115 'The London Charivari: Theatre', *Punch*, 18 October 1967.
116 Clive Barnes, 'Play by Tom Stoppard Opens at the Alvin', *New York Times*, 17 October 1967.
117 Walter Kerr, 'Taking Revenge On Life', *New York Times*, 29 October 1967.
118 Jack Kroll, 'R and G', *Newsweek*, 30 October 1967.
119 Nadel, *Double Life*, 193.
120 NT Accounts, Playing Year 1967/8.
121 Stoppard, *Rosencrantz and Guildenstern are Dead*, 21.
122 'Court Circular', *The Times*, 17 January 1968.
123 This was the performance preserved in the British Library National Sound Archive, and by the sound of it, it went down very well (whatever business was taking place during 'It was a lover and his lass', it was obviously a hoot). Cecil Day-Lewis's prologue is reproduced in the Appendix.
124 'Court Circular', *The Times*, 16 May 1968.
125 'Paris Students March as Strikes Spread through Industry', *The Times*, 17 May 1968.
126 Nadel, *Double Life*, 199.
127 Notes on Income and Expenditure – Financial Year 1967/8, 1 December 1967.
128 Garry O'Connor, 'Stoppard and Savary', *Financial Times*, 18 October 1967.
129 Our Special Correspondent, 'Female Rosencrantz in Stoppard Play', *The Times*, 22 February 1968.
130 Peter Brook, *The Empty Space* (Harmondsworth: Penguin, 1972), 1–2.

131 H. R., 'Spoken As You Like It', *The Times*, 19 September 1968.
132 *As You Like It*, dir. Clifford Williams (National Theatre at the Old Vic, 1968), Show Report Nos. 52, 53, 54, 55, 56, 57, 58, 59 ('Set + 6'), 60 and 61; 28 September–10 October.
133 David Merrick, Letter to Rowbottom, 15 July 1969.
134 Kenneth Ewing, Letter to Rowbottom, 7 May 1968; Rowbottom, Letter to Ewing, 10 May 1968.
135 Robert Chartoff, Lee International Film Studios, Letter to Laurie Evans, London International, 1 December 1969; NT Board Minutes, 10 February 1969.
136 N. V. Linklater, Letter to Antony Easterbrook, 16 January 1970.
137 Easterbrook, Letter to Linklater, 20 January 1970.
138 Ewing, Letter to Easterbrook, 30 April 1970.
139 Derek Goldby, Letter to Elspeth Cochrane, 7 July 1967.
140 Easterbrook, Memo to Olivier and Dunlop, 7 August 1970.
141 Jill Foster, Letter to Easterbrook, 5 April 1971.
142 Easterbrook, Letter to Foster, 15 April 1971.
143 Foster, Letter to Easterbrook, 22 October 1971.
144 Tyrone Guthrie, *In Various Directions: A View of Theatre* (London: Michael Joseph, 1965), 72.
145 Easterbrook, Letter to Ewing, 16 June 1972.
146 Ewing, Letter to Easterbrook, 19 June 1972.
147 Paine Knickerbocker, 'Splendid Male "As You Like It"', *San Francisco Chronicle*, 18 July 1974.
148 Stanley Eichenbaum, 'A Stunning Switch on "As You Like it"', *San Francisco Examiner*, 18 July 1974.
149 Martin Gottfried, 'All-Male Shakespeare', *New York Post*, 4 December 1974.
150 Clive Barnes, 'Saving the Metropolitan', *The Times*, 14 December 1974.
151 Clifford Williams, 'All-Male "As You Like It"', *The Times*, 27 December 1974.

Chapter 3

1 *Romeo and Juliet*, dir. Franco Zeffirelli (Old Vic, 1960), Programme.
2 Franco Zeffirelli, *The Autobiography of Franco Zeffirelli* (London: Weidenfeld and Nicholson, 1986), 156.

3 *Romeo and Juliet*, Programme.
4 Kenneth Tynan, 'The Straight Answer' *Observer*, 9 October 1960.
5 T. C. Worsley, 'Romeo and Juliet', *Financial Times*, 6 October 1960.
6 Our Special Correspondent – Rome, 'Mr Franco Zeffirelli Modernizes Hamlet', *The Times*, 3 February 1964.
7 Bamber Gascoigne, 'Drama, Italian style', *Observer*, 8 March 1964.
8 'Zeffirelli's Hamlet for National Theatre', *The Times*, 21 March 1964.
9 Tynan, *Tynan on Theatre*, 240–1, 276.
10 Ion Trewin, 'Peter Daubeny, World Theatre's Inspiration', *The Times*, 3 March 1973.
11 B. A. Young, 'Amleto', *Financial Times*, 25 September 1964.
12 Herbert Kretzmer, 'A Feast for the Parliamo Italiano Fans', *Daily Express*, 16 September 1964.
13 Young, 'Amleto'.
14 Bernard Levin, 'Nightmare Grip of Zeffirelli Hamlet', *Daily Mail*, 16 September 1964.
15 Our Dramatic Critic, 'Hamlet as a Modern Man', *The Times*, 16 September 1964.
16 Ibid.
17 Ibid.
18 J. C. Trewin, 'Theatre', *Illustrated London News*, 26 September 1964.
19 B. A. Young, 'Amleto Again', *Financial Times*, 26 September 1964.
20 Our Dramatic Critic, 'Hamlet as a Modern Man'.
21 Ronald Bryden, 'Somebodaddy', *New Statesman*, 25 September 1964. One wonders how Bryden would have reacted had he been told that Finney would play Hamlet at the National within a decade.
22 Levin, 'Nightmare Grip'; Kretzmer, 'A Feast'; Trewin, 'Theatre'.
23 Our Dramatic Critic, 'Hamlet as a Modern Man'.
24 Young, 'Amleto'.
25 Levin, 'Nightmare Grip'.
26 Harold Hobson, 'A New Kind of Hamlet', *Sunday Times*, 20 September 1964.
27 Kretzmer, 'A Feast'.

28   Young, 'Amleto Again'.
29   Young, 'Amleto'.
30   B. A. Young, 'Widened Horizons', *Financial Times*, 24 June 1968.
31   NT Board Minutes, 14 September 1964.
32   NT Board Minutes, 12 October 1964.
33   'As Busy as he is Inventive', *Sunday Times*, 14 February 1965.
34   Tom Matheson, 'Franco Zeffirelli', in *The Routledge Companion to Directors' Shakespeare*, ed. John Russell Brown (Abingdon: Routledge, 2008), 541.
35   Harold Hobson, 'It's Great After the Fiesta', *Sunday Times*, 21 February 1965.
36   B. A. Young, 'Much Ado about Nothing', *Financial Times*, 18 February 1965.
37   Penelope Gilliatt, 'A Merry War in Messina', *Observer*, 21 February 1965.
38   Malcolm Rutherford, 'Show Business', *Spectator*, 26 February 1965. Our Dramatic Critic in *The Times*, perhaps seeing a more astringent Beatrice, recorded 'a quilt in which she delves for a cup of coffee' ('It All Ends on a Note of Magic', 17 February 1965). In an unpublished interview with Daniel Rosenthal (28 September 2009), Smith confirmed that it was coffee, not chocolate: 'I had an eiderdown and a cup of black coffee because, look, it's four o'clock in the morning – coz you've got to get up. She's very unhappy'. My thanks to Daniel Rosenthal for sharing this story with me.
39   Our Dramatic Critic, 'It All Ends'.
40   Gilliatt, 'A Merry War'.
41   W. A. Darlington, 'Pure Delight in Zeffirelli's "Much Ado"', *Daily Telegraph*, 17 February 1965.
42   Michael Coveney, *Maggie Smith: A Bright Particular Star* (London: Victor Gollancz, 1992), 115.
43   Philip Hope-Wallace, 'Zeffirelli's Much Ado at the National Theatre', *Guardian*, 17 February 1965.
44   J. C. Trewin, 'A Director's Night', *Illustrated London News*, 27 February 1965.
45   John F. Cox, *Shakespeare in Production: Much Ado about Nothing* (Cambridge: Cambridge University Press, 1997), 131.
46   *Much Ado about Nothing*, dir. Franco Zeffirelli (National Theatre at the Old Vic, 1965), Promptbook.

47 Cox, *Shakespeare in Production*, 157, 164.
48 Jeremy Kingston, 'Theatre', *Punch*, 24 February 1965.
49 David Nathan, 'Too Much Ado about Words', *The Sun*, 17 February 1965.
50 Herbert Kretzmer, 'Much Ado with a Taste of Candy Floss', *Daily Express*, 17 February 1965.
51 Bernard Levin, 'Mucking about with Shakespeare', *Daily Mail*, 17 February 1965.
52 'Olivier on Choosing an Accent for Shakespeare's Peasants', *The Times*, 18 February 1965.
53 Levin, 'Mucking about'.
54 Zeffirelli, *Autobiography*, 202.
55 Kretzmer, 'Much Ado'.
56 Our Dramatic Critic, 'It All Ends'.
57 Tynan, Letters, 303.
58 Robert Graves, 'Making Sound Sense of Shakespeare', *Sunday Times*, 14 February 1965.
59 Robert Graves, 'The Textual Changes', *Much Ado about Nothing*, dir. Zeffirelli (National Theatre at the Old Vic, 1965), Programme.
60 NT Board Minutes, 12 October 1964.
61 Tynan, *Tynan on Theatre*, 42.
62 Graves, 'Making Sound'.
63 Graves, 'Textual Changes'.
64 Ibid.
65 Graves, 'Making Sound'.
66 Ibid.
67 Ibid.
68 Gilliatt, 'A Merry War'.
69 Levin, 'Mucking about'.
70 Miss B. Crawter, Letter to George Rowbottom, 1 May 1965; Rowbottom, Letter to Crawter, 5 May 1965.
71 George Bernard Shaw, 'Much Ado about Nothing', in *Shaw on Shakespeare*, ed. Edwin Wilson (Harmondsworth: Penguin, 1969), 155–7.
72 Zeffirelli, *Autobiography*, 202.
73 Stephens, *Knight Errant*, 82.
74 Ibid., 83.
75 'Miss Plowright impresses', *The Times*, 22 March 1967.
76 Stephens, *Knight Errant*, 82–3.

77 'Sold', *The Sun*, 6 August 1965.
78 R. B. Marriott, 'The Berliner Ensemble', *The Stage*, 5 August 1965.
79 Sean Day-Lewis, 'The Berlin Brecht', *Daily Telegraph*, 7 August 1965.
80 *Mother Courage*, dir. William Gaskill (National Theatre at the Old Vic, 1965), Programme.
81 Our Dramatic Critic, 'Brecht Production a Wise Choice', *The Times*, 13 May 1965.
82 Penelope Gilliatt, 'Mother Courage Marches On', *Observer*, 16 May 1965.
83 Harold Hobson, 'Brecht, the Misunderstood', *Sunday Times*, 16 May 1965.
84 Bernard Levin, 'Forget the Drivel, Brecht is Great', *Daily Mail*, 13 May 1965.
85 James Smith, 'Brecht, the Berliner Ensemble, and the British Government', *New Theatre Quarterly*, 22.4 (2000), 320.
86 NT Board Minutes, 19 November 1963.
87 NT Board Minutes, 13 January 1964. The minute concerning the 'political implications' is a supplement to this document, in the form of a slip of paper pasted, irremovably, over the original text. We can only speculate as to the content of this.
88 NT Board Minutes, 10 February 1964.
89 NT Board Minutes, 11 May 1964.
90 Ibid.
91 Philip Hope-Wallace, 'The Berliner Ensemble at the National Theatre', *Guardian*, 10 August 1965.
92 Herbert Kretzmer, 'It's Hitler Again – in Chicago's Gangland', *Daily Express*, 10 August 1965.
93 David Benedictus, 'We Came, We Saw, We Concurred', *Spectator*, 20 August 1965.
94 Penelope Gilliatt, 'Brecht and Company', *Observer*, 15 August 1965.
95 Alan Brien, 'A Massive Dose of Brecht', *Sunday Telegraph*, 15 August 1965.
96 Milton Shulman, 'Brecht – So Happy in his Soho Days', *Evening Standard*, 12 August 1965.
97 Ralph Manheim and John Willett (eds), *Bertolt Brecht: Collected Plays*, vol. 9 (New York: Vintage, 1972), 396.

98 Brecht, *Coriolan*, 3.2.70–3, in *Gesammelte Werke*, vol. 6 (Frankfurt: Suhrkamp Verlag, 1967), 2459.
99 Brecht, *Coriolanus*, 3.2.70–3, in Manheim and Willett, *Bertolt Brecht: Collected Plays*, vol. 9, 113.
100 *Coriolanus*, 3.3.135, in *Shakespeares Werke, Englisch und Deutsch*, vol. 5, ed. L. L. Schücking (Berlin and Darmstadt: Tempel-Verlag, 1965), 330.
101 Brecht, *Coriolan*, 2460.
102 Brecht, 'Enjoying the Hero', in Manheim and Willett, *Bertolt Brecht: Collected Plays*, vol. 9, 374.
103 Brecht, 'Four Short Notes', in Manheim and Willett, *Bertolt Brecht: Collected Plays*, vol. 9, 377.
104 Bertolt Brecht, 'Study of the First Scene of Shakespeare's "Coriolanus"', in *Brecht on Theatre*, ed. John Willett (London: Methuen, 1964), 252–65, 257, 264.
105 Ibid., 265.
106 Brecht, *Coriolan*, 2597.
107 Brecht, *Coriolanus*, 59.
108 Brecht, *Coriolan*, 2478.
109 Brecht, *Coriolanus*, 130.
110 Brecht, *Coriolan*, 2492.
111 Brecht, *Coriolanus*, 142.
112 Peter Holland (ed.), *Coriolanus*, The Arden Shakespeare, Third Series (London: Bloomsbury, 2013), 120.
113 Brecht, *Coriolan*, 2495.
114 Ibid., 2497.
115 Brecht, *Coriolanus*, 146.
116 Manheim in Brecht, *Coriolanus*, 70.
117 'Version of the Berliner Ensemble', *Coriolanus*, dir. Manfred Wekwerth and Joachim Tenschert (National Theatre at the Old Vic, 1965), Programme.
118 David Barnett, *A History of the Berliner Ensemble* (Cambridge: Cambridge University Press, 2015), 185.
119 'Version of the Berliner Ensemble', Programme.
120 '*Coriolanus*: History and Versions', *Coriolanus*, dir. Manfred Wekworth and Joachim Tenschert (National Theatre at the Old Voc, 1965), Programme.
121 Philip Hope-Wallace, 'The Berliner Ensemble at the Old Vic', *Guardian*, 13 August 1965.
122 Our Dramatic Critic, 'Shakespeare Remodelled by Brecht', *The Times*, 11 August 1965.

123 Gilliatt, 'Brecht and Company'.
124 Benedictus, 'We Came, We Saw'.
125 Barnett, *A History*, 186.
126 Gilliatt, 'Brecht and Company'.
127 B. A. Young, 'Coriolanus at the Old Vic', *Financial Times*, 12 August 1965.
128 Gilliatt, 'Brecht and Company'.
129 Bob Leeson, 'Faces in the Crowd', *Daily Worker*, 12 August 1965.
130 Ronald Bryden, 'The Brechts of the Apostles', *New Statesman*, 20 August 1965.
131 W. A. Darlington, 'Travesty of "Coriolanus" by Brecht', *The Times*, 11 August 1965.
132 Julian Holland, 'The Man Who Made the Bard a Bore', *Daily Mail*, 11 August 1965.
133 Our Dramatic Critic, 'Shakespeare Remodelled'.
134 Benedictus, 'We Came, We Saw'.
135 Hope-Wallace, 'The Berliner Ensemble at the Old Vic'.
136 Gilliatt, 'Brecht and Company'.
137 Hope-Wallace, 'The Berliner Ensemble at the Old Vic'.
138 Our Dramatic Critic', 'Shakespeare Remodelled'.
139 Barnett, *Berliner Ensemble*, 189.
140 'Two Berliner Ensemble Men Defect', *The Times*, 30 August 1965.
141 'Actor Returns to E. Germany', *The Times*, 15 September 1965.
142 'A Threepenny Tragedy', *Time*, 5 November 1965.
143 Smith, 'Brecht, the Berliner Ensemble, and the British Government', 321.
144 'Actor Found Dead in Church', *The Times*, 26 October 1965.
145 Peter Waymark, 'Sir Laurence Told Not to Act for a Year', 30 September 1970.
146 Plummer, *In Spite of Myself,* 521.
147 Ibid., 522
148 Ibid., 523.
149 Ibid., 524.
150 Ibid., 525.
151 John Lahr (ed.), *The Diaries of Kenneth Tynan* (London: Bloomsbury, 2001).
152 P.H.S., 'The Times Diary', *The Times*, 14 April 1971.
153 Denis Quilley, *Happiness Indeed: An Actor's Life* (London: Oberon, 2004), 138–40.

154 Ronald Bryden, 'Off the Peg Coriolanus', *Observer*, 9 May 1971.
155 Philip Hope-Wallace, 'Coriolanus at the Old Vic', *Guardian*, 7 May 1971.
156 Irving Wardle, 'Coriolanus', *The Times*, 7 May 1971.
157 Alan Clarke, 'What "Coriolanus" has to Say to a Modern Audience', *Morning Star*, 4 May 1971.
158 Miss Constance Cummings and others, '"Coriolanus" at the Old Vic', *The Times*, 14 May 1971.
159 Quilley, *Happiness Indeed*, 140.
160 Peter Lewis, 'Shakespeare Hammered into Two Dimensions', *Daily Mail*, 7 May.
161 Bryden, 'Off the Peg Coriolanus'.
162 J. W. Lambert, 'Opposite Numbers', *Sunday Times*, 9 May 1971.
163 B. A. Young, 'Coriolanus', *Financial Times*, 7 May.
164 NT Board Minutes, 5 October 1971.
165 Holland, *Coriolanus*, 124–5.
166 Lambert, 'Opposite Numbers'.
167 Kenneth Hurren, 'National Disasters', *Spectator*, 15 May 1971.
168 Quilley, *Happiness Indeed*, 140.
169 *Coriolanus*, dir. Manfred Wekwerth and Joachim Tenschert (National Theatre at the Old Vic, 1971), Promptbook, Scene Twelve.
170 Felix Barker, 'Heard the One About Coriolanus?' *Evening News*, 7 May 1971.
171 Frank Marcus, 'The Brechtian Bard', *Sunday Telegraph*, 9 May 1971.
172 *Coriolanus*, Promptbook, Scene Twenty-Four.
173 Wardle, 'Coriolanus'.
174 Catullus, *The Complete Poems*, trans. Guy Lee (Oxford: Oxford University Press, 1990), 73.
175 Bertolt Brecht, *Life of Galileo*, ed. and trans. John Willett and Ralph Manheim, trans. John Willett (London: Methuen, 1980).
176 *Coriolanus*, Promptbook, Scene Three. The first four lines are from *Antony and Cleopatra*, 4.4.15–18; the last three from *Coriolanus* in the scene following his banishment, 4.1.48–50.
177 *Coriolanus*, Programme.
178 Wardle, 'Coriolanus'.
179 Bryden, 'Off the Peg Coriolanus'.
180 Hope-Wallace, 'Coriolanus at the Old Vic'.

181 Lambert, 'Opposite Numbers'.
182 Lewis, 'Shakespeare Hammered'.
183 Bryden, 'Off the Peg Coriolanus'.
184 Benedict Nightingale, 'Manly Hopkins', *New Statesman*, 14 May 1971.
185 Hurren, 'National disasters'.
186 Bryden, 'Off the peg Coriolanus'.
187 Wardle, 'Coriolanus'.
188 Robert Cushman, 'Coriolanus', *Plays and Players*, July 1971, 59.
189 Callow, *The National*, 64.

Chapter 4

1 Goodwin, *Peter Hall's Diaries,* 61.
2 Marc Wilkinson, Letter to Paul Conroy, Charisma Artists, 27 September 1973.
3 Goodwin, *Peter Hall's Diaries*, 76.
4 Derek Jewell, *The Tempest*, dir. Peter Hall (National Theatre at the Old Vic, 1974), Programme.
5 Robert Speaight, 'Shakespeare in Britain, 1974', *Shakespeare Quarterly*, 25, no. 4 (1974), 389–94: 393.
6 Irving Wardle, 'Prospero's Novel Masque', *The Times*, 6 March 1974.
7 Goodwin, *Peter Hall's Diaries*, 106, 111, 113, 109. The play was *No Man's Land*, which opened on 23 April 1975.
8 Peter Hall, *Making an Exhibition of Myself* (London: Sinclair-Stevenson, 1993), 201.
9 Ibid., 262.
10 Goodwin, *Peter Hall's Diaries*, xi.
11 Olivier, *Confessions*, 245.
12 Ibid., 247.
13 Goodwin, *Peter Hall's Diaries*, xii.
14 Ibid., 31, 34, 35.
15 Ibid., 8.
16 Ibid., 32.
17 Ibid., 38.
18 Laurence Olivier, 'RSC and the National Theatre', *The Times*, 18 April 1973.
19 Goodwin, *Peter Hall's Diaries*, 42.

20 'National Merger with Royal Shakespeare Off', *The Times*, 24 October 1973.
21 Hall, *Making an Exhibition*, 263.
22 Callow, *The National*, 34.
23 Goodwin, *Peter Hall's Diaries*, 11.
24 Ibid., 12.
25 Hall, *Making an Exhibition*, 267.
26 Michael Blakemore, *Stage Blood: Five Tempestuous Years in the Early Life of the National Theatre* (London: Faber and Faber, 2014).
27 Goodwin, *Peter Hall's Diaries*, 80.
28 Harold Pinter, Letter to Peter Hall, 24 April 1973. Neither saw the light of day, and, regrettably, Pinter never directed a Shakespeare play.
29 Hall, *Making an Exhibition*, 267.
30 Goodwin, *Peter Hall's Diaries*, 135.
31 Ibid., 186. Lord (John) Reith was the broadcasting executive who founded the BBC. *The Reith Diaries*, edited by C. H. Stuart, was published by Collins in 1975.
32 Hilary Spurling, 'A Touch of Tamburlaine', *Observer*, 25 September 1983. The graduation ceremony is recounted in the entry for 12 July 1974.
33 Michael Blakemore, 'Elsinore Takes Over at the National', *Observer*, 2 October 1983.
34 Goodwin, *Peter Hall's Diaries*, 12.
35 Ibid., 18.
36 Ibid., 36.
37 Ibid., 43.
38 Ibid., 48.
39 *Red Queen to Gryphon Three*, a four-track concept album deploying the theme of a chess game, was released by Transatlantic Records in December 1974. The image of the album cover can be found online.
40 Goodwin, *Peter Hall's Diaries*, 52. It is difficult to determine what Hall is worried about here. The music for the 1963 *Hamlet* had been composed by John Addison, *Othello* by Richard Hampton, *Much Ado* by Nino Rota and *Merchant* by Carl Davis. Marc Wilkinson, director of music from 1965 to 1975, composed the scores for *As You Like It*, *Rosencrantz and Guildenstern* and *Love's Labour's Lost*. An exception was

the 1971 *Coriolanus*, which used recordings of Paul Dessau's angular, electronically-scored music from the original Berliner Ensemble production. For his *Hamlet*, Hall commissioned Harrison Birtwistle, a composer not renowned for his mainstream easy listening qualities.

41 Goodwin, *Peter Hall's Diaries*, 52.
42 Ibid., 49.
43 Ibid., 57. The Gradgrindery is unexpected, though as Spurling recognized in her review, 'the only hint of recreation in these pages is a massive reading programme. No wonder people found him hard to work with' ('A Touch of Tamburlaine'). See Roy Strong and Stephen Orgel, *Inigo Jones: The Theatre of the Stuart Court* (London: Sotheby Park Bernet, 1973).
44 Stephen Orgel, *The Illusion of Power: Political Theater in the English Renaissance* (Berkeley and Los Angeles: University of California Press, 1975), 87.
45 Goodwin, *Peter Hall's Diaries*, 59.
46 James Shapiro, *1606: Shakespeare and the Year of Lear* (London: Faber and Faber, 2016), 3.
47 Goodwin, *Peter Hall's Diaries*, 69.
48 Ibid., 66–7.
49 Ibid., 65.
50 Robert Shelton, 'Yes', *The Times*, 21 November 1973. The discourse innocently anticipates that of Rob Reiner's 1984 brilliant spoof 'rockumentary' *This is Spinal Tap*, and legend has it that the film's Stonehenge sequence was inspired by Yes's stage shows.
51 Tony Palmer, 'No Exactly Yes', *Observer*, 25 November 1973.
52 Donald Lehmkuhl, Dominy Hamilton and Carla Capalbo, *Roger Dean: Views* (London: Dragon's Dream, 1975), 122, quoted in Edward Macan, *Rocking the Classics: English Progressive Rock and the Counter-Culture* (New York and Oxford: Oxford University Press, 1997), 63.
53 Shelton, 'Yes'.
54 Macan, *Rocking the Classics*, 13.
55 Hall quoted in David Addenbrooke, *The Royal Shakespeare Company: The Peter Hall Years* (London: William Kimber, 1974), 63, 112.
56 Peter Hall, 'Shakespeare and the Modern Director', in *Royal Shakespeare Company 1960–1963*, ed. John Goodwin (London: Max Reinhardt, 1964), 47.

57 Alan Sinfield, 'Royal Shakespeare; Theatre and the Making of Ideology', in *Political Shakespeare: Essays in Cultural Materialism*, 2nd edn, ed. Jonathan Dollimore and Alan Sinfield (Manchester: Manchester University Press, 1994), 183.
58 Hampton-Reeves, 'Peter Hall', 64.
59 Godwin, *Peter Hall's Diaries*, 50.
60 Keith Hack quoted in Peter Ansorge, 'Showman for the 70s', *Plays and Players*, April 1973. The production opened at The Place in London before transferring to Stratford.
61 Goodwin, *Peter Hall's Diaries*, 75.
62 Ibid.
63 Wardle, 'Prospero's Novel Masque'.
64 Benedict Nightingale, 'Wrong Side of the Barrier', *New Statesman*, 15 March 1974.
65 Goodwin, *Peter Hall's Diaries*, 76.
66 Ibid., 78.
67 Ibid., 80.
68 Ibid., 81.
69 Hall, quoted in John Higgins, 'The Theatre of Heaven and Earth', *The Times*, 9 March 1974.
70 Goodwin, *Peter Hall's Diaries*, 83.
71 Ibid., 84.
72 Michael Billington, '*The Tempest* at the Old Vic', *Guardian*, 6 March 1974.
73 Wardle, 'Prospero's Novel Masque'.
74 Ibid., 85.
75 Frank Marcus, 'Tract for Our Time', *Sunday Telegraph*, 10 March 1974.
76 Harold Hobson, 'Field of Fire', *Sunday Times*, 10 March 1974.
77 Nightingale, 'Wrong Side of the Barrier'. Emily Post (1872–1960) was the legendary American author known for her guidance on etiquette, made famous in her best-selling *Etiquette in Society, in Business, in Politics, and at Home* (New York: Funk and Wagnalls, 1922; *Emily Post's Etiquette, 18th Edition: Manners for a New World*, eds Peggy Post, Anna Post, Lizzie Post and Daniel Post Senning, New York: William Morrow, 2011). I checked, and neither 'salamander' nor 'penis' rate entries in the index of the most recent edition: 'pe ...' passes from 'peacemaker' to 'pepper and salt' (714), 'sa' follows 'salad plate' with 'salary discussion' (717); 'soup eating' (718), however, merits three entries.

78 Robert Cushman, 'The National's Great "Tempest"', *Observer*, 10 March 1974.
79 Michael Billington, 'Are we Hung up on Words to the Exclusion of Images?', *Guardian*, 20 March 1974.
80 Orgel and Strong, *Inigo Jones*, 1, 13.
81 Peter Thomson, 'Towards a Poor Shakespeare: The Royal Shakespeare Company at Stratford in 1975', *Shakespeare Survey*, 29 (1976), 151–6.
82 *The Tempest*, dir. Peter Hall (National Theatre at the Old Vic, 1974), Show Report No. 10, 14 March 1974.
83 *The Tempest*, Show Report No. 18, 28 March 1974.
84 Jackie Harvey, Notes from Peter Hall, 14 March 1974.
85 *The Tempest*, Show Report No. 47, 22 June 1974.
86 *The Tempest*, Show report No. 6, 6 March 1974.
87 *The Tempest*, Show Report No. 52, 28 June 1974.
88 Douglas Cornelissen, Memo to Tom Pate, 24 February 1974.
89 Jason Barnes, Memo to Jackie Harvey, 13 March 1974.
90 *The Tempest*, Show Report No. 23, 13 March 1974.
91 *The Tempest*, Show Report No. 54, 29 June 1974.
92 *The Tempest*, Show Report No. 30, 23 April 1974.
93 Mary Walker, Letter to Messrs. Peter Hall AND John Bury – copy Sir John Gielgud, 18 April 1974.
94 Fran Marsh, Memo to Hall, 24 April 1974.
95 Higgins, 'The Theatre of Heaven and Earth'. When Gryphon's Old Vic performance of music derived from the *Tempest* score was announced, it was 'to mark the end of its first run' ('Briefing', *Observer*, 7 July 1974).
96 Goodwin, *Peter Hall's Diaries*, 162–3.
97 Ibid., 95.
98 Ibid., 85.
99 Ibid., 89, 100, 105.
100 Callow, *The National*, 44.
101 Higgins, 'The Theatre of Heaven and Earth'.
102 Nightingale, 'Wrong Side of the Barrier'.
103 Speaight, 'Shakespeare in Britain, 1974', 393–4.
104 Sheridan Morley, 'Arthur Lowe: Keeping at It', *The Times*, 10 August 1974.
105 Goodwin, *Peter Hall's Diaries*, 117.
106 Hall, Letter to Edward Bond, 4 April 1973; Bond, Postcard to Hall, 12 April 1973.

107 Malcolm Hay and Phillip Roberts, *Bond: A Study of his Plays* (London: Eyre Methuen, 1980), 183.
108 Hall, Memo to John Russell Brown, 11 December 1973; Brown, Memo to Hall, 17 December 1973.
109 See, for example, *Shakespeare's Plays in Performance* (London: Edward Arnold, 1966), *Drama* (London: Heinemann, 1968), *Theatre Language: A Study of Arden, Osborne, Pinter and Wesker* (London: Allen Lane, 1972), *Free Shakespeare* (London: Heinemann, 1974) and, as editor, *The Merchant of Venice*, The Arden Shakespeare, Second Series (London: Methuen, 1955).
110 Goodwin, *Peter Hall's Diaries*, 64, 89.
111 Hall, Letter to Oscar Lewenstein, 15 August 1974.
112 Bond, Postcard to Hall, 16 August 1974.
113 Hall, Memo to All Associate Directors, 22 August 1974.
114 Hall, Letter to Bond, 23 August 1974.
115 Hall, Memo to Bill Bryden, 23 August 1974.
116 Peter Stevens, Letter to Lewenstein, 30 August 1974.
117 Eddie Kulukundis, Letter to Stevens, 18 September 1974.
118 Stevens, Letter to Kulukundis, 23 September 1974.
119 Stevens, Letter to Kulukundis, 4 October 1974.
120 Stevens, Letter to Kulukundis, 16 October 1974.
121 Hall, Letter to Bond, 17 October 1974.
122 Brown, Prospectus for the 1977/76 Repertory, presented to the Policy Meeting on 3 January 1974.
123 Hall, Memo to Brown, 14 January 1974.
124 Hall, Memo to Brown, 28 January 1974.
125 Brown, Memo to Hall, 30 January 1974.
126 Goodwin, *Peter Hall's Diaries*, 106.
127 Ibid., 163.
128 Hall, Letter to Giorgio Strehler, 22 July 1974.
129 Hall, Letter to Strehler, 22 August 1974, Letter to Strehler, 3 September 1974.
130 Emy Moresco, Letter to Hall, 6 December 1974.
131 Goodwin, *Peter Hall's Diaries*, 176.
132 Ibid., 171.
133 Peter Holland, 'Peter Hall', in Brown (ed.), *The Routledge Companion to Directors' Shakespeare*, 147.
134 Peter Ansorge, 'Measure for Measure', *Plays and Players*, March 1974.

135 Goodwin, *Peter Hall's Diaries*, 64.
136 Ibid., 177.
137 Holland, 'Peter Hall', 143.
138 Michael Hallifax, Memo to Hall, 28 August 1975.
139 Michael Hallifax, Memo to Peter Hall and Birkett, 1 September 1975. I have no idea what 'chicken wallop' was, but it sounds ominous.
140 Goodwin, *Peter Hall's Diaries*, 180.
141 Hall, Memo to Brown, 27 October 1975.
142 Goodwin, *Peter Hall's Diaries*, 185.
143 Ibid., 188.
144 Ibid., 189.
145 Ibid., 190.
146 Ibid., 191.
147 Ibid., 193.
148 Ibid., 195–6.
149 Ibid., 198.
150 Ibid., 199.
151 Ibid., 200.
152 Bill Hagerty, 'Hamlet in the Rough', *Daily Mirror*, 11 December 1975.
153 Michael Billington, 'Hamlet', *Guardian*, 11 December 1975.
154 Herbert Kretzmer, 'Fiery Finney Lights up the Danish Court', *Daily Express*, 11 December 1975.
155 Robert Cushman, 'The Whole Hamlet', *Observer*, 14 December 1975.
156 Benedict Nightingale, 'Unfit for a King', *New Statesman*, 19 December 1975.
157 Jack Tinker, 'Alas, Poor Finney! He's Wasted in this State of Denmark', *Daily Mail*, 11 December 1975.
158 Irving Wardle, 'Hamlet and "Shakespearean Intentions"', *The Times*, 11 December 1975.
159 Kenneth Hurren, 'Hare Splitting and Fox Hunting', *Spectator*, 16 March 1974.
160 Kenneth Hurren, 'National Disaster', *Spectator*, 20 December 1975.
161 Goodwin, *Peter Hall's Diaries*, 200.
162 Harold Hobson, 'Private Lives', *Sunday Times*, 14 December 1975.

163 *Hamlet*, dir. Peter Hall (National Theatre at the Old Vic, 1975), Programme. The quotation is from 'A Short Organum for the Theatre', *Brecht on Theatre*, 201–2.
164 Michael White, 'London Letter', *Guardian*, 20 December 1975.
165 Goodwin, *Peter Hall's Diaries*, 205.
166 Ibid., 214.
167 Ibid., 220.
168 Peter Holland, 'National Theatre's New Ticket Scheme', *The Times*, 6 February 1976.
169 Harold Hobson, 'The Doors are Open', *Sunday Times*, 14 March 1976.
170 Robert Cushman, 'First Impressions', *Observer*, 14 March 1976.
171 Irving Wardle, 'The National Theatre Comes True', *The Times*, 12 March 1976.
172 Richard David, *Shakespeare in the Theatre* (Cambridge: Cambridge University Press, 1978), 67, 70, 83.
173 Ibid., 83.
174 Ibid., 77.
175 Ibid., 77.
176 Milton Shulman, 'Drawbacks at Elsinore', *Evening Standard*, 11 December 1975.

Conclusion

1 Hall, *Making an Exhibition of Myself*, 272.
2 Sydney Edwards, 'A Line of History', *Evening Standard*, 19 December 1975.
3 See Abigail Rokison-Woodall, *Shakespeare in the Theatre: Nicholas Hytner* (London: Bloomsbury Arden Shakespeare, 2017).

BIBLIOGRAPHY

Adams Schmidt, Dana. 'Male Cast Opens in "As You Like It": Londoners Applaud Old Vic Version in Modern Spirit'. *New York Times*, 6 October 1967.

Addenbrooke, David. *The Royal Shakespeare Company: The Peter Hall Years*. London: William Kimber, 1974.

Ansorge, Peter. 'Showman for the 70s'. *Plays and Players*, April 1973.

Ansorge, Peter. 'Measure for Measure'. *Plays and Players*, March 1974.

Archer, William, and Harley Granville Barker. *A National Theatre: Schemes and Estimates*. London: Duckworth and Co., 1907.

Backemayer, Syliva (ed.). *Ralph Koltai: Designer for the Stage*. 3rd edn. London: Nick Hern Books, 2003.

Baker, Richard Anthony. 'Dan Meaden, Stage, Film and Television Actor'. *The Stage*, 10 January 2012.

Barker, Felix. 'Heard the One About Coriolanus?' *Evening News*, 7 May 1971.

Barnes, Clive. 'Play by Tom Stoppard Opens at the Alvin'. *New York Times*, 17 October 1967.

Barnes, Clive. 'Saving the Metropolitan'. *The Times*, 14 December 1974.

Barnett, David. *A History of the Berliner Ensemble*. Cambridge: Cambridge University Press, 2015.

Beeton, Isabella. *Mrs Beeton's Book of Household Management: A Guide to Cookery in all Branches*. London: Ward Lock, 1861.

Benedictus, David. 'We Came, We Saw, We Concurred'. *Spectator*, 20 August 1965.

Billington, Michael. *The Modern Actor*. London: Hamish Hamilton, 1973.

Billington, Michael. 'The Tempest at the Old Vic'. *Guardian*, 6 March 1974.

Billington, Michael. 'Are We Hung up on Words to the Exclusion of Images?' *Guardian*, 20 March 1974.

Billington, Michael. 'Hamlet'. *Guardian*, 11 December 1975.
Blakemore, Michael. 'Elsinore Takes Over at the National'. *Observer*, 2 October 1983.
Blakemore, Michael. *Stage Blood: Five Tempestuous Years in the Early Life of the National Theatre*. London: Faber and Faber, 2014.
Boose, Lynda E., and Burt Richard (eds). *Shakespeare, The Movie: Popularizing the Plays on Film, TV, and Video*. London and New York: Routledge, 1997.
Breach, Ian. 'Carmell Jones at Club 43, Manchester'. *Guardian*, 9 June 1967.
Brecht, Bertolt. *Gesammelte Werke*, vol. 6. Frankfurt: Suhrkamp Verlag, 1967.
Brecht, Bertolt. *Life of Galileo*, edited by John Willett and Ralph Manheim, translated by John Willett. London: Methuen, 1980.
Brien, Alan. 'Moody Prince Charming'. *Sunday Telegraph*, 27 October 1963.
Brien, Alan. 'Scenes from Olivier'. *Sunday Telegraph*, 26 April 1964.
Brien, Alan. 'A Massive Dose of Brecht'. *Sunday Telegraph*, 15 August 1965.
Brook, Peter. *The Empty Space*. Harmondsworth: Penguin, 1972.
Brown, John Russell (ed.). *The Merchant of Venice*. The Arden Shakespeare, Second Series. London: Methuen, 1955.
Brown, John Russell. *Shakespeare's Plays in Performance*. London: Edward Arnold, 1966.
Brown, John Russell. *Drama*. London: Heinemann, 1968.
Brown, John Russell. *Theatre Language: A Study of Osborne, Pinter and Wesker*. London: Allen Lane, 1972.
Brown, John Russell. *Free Shakespeare*. London: Heinemann, 1974.
Brown, John Russell (ed.). *The Routledge Companion to Directors' Shakespeare*. Abingdon: Routledge, 2008.
Bryden, Ronald. 'Olivier's Moor'. *New Statesman*, 1 May 1964.
Bryden, Ronald. 'Somebodaddy'. *New Statesman*, 25 September 1964.
Bryden, Ronald. 'The Brechts of the Apostles'. *New Statesman*, 20 August 1965.
Bryden, Ronald. 'Out of Their World'. *Observer*, 16 April 1967.
Bryden, Ronald. 'The Wrong Kind of Achievement'. *Observer*, 8 October 1967.
Bryden, Ronald. 'The Jew Among the Gentlemen'. *Observer*, 3 May 1970.

Bryden, Ronald. 'Off the Peg Coriolanus'. *Observer*, 9 May 1971.
Bulman, James C. *Shakespeare in Performance: The Merchant of Venice*. Manchester: Manchester University Press, 1991.
Callow, Simon. *The National: The Theatre and its Work 1963–1997*. London: Nick Hern, 1997.
Cashin, Fergus. 'Olivier – But with a Look of Jolson'. *Daily Sketch*, 22 April 1964.
Catullus. *The Complete Poems*, translated by Guy Lee. Oxford: Oxford University Press, 1990.
Clarke, Alan. 'What "Coriolanus" has to Say to a Modern Audience'. *Morning Star*, 4 May 1971.
Coveney, Michael. *Maggie Smith: A Bright Particular Star*. London: Victor Gollancz, 1992.
Coveney, Michael. 'Graham Crowden Obituary'. *Guardian*, 22 October 2010.
Cox, John F. *Shakespeare in Production: Much Ado about Nothing*. Cambridge: Cambridge University Press, 1997.
Crowther, Bosley. 'Minstrel Show "Othello"; Radical Makeup Marks Olivier's Interpretation'. *New York Times*, 2 February 1966.
Cummings, Constance and others. '"Coriolanus" at the Old Vic'. *The Times*, 14 May 1971.
Cushman, Robert. 'Coriolanus'. *Plays and Players*, July 1971.
Cushman, Robert. 'The National's Great "Tempest"'. *Observer*, 10 March 1974.
Cushman, Robert. 'The Whole Hamlet'. *Observer*, 14 December 1975.
Cushman, Robert. 'First Impressions'. *Observer*, 14 March 1976.
Daily Sketch. 'A Hamlet to Cheer'. 23 October 1963.
Daily Telegraph. 'Women for "Hamlet" – But not for Speeches'. 18 November 1963.
Darlington, W. A. 'Black, but Comely'. *Daily Telegraph*, 18 May 1964.
Darlington, W. A. 'Pure Delight in Zeffirelli's "Much Ado"'. *Daily Telegraph*, 17 February 1965.
Darlington, W. A. 'Travesty of "Coriolanus" by Brecht'. *Daily Telegraph*, 11 August 1965.
Darlington, W. A. 'Two Characters in a Dreadful Limbo'. *Daily Telegraph*, 12 April 1967.
Darlington, W. A. 'Experiment Comes off Brilliantly'. *Daily Telegraph*, 4 October 1967.

David, Richard. *Shakespeare in the Theatre*. Cambridge: Cambridge University Press, 1978.

Day-Lewis, Sean. 'The Berlin Brecht'. *Daily Telegraph*, 7 August 1965.

Dent, Alan. 'The Olivier Othello'. *Financial Times*, 23 April 1964.

Dexter, John. *The Honourable Beast: A Posthumous Autobiography*. London: Nick Hern Books, 1993.

Dollimore, Jonathan, and Alan Sinfield (eds). *Political Shakespeare: Essays in Cultural Materialism*. 2nd edn. Manchester: Manchester University Press, 1994.

Dunn, Cyril. 'Briefing: Footnote to the Bard'. *Observer*, 9 April 1967.

Edwards, Sydney. 'A Line of History'. *Evening Standard*, 19 December 1975.

Eichenbaum, Stanley. 'A Stunning Switch on "As You Like It"'. *San Francisco Examiner*, 18 July 1974.

Ellis, Samantha. 'Hamlet, National Theatre, October 1963'. *Guardian*, 12 March 2003.

Esslin, Martin. 'Theater in London: "As You Like It", or Boy Meets Boy'. *New York Times*, 15 October 1967.

Evans, Peter. 'An Historic Performance'. *Southern Evening News*, 24 July 1964.

Foster, Susan Leigh. *Choreographing Empathy: Kinaesthesia in Performance*. London and New York: Routledge, 2011.

Gardner, John. 'The Plain Man's Guide to Hamlet'. *Stratford-upon-Avon Herald*, 25 October 1963.

Gardner, John. 'Othello's Olivier'. *Stratford-upon-Avon Herald*, 1 May 1964.

Gascoigne, Bamber. 'Extrovert at Elsinore (S. E.)'. *Observer*, 27 October 1963.

Gascoigne, Bamber. 'Drama, Italian Style'. *Observer*, 8 March 1964.

Gascoigne, Bamber. 'A Moor for All Time'. *Observer*, 26 April 1964.

Gellert, Roger. 'Without the Prince'. *New Statesman*, 1 November 1963.

Gillett, Eric. 'Exciting "Hamlet" by O'Toole'. *Yorkshire Post*, 23 October 1963.

Gilliatt, Penelope. 'A Merry War in Messina'. *Observer*, 21 February 1965.

Gilliatt, Penelope. 'Mother Courage Marches On'. *Observer*, 16 May 1965.

Gilliatt, Penelope, 'Brecht and Company'. *Observer*, 15 August 1965.
Goodwin, John (ed.). *Royal Shakespeare Company 1960–1963*. London: Max Reinhardt, 1964.
Goodwin, John (ed.). *Peter Hall's Diaries: The Story of a Dramatic Battle*. London: Hamish Hamilton, 1983.
Gottfried, Martin. 'All-Male Shakespeare'. *New York Post*, 4 December 1974.
Graves, Robert. 'Making Sound Sense of Shakespeare'. *Sunday Times*, 14 February 1965.
Green, Benny. 'Hushing up the Audience'. *Observer*, 11 June 1967.
Guardian. 'Desperate Calm of First Night'. 23 October 1963.
Guthrie, Tyrone. *In Various Directions: A View of Theatre*. London: Michael Joseph, 1965.
H. R. 'Spoken As You Like It'. *The Times*, 19 September 1968.
Hagerty, Bill. 'Hamlet in the Rough'. *Daily Mirror*, 11 December 1975.
Haill, Lyn (ed.). *Olivier at Work: The National Years*. London: Nick Hern Books/NT Publications, 1989.
Hall, Peter. *Making an Exhibition of Myself*. London: Sinclair-Stevenson, 1993.
Harper, Keith. 'The Devious Route to Waterloo Road'. *Guardian*, 12 April 1967.
Hay, Malcolm, and Phillip Roberts. *Bond: A Study of his Plays*. London: Eyre Methuen, 1980.
Higgins, John. 'The Theatre of Heaven and Earth'. *The Times*, 9 March 1974.
Hobson, Harold. 'A Hand Upon the Royalty'. *Sunday Times*, 27 October 1963.
Hobson, Harold. 'A New Kind of Hamlet'. *Sunday Times*, 20 September 1964.
Hobson, Harold. 'It's Great After the Fiesta'. *Sunday Times*, 21 February 1965.
Hobson, Harold. 'Brecht, the Misunderstood'. *Sunday Times*, 16 May 1965.
Hobson, Harold. 'Educating Edinburgh'. *Sunday Times*, 4 September 1966.
Hobson, Harold. 'A Fearful Summons'. *Sunday Times*, 16 April 1967.
Hobson, Harold. 'Absorbed in Sweet Propriety'. *Sunday Times*, 8 October 1967.

Hobson, Harold. 'Paths of Dalliance'. *Sunday Times*, 22 December 1968.
Hobson, Harold. 'Field of Fire'. *Sunday Times*, 10 March 1974.
Hobson, Harold. 'Private Lives'. *Sunday Times*, 14 December 1975.
Hobson, Harold. 'The Doors are Open'. *Sunday Times*, 14 March 1976.
Holland, Julian. 'The Man Who Made the Bard a Bore'. *Daily Mail*, 11 August 1965.
Holland, Peter. 'National Theatre's New Ticket Scheme'. *The Times*, 6 February 1976.
Holland, Peter (ed.). *Coriolanus*. The Arden Shakespeare, Third Series. London: Bloomsbury Arden Shakespeare, 2013.
Holland, Peter (ed.). *Great Shakespeareans, Volume XVIII: Brook, Hall, Ninagawa. Lepage*. London: Bloomsbury Arden Shakespeare, 2013.
Hope-Wallace, Phillip. 'Ghosts afoot at the Old Vic'. *Guardian*, 23 October 1963.
Hope-Wallace, Phillip. 'Othello at the National Theatre'. *Guardian*, 22 April 1964.
Hope-Wallace, Phillip. 'Zeffirelli's Much Ado at the National Theatre'. *Guardian*, 17 February 1965.
Hope-Wallace, Phillip. 'The Berliner Ensemble at the National Theatre'. *Guardian*, 10 August 1965.
Hope-Wallace, Phillip. 'The Berliner Ensemble at the Old Vic'. *Guardian*, 13 August 1965.
Hope-Wallace, Phillip. 'As You Like It at the Old Vic'. *Guardian*, 4 October 1967.
Hope-Wallace, Phillip. 'Coriolanus at the Old Vic'. *Guardian*, 7 May 1971.
Hurren, Kenneth. 'National Disasters'. *Spectator*, 15 May 1971.
Hurren, Kenneth. 'Hare Splitting and Fox Hunting'. *Spectator*, 16 March 1974.
Hurren, Kenneth. 'National Disaster'. *Spectator*, 20 December 1975.
Jackson, Russell (ed.). *Great Shakespeareans, Volume XVI: Gielgud, Olivier, Ashcroft, Dench*. London: Bloomsbury Arden Shakespeare, 2013.
Jones, D. A. N. 'Safe Play'. *New Statesman*, 5 May 1967.
Jones, D. A. N. 'Spear-carriers'. *New Statesman*, 21 April 1967.
Jones, D. A. N. 'Disguises'. *Listener*, 9 November 1967.

Kerr, Walter. 'Taking Revenge On Life'. *New York Times*, 29 October 1967.
Kingston, Jeremy. 'Theatre'. *Punch*, 24 February 1965.
Kingston, Jeremy. 'Theatre'. *Punch*, 19 April 1967.
Kingston, Jeremy. 'Theatre'. *Punch*, 11 October 1967.
Kingston, Jeremy. 'At the Theatre'. *Punch*, 1 January 1968.
Klein, Richard. *Cigarettes are Sublime*. Durham and London: Duke University Press, 1993.
Knickerbocker, Paine. 'Splendid Male "As You Like It"'. *San Francisco Chronicle*, 18 July 1974.
Knickerbocker, Paine. '"As You Like It" Was Not to Be a Female Impersonation'. *San Francisco Sunday Examiner and Chronicle*, 21 July 1974.
Kretzmer, Herbert. 'I Shall Dream of this Othello for Years'. *Daily Express*, 22 April 1964.
Kretzmer, Herbert. 'A Feast for the Parliamo Italiano Fans'. *Daily Express*, 16 September 1964.
Kretzmer, Herbert. 'Much Ado with a Taste of Candy Floss'. *Daily Express*, 17 February 1965.
Kretzmer, Herbert. 'It's Hitler Again – In Chicago's Gangland'. *Daily Express*, 10 August 1965.
Kretzmer, Herbert. 'A Triumph for the National Theatre'. *Daily Express*, 4 October 1967.
Kretzmer, Herbert. 'Fiery Finney Lights up the Danish Court'. *Daily Express*, 11 December 1975.
Kroll, Jack. 'R and G'. *Newsweek*, 30 October 1967.
Lahr, John (ed.). *The Orton Diaries*. London: Methuen, 1987.
Lahr, John (ed.). *The Diaries of Kenneth Tynan*. London: Bloomsbury, 2001.
Laity, Paul. 'A Life in Writing: Hilary Spurling'. *Guardian*, 17 April 2010.
Lambert, J. W. 'Opposite Numbers'. *Sunday Times*, 9 May 1971.
Larner, Gerald. 'David Jordan and the RMCM Orchestra at the Free Trade Hall'. *Guardian*, 9 June 1967.
Leavis, F. R. *The Common Pursuit*. Harmondsworth: Penguin, 1962.
Leeson, Bob. 'Faces in the Crowd'. *Daily Worker*, 12 August 1965.
Leigh Foster, Susan. *Choreographing Empathy: Kinesthesia in Performance*. London and New York: Routledge, 2011.
Levin, Bernard. 'After a Wait of 100 Years, this will do for a Start'. *Daily Mail*, 23 October 1963.

Levin, Bernard. 'And Now Othello Falls to Sir Laurence'. *Daily Mail*, 22 April 1964.

Levin, Bernard. 'Nightmare Grip of Zeffirelli's Hamlet'. *Daily Mail*, 16 September 1964.

Levin, Bernard. 'Mucking about with Shakespeare'. *Daily Mail*, 17 February 1965.

Levin, Bernard. 'Forget the Drivel, Brecht is Great'. *Daily Mail*, 13 May 1965.

Lewis, Peter. 'Faces in the Crowd are Lords at Last'. *Daily Mail*, 12 April 1967.

Lewis, Peter. 'Taking a Dream Trip with the Bard'. *Daily Mail*, 4 October 1967.

Lewis, Peter. 'Shakespeare Hammered into Two Dimensions'. *Daily Mail*, 7 May 1971.

Macan, Edward. *Rocking the Classics: English Progressive Rock and the Counter-Culture*. New York and Oxford: Oxford University Press, 1997.

Manheim, Ralph, and John Willett (eds). *Bertolt Brecht: Collected Plays*, vol. 9. New York: Vintage, 1972.

Mann, William. 'Opera Restored for Berlioz Celebrations'. *The Times*, 21 May 1969.

Marcus, Frank. 'Modern Arcadia'. *Plays and Players*, October 1967.

Marcus, Frank. 'The Brechtian Bard'. *Sunday Telegraph*, 9 May 1971.

Marcus, Frank. 'Tract for our Time'. *Sunday Telegraph*, 10 March 1974.

Marriott, R. B. 'The Berliner Ensemble'. *The Stage*, 5 August 1965.

Marriott, R. B. 'Imaginative, Witty and Tender "Love's Labour's Lost"'. *Stage and Television Today*, 24 December 1968.

Mellers, Wilfred. 'Pop Mod'. *New Statesman*, 9 June 1967.

Menzer, Paul. *Anecdotal Shakespeare: A New Performance History*. London: Bloomsbury Arden Shakespeare, 2015.

Miller, Jonathan. *Subsequent Performances*. London: Faber and Faber, 1986.

Morley, Sheridan. 'Arthur Lowe: Keeping at It'. *The Times*, 10 August 1974.

Morley, Sheridan. 'New Challenge for Non-Stop Trevor Nunn'. *The Times*, 28 June 1977.

Nadel, Ira. *Double Act: A Life of Tom Stoppard*. London: Methuen, 2002.

Nathan, David. 'Too Much Ado about Words'. *The Sun*, 17 February 1965.
Nathan, David. 'Success for the Boys'. *The Sun*, 4 October 1967.
Nightingale, Benedict. 'Tribal Behaviour'. *New Statesman*, 8 May 1970.
Nightingale, Benedict. 'Manly Hopkins'. *New Statesman*, 14 May 1971.
Nightingale, Benedict. 'Wrong Side of the Barrier'. *New Statesman*, 15 March 1974.
Nightingale, Benedict. 'Unfit for a King'. *New Statesman*, 19 December 1975.
Norman, Barry. 'O'Toole's Hamlet'. *Daily Mail*, 22 October 1963.
Norman, Barry. 'Olivier's Challenge'. *Daily Mail*, 14 April 1964.
Observer. 'A National Refresher'. 20 October 1963.
Observer. 'Briefing'. 7 July 1974.
O'Connor, Garry. 'Stoppard and Savary'. *Financial Times*, 18 October 1967.
Odam, George. 'The Aeolian Quartet at the Bath Festival'. *Guardian*, 9 June 1967.
Olivier, Laurence. 'RSC and the National Theatre'. *The Times*, 18 April 1973.
Olivier, Laurence. *Confessions of an Actor*. London: Weidenfeld and Nicholson, 1982.
Olivier, Laurence. *On Acting*. London: Sceptre, 1987.
Orgel, Stephen. *The Illusion of Power: Political Theater in the English Renaissance*. Berkeley and Los Angeles: University of California Press, 1975.
Our Dramatic Critic. 'Routine Performance of Hamlet'. *The Times*, 23 October 1963.
Our Dramatic Critic. 'The Moor Built Up at Iago's Expense'. *The Times*, 22 April 1964.
Our Dramatic Critic. 'Hamlet as a Modern Man'. *The Times*, 16 September 1964.
Our Dramatic Critic. 'It All Ends on a Note of Magic'. *The Times*, 17 February 1965.
Our Dramatic Critic. 'Brecht Production a Wise Choice'. *The Times*, 13 May 1965.
Our Dramatic Critic. 'Shakespeare Remodelled by Brecht'. *The Times*, 11 August 1965.
Our London Drama Critic. 'Sir Laurence Olivier a Superb Othello'. *Glasgow Herald*, 23 April 1964.

Our New York Dramatic Critic. 'Kazan Defeated by the Changeling'. *The Times*, 23 December 1964.
Our Special Correspondent. 'Female Rosencrantz in Stoppard Play'. *The Times*, 22 February 1968.
Our Special Correspondent – Rome. 'Mr Franco Zeffirelli Modernizes Hamlet'. *The Times*, 3 February 1964.
P.H.S. 'The Times Diary'. *The Times*, 12 June 1967.
P.H.S. 'The Times Diary'. *The Times*, 14 April 1971.
Palmer, Tony. 'Not Exactly Yes'. *Observer*, 25 November 1973.
Parliamentary Debates: House of Commons (Hansard), 1948–9. London: HMSO, 1949.
Patton, Alec. 'How *The National Health* Improved the Nation's Health: Peter Nichols, Michael Blakemore, and the National Theatre Company'. *Theatre Journal*, 61, no. 3 (2009): 443–62.
Pearson, Kenneth. 'The Man Who Plays Rosalind'. *Sunday Times*, 1 October 1967.
Plowright, Joan. *And That's Not All*. London: Weidenfeld and Nicholson, 2001.
Plummer, Christopher. *In Spite of Myself: A Memoir*. New York: Alfred A. Knopf, 2008.
Post, Peggy, Anna Post, Lizzie Post and Daniel Post Sennng (eds). *Emily Post's Etiquette, 18th Edition: Manners for a Modern World*. New York: William Morrow, 2011.
Pryce-Jones, David. 'Son et lumière'. *Spectator*, 1 November 1963.
Pryce-Jones, David. 'Olivier'. *Spectator*, 1 May 1964.
Punch. 'The London Charivari: Theatre'. 12 April 1967.
Punch. 'The London Charivari: Theatre'. 26 April 1967.
Punch. 'The London Charivari: Theatre'. 4 October 1967.
Punch. 'The London Charivari: Theatre'. 18 October 1967.
Quilley, Denis. *Happiness Indeed: An Actors' Life*. London: Oberon, 2004.
Reid, Charles. 'Sir William's Bear'. *Spectator*, 9 June 1967.
Ridout, Nicholas. *Stage Fright, Animals, and Other Theatrical Problems*. Cambridge: Cambridge University Press, 2006.
Rokison-Woodall, Abigail. *Shakespeare in the Theatre: Nicholas Hytner*. London: Bloomsbury Arden Shakespeare, 2017.
Rosenthal, Daniel, *The National Theatre Story*. London: Oberon, 2013.
Rutherford, Malcolm. 'Show Business'. *Spectator*, 26 February 1965.
Sandbrook, Dominic. *Never Had It So Good: A History of Britain from Suez to the Beatles*. London: Abacus, 2006.

Schücking, L.L. (ed.). *Shakespeares Werke, Englisch und Deutsch*, vol. 5. Berlin and Darmstadt: Tempel-Verlag, 1965.

Shapiro, James. *1606: Shakespeare and the Year of Lear*. London: Faber and Faber, 2016.

Shaughnessy, Robert. *Shakespeare in Performance: As You Like It*. Manchester: Manchester University Press, 2018.

Shelton, Robert. 'Yes'. *The Times*, 21 November 1973.

Shulman, Milton. 'Olivier Sniffs a Rose, and so Begins a Landmark of Acting'. *Evening Standard*, 22 July 1964.

Shulman, Milton. 'Brecht – So Happy in his Soho Days'. *Evening Standard*, 12 August 1965.

Shulman, Milton. 'Delicious – But I Still Prefer Vanessa'. *Evening Standard*, 4 October 1967.

Shulman, Milton. 'Drawbacks at Elsinore'. *Evening Standard*, 11 December 1975.

Smith, James. 'Brecht, the Berliner Ensemble, and the British Government'. *New Theatre Quarterly*, 22.4 (2000): 307–23.

Solomos, John. *Race and Racism in Britain*. 3rd edn. Basingstoke: Palgrave Macmillan, 2003.

Speaight, Robert. 'Shakespeare in Britain'. *Shakespeare Quarterly*, 15, no. 4 (1964): 377–89.

Speaight, Robert. 'Shakespeare in Britain, 1974'. *Shakespeare Quarterly*, 25, no. 4 (1974): 389–94.

Spurling, Hilary. 'Prints of the Japanese Buskin'. *Spectator*, 21 April 1967.

Spurling, Hilary. 'Dan Dare's Arden'. *Spectator*, 13 October 1967.

Spurling, Hilary. 'Sugar is Sweet'. *Spectator*, 27 December 1968.

Spurling, Hilary. 'Strangers in Belmont'. *Spectator*, 9 May 1970.

Spurling, Hilary. 'A Touch of Tamburlaine'. *Observer*, 25 September 1983.

Stephens, Robert. *Knight Errant: Memoirs of a Vagabond Actor*. London: Sceptre, 1996.

Stoppard, Tom. *Rosencrantz and Guildenstern are Dead*. London: Faber, 1968.

Strong, Roy, and Stephen Orgel. *Inigo Jones: The Theatre of the Stuart Court*. London: Sotheby Park Bernet, 1973.

Sunday Times. 'As Busy as he is Inventive'. 14 February 1965.

Suskind, Jacob. 'Olivier's Othello A Masterpiece'. *Montreal Star*, 5 May 1964.

Taylor, John Russell. *Anger and After: A Guide to the New British Drama*. Harmondsworth: Penguin, 1963.

Taylor, John Russell. 'Rosencrantz and Guildenstern are Dead'. *Plays and Players*, June 1967.
The Sun. 'Sold'. 6 August 1965.
The Times. 'La Comédie Française at the Gaiety'. 3 June 1879.
The Times. 'Zeffirelli's Hamlet for the National Theatre'. 21 March 1964.
The Times. 'Helping Playwrights Get Ideas'. 11 September 1964.
The Times. 'Olivier on Choosing an Accent for Shakespeare's Peasants'. 18 February 1965.
The Times. 'Two Berliner Ensemble Men Defect'. 30 August 1965.
The Times. 'Actor Returns to E. Germany'. 15 September 1965.
The Times. 'Actor Found Dead in Church'. 26 October 1965.
The Times. 'The Moor of Waterloo Road'. 28 April 1966.
The Times. 'Britten Opera Strikingly Produced'. 24 February 1967.
The Times. 'Miss Plowright impresses'. 22 March 1967.
The Times. 'Dexter Dispute Over "As You Like It"'. 23 March 1967.
The Times. 'The Old Way with Shakespeare'. 7 August 1967.
The Times. 'All-Male Cast for As You Like It'. 24 August 1967.
The Times. 'National Theatre's "Fringe" Play'. 14 December 1967.
The Times. 'Court Circular'. 17 January 1968.
The Times. 'Court Circular'. 16 May 1968.
The Times. 'Paris Students March as Strikes Spread through Industry'. 17 May 1968.
The Times. 'National Merger with Royal Shakespeare Off'. 24 October 1973.
Thompson, Ann, David Scott Kastan and Richard Proudfoot (eds). *The Arden Shakespeare: Complete Works*. Rev. edn. London: Arden Shakespeare, 2011.
Thomson, Peter. 'Towards a Poor Shakespeare: The Royal Shakespeare Company at Stratford in 1975'. *Shakespeare Survey*, 29 (1976): 151–6.
Time. 'A Threepenny Tragedy'. 14 April 1971.
Tinker, Jack. 'Alas, Poor Finney! He's Wasted in this State of Denmark'. *Daily Mail*, 11 December 1975.
Trewin, Ion. 'Peter Daubeny, World Theatre's Inspiration'. *The Times*, 3 March 1973.
Trewin, J. C. 'First Night'. *Illustrated London News*, 2 November 1963.
Trewin, J. C. 'Standing Ovation for Olivier'. *Birmingham Post*, 22 April 1964.

Trewin, J. C. 'Olivier's Othello'. *Illustrated London News*, 2 May 1964.
Trewin, J. C. 'Theatre'. *Illustrated London News*, 26 September 1964.
Trewin, J. C. 'A Director's Night'. *Illustrated London News*, 27 February 1965.
Trewin, J. C. 'Sir Laurence as the Jew of Venice'. *Illustrated London News*, 9 May 1970.
Trueman, Matt. 'A Princess and a Lackey: The Actors' Guide to Rosalind in *As You Like It*'. *Guardian*, 13 July 2015.
Tynan, Kenneth. 'The Straight Answer'. *Observer*, 9 October 1960.
Tynan, Kenneth. *Tynan on Theatre*. Harmondsworth: Penguin, 1964.
Tynan, Kenneth. *Letters*, edited by Kathleen Tynan. London: Weidenfeld and Nicholson, 1994.
Wallace, Pat. 'That Old Black Magic'. *Tatler*, 13 May 1964.
Wardle, Irving. 'National Theatre Avoids the Pitfalls of Privilege'. *The Times*, 11 March 1967.
Wardle, Irving. 'Drama Unearthed from Elsinore's Depths'. *The Times*, 12 April 1967.
Wardle, Irving. 'Comic Result When Men Take over From Actresses'. *The Times*, 4 October 1967.
Wardle, Irving. 'Gentle Enchantment of Olivier Production'. *The Times*, 20 December 1968.
Wardle, Irving. 'Merchants all'. *The Times*, 29 April 1970.
Wardle, Irving. 'Coriolanus'. *The Times*, 7 May 1971.
Wardle, Irving. 'Prospero's Novel Masque'. *The Times*, 6 March 1974.
Wardle, Irving. 'Hamlet and "Shakespearean Intentions"'. *The Times*, 11 December 1975.
Wardle, Irving. 'The National Theatre Comes True'. *The Times*, 12 March 1976.
Waymark, Peter. 'Sir Laurence Told Not to Act for a Year'. *The Times*, 30 September 1970.
White, Michael. 'London Letter'. *Guardian*, 20 December 1975.
Whitelaw, Billie. ...*Who He?* London: Hodder and Stoughton, 1995.
Whitworth, Charles. *The Making of a National Theatre*. London: Faber and Faber, 1951.
Willett, John (ed.). *Brecht on Theatre*. London: Methuen, 1964.
Williams, Clifford. 'All-Male "As You Like It"'. *The Times*, 27 December 1974.
Wilson, Edwin (ed.). *Shaw on Shakespeare*. Harmondsworth: Penguin, 1969.

Worsley, T. C. 'Romeo and Juliet'. *Financial Times*, 6 October 1960.
Worsley, T. C. 'Hamlet'. *Financial Times*, 24 October 1963.
Yorkshire Evening Post. 'What's on in Town'. 22 April 1964.
Yorkshire Evening Post. 'Olivier as Superb Othello'. 23 April 1964.
Young, B. A. 'At the Play'. *Punch*, 30 October 1963.
Young, B. A. 'Othello'. *Financial Times*, 23 July 1964.
Young, B. A. 'Amleto'. *Financial Times*, 25 September 1964.
Young, B. A. 'Amleto Again'. *Financial Times*, 26 September 1964.
Young, B. A. 'Much Ado about Nothing'. *Financial Times*, 18 February 1965.
Young, B. A. 'Coriolanus at the Old Vic'. *Financial Times*, 12 August 1965.
Young, B. A. 'Rosencrantz and Guildenstern Are Dead'. *Financial Times*, 12 April 1967.
Young, B. A. 'Widened Horizons'. *Financial Times*, 24 June 1968.
Young, B. A. 'Love's Labour's Lost'. *Financial Times*, 20 December 1968.
Young, B. A. 'The Merchant of Venice'. *Financial Times*, 29 April 1970.
Young, B. A. 'Coriolanus'. *Financial Times*, 9 May 1971.
Zeffirelli, Franco. *The Autobiography of Franco Zeffirelli*. London: Weidenfeld and Nicholson, 1986.

INDEX

Adaré, Elizabeth, 197 n.150
Addison, John, 214 n.40
Adrian, Max, 12
Agutter, Jenny, 155, 160
Albertazzi, Giorgio, 98–102
Aldwych Theatre, 4, 17, 58, 64, 99, 147
Ansorge, Peter, 172
Archer, William, 2, 187
Arden, John, 59, 154
  Armstrong's Last Goodnight, 111
Arden Shakespeare, 109, 168
Armstrong, Louis, 26–7
Arnold, Matthew, 1
Arrabal, Fernando
  The Architect and the Emperor of Assyria, 142
Arts Council, 3, 97, 145, 150, 165
Arts Lab, 91
Arts Theatre, 99
Ashcroft, Peggy, 3, 166, 181, 187

Bacall, Lauren, 35
Bach, Johann Sebastian, 153
Baker, Tom, 52
Barbican Theatre, 147
Barker, Harley Granville, 2, 187
Barker, Petronella, 196 n.107
Barnes, Clive, 85–6, 95
Barnes, Jason, 163

Barrault, Jean-Louis, 89, 99
Barrie, Frank, 6–7
Barrie, J. M., 3
Barton, John, 110
Bassey, Shirley, 9
Baylis, Lilian, 3, 166, 190
BBC television, 155
BBC/Time-Life Television Shakespeare, 16
The Beatles 28, 68
  'Ain't She Sweet', 144
  Revolver, 73
  Sgt. Pepper's Lonely Hearts Club Band, 68–9, 73, 82, 152
Beaton, Norman, 52
Beckett, Samuel, 19, 70, 154
  Happy Days, 187
  Play, 19
  Waiting for Godot, 64–6
Beeton, Isabella, 42
Behrens, Manja, 129
Bell, Marie, 99
Bellini, Giovanni, 157
Benny, Jack, 26
Benthall, Michael, 97
Berghaus, Ruth, 124
Berliner Ensemble, 99, 113–30, 132, 135, 139
Berlioz, Hector
  Beatrice and Benedick, 74
Berman, Ed, 43, 91
Berry, Cicely, 188

Betterton, Thomas, 180
Big Bad Mouse, 64, 79
Billington, Michael, 48, 157, 158, 161, 176, 177
Birtwhistle, Harrison, 215 n.40
The Black and White Minstrel Show, 23, 26, 52
Blakemore, Michael, 145, 148–50, 157, 181
Bogart, Humphrey, 35
Bond, Edward
    Bingo, 7, 166–9
    Saved, 60
Boorman, John, 92
Bourne, Helen, 191 n.12
Bowie, David
    The Rise and Fall of Ziggy Stardust and the Spiders from Mars, 158
Brecht, Bertolt, 61, 74–5, 98–9, 180
    Coriolanus, 113–30, 132–40
    The Days of the Commune, 113, 116
    Don Juan, 117
    Life of Galileo, 139
    Mother Courage, 111, 113, 114, 126
    The Resistible Rise of Arturo Ui, 113, 116
    The Rise and Fall of the City of Mahagonny, 74–5
    The Threepenny Opera, 113, 116–17
    Trumpets and Drums, 117
    The Tutor, 117
Bremen Theatre, 115–16
Brett, Jeremy, 40, 44, 73, 76, 83–4, 112
Brien, Alan, 13, 26–8, 116

Bristol Old Vic, 104
Britten, Benjamin
    The Turn of the Screw, 74
Brook, Natasha (Natasha Parry), 156
Brook, Peter, 60, 91, 95, 156, 188
Brooks, Jeremy, 59
Brown, John Russell, 167–70, 173
Bryan, Dora, 64
Bryden, Bill, 168
Bryden, Ronald, 21–2, 59, 65, 80, 84, 101–2, 126, 133, 135, 141
Burbage, Richard, 25, 180
Burge, Stuart, 20, 31, 36–7
Bury, John, 151, 157, 159, 163–4, 177, 182
Byrne, Michael, 112

Cactus Flower, 64, 79
Caine, Michael, 7
Callow, Simon, 16, 147, 166
Captain Scarlet and the Mysterons, 89
Casablanca, 35
Catullus, 138
Cellier, Peter, 62
CEMA, 3
Chaplin, Charles, 50
Charon, Jacques, 111
Chekhov, Anton
    Three Sisters, 64, 80, 87, 89, 189
    Uncle Vanya, 19
Chichester Festival Theatre, 4, 26, 39, 111
Church, Tony, 93
Churchill, Winston, 60, 150

Clark, Kenneth, 115
Cochrane, Elspeth, 93
Come Spy with Me, 64, 79
Comédie-Française, 1, 99, 111
Comedy Theatre, 157
Compagnia dei Quattro, 90
Congreve, William
  Love for Love, 111
Copeau, Jaques, 99
Cordon, Michael, 200 n.46
Cornelissen, Douglas, 163
Cotton, Oliver, 184
Coveney, Michael, 105
Covington, Julie, 158
Coward, Noel
  Hay Fever, 70, 111
Cranston Street Hall, 59
Crawter, B., 110
Crowden, Graham, 62, 112
Crowther, Bosley, 31
Culver, Roland, 178
Cummings, Constance, 134–5, 141
Cunningham, Margo, 196 n.107
Curtis, Tony, 81
Cusack, Cyril, 159
Cushman, Robert, 141, 158–61, 164, 176–7, 182, 183

Dad's Army, 155
Darlington, W. A., 20, 64, 84–5, 126
Dastoor, Sam, 112
Daubeny, Peter, 99
David, Richard, 182–5
Davis, Carl, 44
Day-Lewis, Cecil, 89, 190
Day-Lewis, Sean, 114
de Filippo, Eduardo

Saturday, Sunday, Monday, 198 n.163
de Vega, Lope
  La Fianza Satisfacha, 111
Dearie, Blossom, 68
della Francesca, Piero, 41
Dench, Judi, 97
Dent, Alan, 35
Dessau, Paul, 125
Devlin, J. G., 178–9
Dexter, John, 16–17, 20, 23, 25, 33, 39, 45, 72–4, 131, 145, 188
Disraeli, Benjamin, 45
Doctor Who, 52
Donizetti, Gaetano, 44
Douglas, Lord Alfred (Bosie), 45
Drabble, Margaret, 40
Droeshout portrait, 166
Drury Lane Theatre, 64
Duffy, Maureen
  Rites, 40
Dunlop, Frank, 93
Dylan, Bob, 68

Easterbrook, Antony, 92–4
Edinburgh Festival, 59
Edwards, Jimmy, 64
Enriquez, Franco, 90
Esslin, Martin, 83, 85
'An Evasion of Women', 40
Ewing, Kenneth, 92–4

Faith, Adam, 12
Farmer, George, 146
Farquhar, George
  The Beaux' Stratagem, 189
  The Recruiting Officer, 15, 39, 117, 189
Feast, Michael, 155, 159

Feydeau, Georges, 65
  A Flea in Her Ear, 80, 112
Finlay, Frank, 12, 35, 37, 53, 105
Finney, Albert, 102, 105, 112, 116, 170, 173–85, 188
Fleetwood, Susan, 178–9
Floy, Gregory, 95
Ford Foundation, 58
Forum Theatre, Berlin, 58
Foster, Jill, 94
Foster, Susan Leigh, 29
Fox, Edward, 16
Frazer, Rupert, 160, 163
Freeman, Gillian, 40
Freud, Sigmund, 102, 122, 172, 180
Fry, Christopher, 67

Gaiety Theatre, 1
Gallie, Kay, 196 n.107
Gambon, Michael, 15
Garcia, Victor, 142
Gardner, John, 26
Garland, Judy, 159
Garrick Theatre, 79
Gascoigne, Bamber, 10, 12, 18, 21, 36, 98–9
Gaskill, William, 64, 114, 189
Gellert, Roger, 12–13, 18
Genet, Jean, 73, 154
Gielgud, John, 3, 7, 20, 89, 98, 150–2, 155–7, 159–61, 163–70, 181, 188
Gillespie, Dana, 157–8
Gilliatt, Penelope, 105, 107, 110, 114, 116, 125, 127
Ginzberg, Natalia
  The Advertisement, 40
Globe Theatre, 64, 99
Godspell, 158

Goldby, Derek, 6, 62–3, 65, 71, 93
Goodbody, Buzz, 154–5, 171–2, 174, 183
Goodman, Lord Arnold, 145
Gottfried, Martin, 95
Graves, Robert, 107–11
The Great Dictator, 50
Green, Benny, 68
Green, Dorothy, 156
Greif, Stephen, 52–3
Griffiths, Mary, 196 n.107
Griffiths, Peter, 23
Griffiths, Trevor
  The Party, 198 n.163
Grotowski, Jerzy, 161
Gryphon, 143–5, 152, 153, 159
  Midnight Mushrumps, 144
  Red Queen to Gryphon Three, 151
Guerrieri, Gerardo, 100
Guinness, Alec, 81, 150
Guthrie, Tyrone, 86, 94, 115

Hack, Keith, 155
Hagerty, Bill, 176
Hair, 91
Hall, Peter, 4–5, 11, 17, 46, 59, 101, 110, 142, 187–9
  Hamlet, 170–86, 187
  The Tempest, 143–70, 172, 178, 179
Hallifax, Michael, 173
Halliwell, Kenneth, 200 n.24
Hampton, Richard, 9–10, 15–16, 17
Hampton-Reeves, Stuart, 154
Hardwicke, Edward, 93
Hare, David
  Knuckle, 157

Harris, Rosemary, 12, 17–19, 36
Harrison, Rex, 76
Harvey, Jackie, 162–3
Haw, G. A., 71–2
Hawkins, Jack, 20
Haynes, Jim, 91
Heeley, Desmond, 62
Hello Dolly!, 64, 79
Herbert, Jocelyn, 74
Hitler, Adolf, 50
Hobson, Harold, 10–11, 42–3, 59, 65–6, 84, 102–3, 114, 157–8, 176, 179–80, 182
Hochhuth, Rolf
  Soldiers, 60
Hodgdon, Barbara, 20, 24
Holland, Julian, 126–7
Holland, Peter, 122, 135, 171–2, 181–2
Holloway, Balliol, 156
Hope-Wallace, Philip, 133–4
Hopkins, Anthony, 16, 77–8, 80, 88, 132, 135, 136, 140–2
Horváth, Ödön von, 142
Hunt, Gareth, 184
Hurren, Kenneth, 141, 176, 178–9
Hytner, Nicholas, 189

Ibsen, Henrik
  John Gabriel Borkman, 189
  The Master Builder, 39, 70
Institute of Contemporary Arts, 43
Irish Republican Army, 175
Irving, Henry, 1–2

Jacobi, Derek, 12, 14, 15, 51, 112
Jagger, Mick, 69

James, Henry
  The Turn of the Screw, 54
Jeanette Cochrane Theatre, 40
Jesus Christ Superstar, 158
Jewell, Derek, 143
John, Caroline, 191 n.12
Jolson, Al, 26
Jones, D. A. N., 66–8, 83
Jones, Inigo, 151, 157, 161
Jonson, Ben, 167

Kafka, Franz, 66
Kaiser, Wolf, 128
Kay, Charles, 77–8, 80, 84, 90, 112, 131
Kay, Richard, 77–8, 84–5, 90
Kean, Charles, 190
Kean, Edmund, 30
Kenny, Sean, 10–11, 15
Kerr, Walter, 86
Kind Hearts and Coronets, 81
King Farouk I, 131
King James I, 161
Kingston, Jeremy, 83–4
Kinnear, Roy, 79
Klein, Richard, 34
Koltai, Ralph, 73–5, 78, 81, 91
Kott, Jan, 73, 77, 81, 180
Kretzmer, Herbert, 100, 103, 107, 116, 176
Kulukundis, Eddie, 169
Kyd, Thomas
  The Spanish Tragedy, 169–70
Kynaston, Edward, 81

La Rue, Danny, 64, 80–1
Labiche, Eugène Marin, 105
  The Italian Straw Hat, 104
Lambert, J. W., 141

Landis, Jeanette, 196 n.107
Lansbury, Angela, 178
Lapotaire, Jane, 52
Lawrence of Arabia, 12, 14
Lawrence, D. H.
   The Daughter-in-Law, 64
Leavis, F. R., 25
Leeson, Bob, 126
Lemmon, Jack, 81
Lenin, Vladimir, 131
Lennon, John, 86
Lenz, Jakob
   The Tutor, 117
Lester, Adrian, 189
Let Sleeping Wives Lie, 79
Levin, Bernard, 10–11, 12, 21–2, 35, 100, 102, 106, 110, 114
Lewenstein, Oscar, 168–9
Lewis, Peter, 65, 67, 82–3, 135
Linklater, N. V., 93
Lloyd, Selwyn, 4, 9
Lomax, Harry, 187
London County Council, 4
London Shakespeare League, 2
London Symphony Orchestra, 152
Losey, Joseph
   Modesty Blaise, 82
Lowe, Arthur, 155, 159, 167
Lyceum Theatre, 2
Lyric Hammersmith, 64

Macan, Edward, 153
Mackay, Sheila, 40
Macmillan, Harold, 4
Magritte, René, 156
Manheim, Ralph, 117–18
Marcus, Frank, 82, 157
Marlowe, Christopher, 81
   Edward II, 88
   Tamburlaine, 149, 170, 188
Marowitz, Charles, 91
Marriott, R. B., 113
Marsh, Fran, 164
Marston, John
   The Dutch Courtesan, 39
Martin, John, 29
Marx, Karl, 61, 120, 127, 137
Maugham, Somerset
   Home and Beauty, 155
Maxwell, Venetia, 202 n.77
Maxwell-Muller, Jo, 6–7
May, Val
   Tribute to the Lady, 166, 181
McCartney, Paul 73
McDowell, Roddy, 33
McEnery, John, 62
McKellen, Ian, 93–4, 112
Meaden, Dan, 9, 15–16, 17
Mei Lanfang, 81
Menzer, Paul, 38
Merrick, David, 71, 92
MGM, 92
Middleton, Thomas
   A Chaste Maid in Cheapside, 39
Miller, Arthur
   The Crucible, 111
Miller, Jonathan, 44–52, 87, 148–9, 172
Mohammed Ali, 32
Moissi, Alexander, 99
Molière, 1, 99
   Don Juan, 117
   Tartuffe, 86
Monteverdi, Claudio, 143
Moriconi, Valeria, 90
Moscow Art Theatre, 99, 116

Mrożek, Slawomir
　Tango, 58
Murray, Brian, 86
Murray, Valerie, 197 n.150

National Gallery, 1
National Theatre Board, 4, 39, 40, 60, 61, 72, 90, 103–4, 108, 115, 135, 145, 169
Never Say Never Again, 16
Nicholls, Anthony, 44
Nichols, Peter
　The National Health, 52, 92, 189
Nightingale, Benedict, 141, 155, 158, 166, 177
Ninagawa, Yukio, 129
Ninchi, Alessandro, 101
Nixon, Richard, 176
Noh Theatre of Japan, 64
Northcott Theatre, 93, 167
NT Mobile, 5, 172, 188
Nunn, Trevor, 59, 146

O'Casey, Sean
　Juno and the Paycock, 112
O'Neill, Eugene
　Long Day's Journey into Night, 198 n.163
O'Toole, Peter, 12–15, 17–18, 27, 62
Obey, André
　Le Viol de Lucrèce, 99
Olivier, Laurence, 3–5, 7, 60, 62, 72–4, 85, 78–9, 81, 85, 92–3, 99, 106, 112, 116, 130–3, 142, 145–8, 150, 155, 167–8, 181, 187–9
　Hamlet, 9–19, 62–3, 187

Love's Labour's Lost, 40–3, 87
The Merchant of Venice, 44–55, 87, 188
Othello, 19–39, 74, 87, 188
The Open Space, 91
Orff, Carl, 68
Orgel, Stephen, 151, 161
Orton, Joe
　Loot, 64
Osborne, John
　A Bond Honoured, 111
　Look Back in Anger, 11, 13, 64, 68, 108

Page, Anthony, 130
Palace Theatre, 99
Palmer, Tony, 153
Parker, Dorothy, 13
Pate, Tom, 163
Pearson, Kenneth, 75–7
Peking Opera, 81, 124
Penderecki, Krzyzstof, 68
Petherbride, Edward, 62, 65, 66
Pickup, Ronald, 72, 76–9, 81, 82–5, 88, 90, 93, 112, 131
Pilbrow, Richard, 86
Pinero, Arthur Wing, 3
　Trelawney of the 'Wells', 111
Pinter, Harold, 70, 145, 148, 154
　The Birthday Party, 65
　The Homecoming, 60
　No Man's Land, 189
Pirandello, Luigi, 65, 66
　The Rules of the Game, 130
Piscator Theatre, 115
Planchon, Roger, 99
Plowright, Joan, 7, 16, 39, 40–2, 44, 51–2, 73, 112

Plummer, Christopher, 7, 27, 37–8, 130–3
Pollock, Jackson, 151
Post, Emily, 158
Powell, Enoch, 89
Prieser, Rolf, 129
Primoli, Giuseppe (Count de), 45
Princess Margaret, 181
Princess Marina, 89
Proclemer-Albertazzi, 98–104
Proclemer, Anna, 98, 101
Prospect Theatre, 93–4
Pryce-Jones, David, 18
Punch, 63–4, 66, 85
Punt, Dacre, 73
Purnell, Louise, 40–1, 52

Quant, Mary, 85
Quayle, Anthony, 20
Queen
  'Bohemian Rhapsody', 175
Queen Victoria, 11
Questors' Theatre, 58–9
Quilley, Denis, 131, 133–6, 141, 155, 159, 177–8, 182

Racine, 1, 98, 99
The Railway Children, 155
Rattigan, Terence, 68
Rayne, Max, 145–6
Rea, Stephen, 178–9
Redgrave, Michael, 12
Redman, Joyce, 36–7
Régy, Claude, 90
Reid, Charles, 68
Reiner, Rob
  This is Spinal Tap, 215 n.50
Reisz, Karl
  Saturday Night and Sunday Morning, 179

Reith, Lord John, 149
Renaud, Madeleine, 99
Richardson, Ralph, 3, 20, 62, 166, 174
Ridout, Nicholas, 53
Riley, Maggie, 196 n.107
Robeson, Paul, 20
Roeg, Nicolas
  Walkabout, 155
The Rolling Stones, 69
Rosenthal, Daniel, 5
Rossini, Gioachino, 104
Rota, Nino, 214 n.40
Rothwell, Michael, 105, 112
The Roundhouse, 183, 185
Rowbottom, George, 71, 92, 110
Royal Court, 60, 62, 64, 167–9
Royal Festival Hall, 59
Royal Shakespeare Company, 4–5, 15–17, 58–9, 60, 64, 74, 79, 91, 98, 101, 110, 146–7, 154–5, 161, 164, 167, 171–2, 177, 188
  The Romans, 188
  The Wars of the Roses, 110, 154, 188
Royal Shakespeare Theatre, 4
Rubens, Peter Paul, 21
Rudman, Michael, 188
Ryall, David, 112

Sadler's Wells, 4, 74–5, 99
St Trinian's films, 38
Sandbrook, Dominic, 19
Scaccio, Mario, 90
Schall, Ekkehard, 127–8, 141
Schell, Maximillian, 142
Schlesinger, John, 148
Schoenberg, Arnold, 68, 125

Scofield, Paul, 31, 130
Seneca, 180
Shaffer, Peter
　Black Comedy, 111
　Equus, 189
　The Royal Hunt of the Sun, 39, 59, 62, 80, 87, 189
Shaftesbury Theatre, 64, 91
Shakespeare Memorial National Theatre Committee, 2–3
Shakespeare Memorial Theatre, 1, 4, 20
Shakespeare, William
　Antony and Cleopatra, 7, 40, 115, 138–9
　As You Like It, 2, 5, 40–2, 60–2, 72–85, 86–92, 95, 148, 154, 188, 190
　The Comedy of Errors, 74
　Coriolanus, 27, 40, 113–42, 145, 149, 178
　Hamlet, 2, 4, 5–7, 9–19, 36, 40, 57–72, 62–3, 66, 67, 75, 90, 91, 94, 97–104, 148–50, 154, 170–86, 187, 188
　Henry IV, Part 1, 2, 188
　Henry IV, Part 2, 2, 188
　Henry V, 2, 16, 49, 104, 115, 188, 189
　Henry VI, Part 1, 110
　Henry VI, Part 2, 110
　Henry VI, Part 3, 110
　Henry VIII, 2
　King Lear, 49, 58, 148, 150, 155, 178, 190
　Love's Labour's Lost, 40–3, 59, 87, 104
　Macbeth, 129, 149, 178
　Measure for Measure, 16, 172, 188
　The Merchant of Venice, 5, 44–55, 87, 115, 168, 188
　The Merry Wives of Windsor, 16
　A Midsummer Night's Dream, 91, 95, 188
　Much Ado about Nothing, 5, 15, 40, 70, 86, 99, 104–12
　Othello, 5, 15, 16–17, 19–45, 47, 48, 50, 52–4, 74, 87, 98, 148, 188
　The Rape of Lucrece, 99
　Richard II, 2, 188
　Richard III, 50, 149
　Romeo and Juliet, 2, 97–8, 100
　The Taming of the Shrew, 2, 79, 81
　The Tempest, 2, 7, 52, 143–70, 172, 178, 179, 188
　Timon of Athens, 2
　Titus Andronicus, 2, 20
　Twelfth Night, 190
Shapiro, James, 151–2
Shaw, George Bernard, 3, 111
　Man and Superman, 17
　Saint Joan, 39
Shelton, Robert, 152–3
Shulman, Milton, 26, 80, 83, 117, 185
Sichel, John, 44
Sim, Alastair, 62
Simpson, N. F.
　One Way Pendulum, 62
Sinfield, Alan, 154

Slade, 143
Smith, Maggie, 16, 32–9, 72, 105, 109, 111, 112, 188
Some Like it Hot, 81
The Sound of Music, 132
Speaight, Robert, 18–19, 144, 166
Spinetti, Victor, 97
Spurling, Hilary, 42–3, 49–51, 62, 66–8, 81, 149
Stanislavsky, Konstantin, 116
Starr, Ringo, 86
Stephens, Robert, 12, 14, 76, 82, 105, 111–12
Stepin Fetchit (Lincoln Perry), 27
Stevens, Peter, 168–9
Stoppard, Tom
   Every Good Boy Deserves Favour, 59
   Lord Malquist and Mr Moon, 59
   The Real Inspector Hound, 201 n.46
   Rosencrantz and Guildenstern are Dead, 5–7, 39–40, 57–72, 80, 82, 85–95, 112, 154, 188
   A Separate Peace, 58
   A Walk on the Water, 58
Strehler, Giorgio, 170–1
Stride, John, 61–2, 65–6, 73, 88, 90, 97
Strindberg, August
   The Dance of Death 80, 87, 112
   Miss Julie, 39
Strong, Roy, 151, 161
Suzman, Janet, 79
Svevo, Italo, 46, 51
Swanson, Gloria, 105

Sykes, Eric, 64
Sylvestre, Cleo, 52

Taylor, John Russell, 69–71
Tearle, Godfrey, 20
Tenschert, Joachim, 123–4, 130–5, 189
Terry, Ellen, 2
Théâtre de l'Odéon, 89
Théâtre Renaud-Barrault, 99
Theatres Act, 91
There's a Girl in My Soup, 64, 79
Thomson, Peter, 161
Thorndike, Daniel, 187
Thorndike, Sybil, 187
Tieck, Dorothea, 117–18, 123
Tinker, Jack, 176, 177
Toms, Carl, 41
Travers, Ben
   Plunder, 181
Trewin, J. C., 10–11, 15, 18, 21, 30–1, 48, 101, 164
Tutin, Dorothy, 79
Twiggy (Lesley Hornby), 78–9
Tynan, Kenneth, 17, 25–6, 39, 48, 59–60, 68, 73, 93, 98, 99, 107, 108, 115–16, 123, 130, 132, 147–8, 167–8, 189

Uproar in the House, 79
US, 60

Valk, Frederick, 20
Van Eyck, Jan, 41
Verdi, Giuseppe, 44, 105
   Otello, 51
   Rigoletto, 50
Victoria Palace Theatre, 23
von Appen, Karl, 125, 135

Wagner, Richard, 153
Wakeman, Rick, 153
Walker, Mary, 163–4
Walker, Rudolph, 52
Walter, Wilfred, 20
Ward, Simon, 184–5
Wardle, Irving, 39, 41, 48, 65, 80, 83, 84, 134, 140–1, 144, 155, 157, 176–7, 182
Warner, David, 101, 171–2, 177, 180
Waugh, Evelyn, 133
Weigel, Helene, 114, 127–9, 130
Weisbrod, Christian, 129–30
Weiss, Peter
  The Investigation, 60
  Marat/Sade, 60
Wekwerth, Manfred, 123–4, 130–5, 189
Welles, Orson, 20
Wenham, Jane, 196 n.107
West Side Story, 106
White, Michael, 180–1
Whitehall Theatre, 64, 79
Whitelaw, Billie, 37–9
Wilde, Oscar, 45, 57
  The Importance of Being Earnest, 148–9
Wilkinson, Marc, 143
Willett, John, 117–18
Williams, Clifford, 73–8, 80–1, 83–5, 95, 148
Wilson, Effingham, 1
Wilson, Harold, 131, 156, 181
Wilson, Robert, 156
Wittgenstein, Ludwig, 57
The Wizard of Oz, 159
Wolfit, Donald, 20
Wood, John, 86
Woodward, Derek, 197 n.150
World Theatre Season, 64, 99
Worsley, T. C., 13
Wylie, Frank, 82
Wynyard, Diana, 12

Yates, Frances, 156
Yes
  Tales from Topographic Oceans, 152–3, 172
Young, B. A., 10, 18, 35–6, 47, 51, 65, 100, 101–3, 141
Young Vic, 16

Zadek, Peter, 115
Zeffirelli, Franco, 5, 40, 86, 115, 189
  Amleto, 97–104, 107
  Much Ado about Nothing, 5, 40, 104–12
Zuckmayer, Carl
  The Captain of Köpenick, 130

www.ingramcontent.com/pod-product-compliance
Lightning Source LLC
Chambersburg PA
CBHW060948230426
43665CB00015B/2104